teaching
adolescent literature

80-667

HAYDEN ENGLISH EDUCATION SERIES

Robert W. Boynton, Consulting Editor

Former Principal, Senior High School
and Chairman, English Department
Germantown Friends School

THE GREAT AMERICAN READING MACHINE
David J. Yarington

QUESTIONS ENGLISH TEACHERS ASK
R. Baird Shuman

TEACHING ADOLESCENT LITERATURE: A Humanistic Approach
Sheila Schwartz

RHETORIC AND COMPOSITION: A Sourcebook for Teachers
Richard L. Graves

UPTAUGHT
Ken Macrorie

A VULNERABLE TEACHER
Ken Macrorie

TEACHING COMPOSING
William E. Coles, Jr.

FREE WRITING! A Group Approach
Joseph Brown et al.

MEDIA & KIDS: Real World Learning in the Schools
James Morrow and Murray Suid

GUIDE TO SHORT FILMS
Jeffrey Schrank

THE CELLULOID CURRICULUM: How to Use Movies in the Classroom
Richard A. Maynard

teaching adolescent literature

A Humanistic Approach

SHEILA SCHWARTZ

Professor of English Education
State University College
at New Paltz

HAYDEN BOOK COMPANY, INC.
Rochelle Park, New Jersey

ISBN 0-8104-6036-X
Library of Congress Catalog Card Number   79-2042

1	2	3	4	5	6	7	8	9	PRINTING
79	80	81	82	83	84	85	86	87	YEAR

contents

To the memory of my beloved daughter,
Nancy Lynn Schwartz, 1952-1978,
whose perceptive criticisms made writing a joy

introduction

In the past, only a set curriculum of "classics" was taught in the secondary school English class, and the same books were used in almost every high school. These books were determined by the questions on the College Board tests and by what publishers put in the fat, chronologically arranged anthologies that were used everywhere. The so-called paperback revolution did not achieve momentum until the 1950s, and it wasn't until the 1970s that schools were willing to buy softcover books for classroom use. Even today many school systems rely mainly on hardcover anthologies, insisting that paperbacks of any kind are too fragile to hold up for more than a year or two. And in many schools the "classics" remain the only literary fare in the classroom.

When I was a secondary school student, books written exclusively for adolescents were the series books, such as Nancy Drew, Sue Barton, Judy Bolton, and the Bobbsey Twins. In school I read works like *Ivanhoe, Julius Caesar, Silas Marner*, and *A Tale of Two Cities*. I was bored by most of the books I read in school and frustrated by those I read at home.

The school books told stories that had happened long ago to characters who bore no relevance to my life. The books I read at home contained contemporary characters so perfect that they set off the imperfections of myself and the people I knew.

There were no Jews in children's books, no Blacks above the menial level, no real Indians but only the fantasies of James Fenimore Cooper. Parents in these books were usually affluent, understanding, and urbane, and the girls were all blue-eyed, golden-haired, exceptionally popular virgins who passed through adolescence without trauma or blemish.

Good contemporary adult books dealing with real problems and believable people seldom got into schools or into the hands of young people. Public libraries gave two classes of cards, and children were forbidden entry to the Adult Section.

In those days, it was considered ill-mannered to talk about one's problems to outsiders. There were no guidance counselors, no school psychologists; psychoanalysis was limited to the affluent. Happiness was generally perceived as more of a rarity than a right. The guideline for acceptable behavior regarding problems was to keep everything inside the family, and the troubled child would be even more troubled if he engaged in disloyal behavior. Books revealing intimate details of family life such as Jill Schary Robinson's *Bed/Time/Story*, Brooke Hayward's *Haywire*, or the books by the Roosevelt sons, which displayed the most intimate flaws and foibles of their famous parents, were rare. The family we read about was the one of *Life with Father*.

In the middle-class mythology that permeated literature and life in the public schools, girls were expected to be virgins when they married, to conceal their intelligence and opt for marriage, to have children as soon as possible, and to embrace willingly the role of housewife. The Nancy Drews never had abortions, got acne, were unpopular, battled with their families, or had a terrible time coming of age.

Nowhere could teenagers find reflections of their own, real problems; nowhere was there help or counseling; nowhere could they find reassurance that the problems of their daily lives were ones faced by many others. Perhaps the greatest contribution of J.D. Salinger is that in *The Catcher in the Rye* he brushed aside the traditional American teenage boy named Andy Hardy and replaced him with a hero who sees, feels, and responds to the real world of the adolescent, who *is* in fact a real adolescent.

Today, because of the burgeoning field of adolescent literature, things are refreshingly different in many schools. It's no revolution, but it is a decided change, and now young people *can* find reflections of what it means to be a teenager in the literature they read. Choice is no longer limited to a few arbitrarily defined classics, for the new literature explores all aspects of the human condition, all races and religions, all problems, societal and personal, all social strata, all nationalities. In one afternoon's visit to an upstate New York school I saw the following books in use: Herman Hesse's *Siddhartha*; Richard Wright's *Black Boy*; Paul Zindel's *The Pigman*; a 1974 non-fiction work about the survival of a rugby team in the Andes, *Alive*; and *Romeo and Juliet*.

The classroom has become a more open, honest place in terms of what may be read and discussed. In addition to books written for adolescents, young people are reading many adult books in paperback. Today's teenagers, far more fortunate than those of my generation, can enjoy the luxury of choice, can find literature that helps them to understand their own problems, to feel communion with the human race, and to see the world as knowable.

What Is Adolescent Literature?

Inclusively, adolescent literature is any literature read by adolescents. During the 1960s, a large number of books began to be published that were written specifically for adolescents. These books rival adult books in their willingness to deal openly with all aspects of modern American life.

They are read by high school students both in and out of the classroom, and in some cases the same books are read by adults. One librarian who catalogues young adult books told me that she had given Isabelle Holland's *The Man Without a Face* to her aged mother to introduce her to the subject of homosexuality.

Each year, the American Library Association (ALA) publishes a list of "Best Books for Young Adults" (see Appendix). These lists contain three categories of books: 1) books written specifically for junior and senior high school students (e.g., Richard Peck's *Introducing Superdoll*); 2) books with adolescent heroes and heroines, written for the general trade market (e.g., *Huckleberry Finn, True Grit, The Catcher in the Rye*); and 3) literature that fits neither of the first two categories but has, in the words of the Young Adult Services Division (YASD) of the ALA, "proven of potential interest to young adults."

Books on the ALA lists are "selected on the basis of young adult appeal; they meet acceptable standards of literary merit and provide a variety of subjects for different reading tastes as well as a broad range of reading levels." If we examine these lists, the wide range of adolescent literature becomes immediately apparent. Let us, for example, look at some of the 1974 list:

BEST BOOKS FOR YOUNG ADULTS, 1974

Books Written Specifically for Adolescents

Bright Candles: A Novel of the Danish Resistance, Nathaniel Benchley. Two teenagers turn from pranks to sabotage in this tense story about the Nazi regime in Denmark.

The Chocolate War: A Novel, Robert Cormier. "Sweets" abound at Trinity High while a schoolmaster feasts on students' fear.

First Person, Singular, Vida Demas. Pam recounts her teenage struggles to find herself.

M. C. Higgins, the Great, Virginia Hamilton. M. C.'s fantasies of escaping the hill country and its threats are shattered, but he gains new insights into his future and that of his family.

Books Written for General Trade Market
Which Have Adolescent Heroes and Heroines

The Launching of Barbara Fabrikant, Louise Blecher Rose. A witty, empathetic and earthy first-person story about the freshman college year of the overweight daughter of a rabbi.

A Cry of Angels, Jeff Fields. The adventures and friendships of a bunch of misfits are woven into a compelling story of a man's capacity for cruelty and love.

General Books of Interest to Young Adults

The Last Butterfly, Michael Jacot. A half-Jewish clown is forced to entertain Jewish children at Terezin before they board trains to Auschwitz.

Alive: The Story of the Andes Survivors, Piers Paul Read. Sixteen rugby players survive a plane crash in the Andes and live for ten weeks on faith, finally using the bodies of their dead comrades for sustenance.

In 1975, the YASD published a bibliography called "Still Alive," listing seventy-two titles published between 1960 and 1974 that were still alive and being read by young adults in 1975. It uses the ALA's three categories of adolescent books and includes titles originally on their annual "Best Books for Young Adults" list as well as titles that had been overlooked (see bibliography).

In the Fall, 1975, issue of the Adolescent Literature Association's *Newsletter*, the editor made the following request of readers: "An inexperienced English teacher asks you to recommend ten adolescent novels worth her/his reading time with enough adolescent appeal to make them attractive to students. The teacher also asks you to recommend ten adult novels using the same criteria."[1] This same request was also sent to 325 English teachers and librarians across the country. Books which received at least ten recommendations were listed in the Spring, 1976, *Newsletter*:

Adolescent Novels

(58) Cormier, *The Chocolate War*
(52) Hinton, *The Outsiders*
     Zindel, *The Pigman*
(48) Peck, *A Day No Pigs Would Die*
(33) Childress, *A Hero Ain't Nothin' But a Sandwich*
     Swarthout, *Bless the Beasts and Children*
(28) Greene, *Summer of My German Soldier*
(27) Kerr, *Dinky Hocker Shoots Smack*
(25) Anonymous, *Go Ask Alice*
     Head, *Mr. and Mrs. Bo Jo Jones*
(23) Hinton, *That Was Then, This Is Now*
(22) Neufeld, *Lisa, Bright and Dark*
(21) Zindel, *My Darling, My Hamburger*
(20) Armstrong, *Sounder*
(19) Holland, *Man Without a Face*
(18) White, *Deathwatch*
(17) Greenberg (Green, pseud.), *I Never Promised You a Rose Garden*
     Hall, *Sticks and Stones*
     Lipsyte, *The Contender*
(16) Mathis, *A Teacup Full of Roses*
(15) Rushing, *Mary Dove*
(14) Guy, *The Friends*
     Tolkien, *The Hobbit*
(13) Bonham, *Durango Street*
     Holman, *Slake's Limbo*
     Sleator, *House of Stairs*
(12) Kerr, *Is That You, Miss Blue?*
     Kerr, *The Son of Someone Famous*
     Taylor, *The Cay*

---

1. Ken Donelson, "Do You Know Any Good Books?" *ALAN Newsletter*, Vol. 3, No. 3, Spring, 1976.

(11) Rawls, *Where the Red Fern Grows*
     White, *The Once and Future King*
(10) Benchley, *Bright Candles*
     Kerr, *If I Love You, Am I Trapped Forever?*

Adult Novels

(43) Benchley, *Jaws*
(39) Adams, *Watership Down*
(38) Craven, *I Heard the Owl Call My Name*
(31) Lee, *To Kill a Mockingbird*
(30) Harris, *Hatter Fox*
(29) Kesey, *One Flew over the Cuckoo's Nest*
(25) Knowles, *A Separate Peace*
(23) Salinger, *The Catcher in the Rye*
(21) Golding, *Lord of the Flies*
(18) Keyes, *Flowers for Algernon*
(16) Bradford, *Red Sky at Morning*
(14) Pirsig, *Zen and the Art of Motorcycle Maintenance*
(13) Borland, *When the Legends Die*
     Potok, *The Chosen*
(12) Trumbo, *Johnny Got His Gun*
     Vonnegut, *Slaughterhouse Five*
(11) Heller, *Catch-22*
     Michener, *Centennial*
     Stein, *The Magician*
     Steinbeck, *The Grapes of Wrath*
     Steinbeck, *Of Mice and Men*
(10) Doctorow, *Ragtime*
     Plath, *The Bell Jar*
     Potok, *My Name Is Asher Lev*

    The NCTE has recently issued two new versions of its bibliographies of books for the junior and senior high schools. The junior high school booklist, entitled *Your Reading*, defines adolescent literature only by inclusion. Neither the acknowledgments nor the introduction helps us understand why a particular book was selected for the junior high school level. The list includes *True Grit*, which was written for the adult market but has a fourteen-year-old heroine, and *To Kill a Mockingbird*, which was also written for the adult market, has a child as protagonist, and is more often taught on the senior high school level.

    Your Reading is not arranged in terms of reading levels but topically in categories that the editors assume are of interest to students of this age group, topics such as "On Being Adventurous," "On Being a Family," "On Being Friends," "On Being in Love."

    The senior high school booklist, entitled *Books for You*, informs the student in the introduction that the sole criterion for inclusion in this list is pleasurable reading. This list is also categorized into topics that are assumed to be of interest to young people; many of the topics are the same as those on the junior high school list: "Coming of Age," "Love," "Science Fiction," etc. Classics such as Wilkie Collins's *The Moonstone* and Dickens's *Bleak House* are included, as well as contemporary fictional works such as Kemelman's *Tuesday, the Rabbi Saw Red.*

It is evident that the range of adolescent literature is somewhat overwhelming. Therefore, I suggest that adolescent literature selected for teaching at the high school or junior high school level should meet the following criteria:

1. It should be literature that helps young people come of age, literature that helps make the world knowable.
2. It should be literature that affirms the best in human beings and asserts the worth of humanistic values, regardless of the failures and problems of society.
3. It should be literature with a high interest factor.
4. It should be literature that gives readers the opportunity to discover themselves, to see and understand themselves in their present and future societal roles.
5. It should be literature that informs its readers about a common humanity by demonstrating that others have encountered similar problems in coming of age.
6. It should be honest literature free from the traditional school avoidance of taboo subjects such as death, illness, and sex.
7. It should be literature that helps students develop moral perspective, respect for individual autonomy, and the ability to reason. It should assist in the forming of moral character.

Teaching Adolescent Literature:
A Humanistic Approach

What is the meaning of the title of this book? It means that literature is read primarily in terms of how it illuminates life.

Let us think for a moment about the traditional way in which literature was taught. In many classrooms, the student was there for the literature rather than the literature serving the student. The purpose of such methodology was usually to take students deeper and deeper into the text. This resulted in impossible exams dealing with minutiae, classes on Shakespeare in which students became so bored with the extensive line-by-line analysis that they could not find either his greatness or his significance to them, and an emphasis solely on the factual and on the convergent.[2]

The purpose and approach to adolescent literature is primarily divergent. Many of the works read or recommended for adolescent litera-

---

2. See the end of this Introduction for an explanation of how I am using these terms (p. 32).

ture are works that have meaning primarily in relation to society rather than as literary exemplars—works such as those about minority groups, addiction, and coming of age. Because of this relation to society, books such as Nat Hentoff's *I'm Really Dragged but Nothing Gets Me Down,* which deals with resistance to the Vietnam War, quickly become dated. In other words, books are of dubious value when their context is no longer significant in the teenager's immediate world.

Lester S. Golub, in an article about literature for today's English classes, underscores the role of literature in relation to currents and developments in contemporary society. He writes:

We can now begin to equate language and literature with national ethnic and moral consciousness. With the rebirth of national ethnic consciousness, with the introduction of the values of a pluralistic and open society, there comes a need to introduce literature written in English which explains cultural experiences of non-Anglo groups who now express their culture and value system in the English language.[3]

The concept of greatest significance is that we must "begin to equate language and literature with national ethnic and moral consciousness." This has not been the goal in the traditional approach to literature, in which the dissection of a literary work was the major activity and literature was viewed as an end in itself.

In addition to focusing on ethnic and moral consciousness, secondary school literature can help students develop sociological and psychological consciousness. *Protokollon*, a guide to a new film series entitled *Responding to Literature*, focuses on what the authors refer to as the "aboutness of literature." "Aboutness is probably what first attracts readers to literature, and what they, in turn, want to talk about. The classroom is the appropriate arena for such talk."[4]

The nature of literature is being questioned today more seriously than ever before as a result of the shift in student allegiance from books to television. Literature is affected by shifts both within the literary world and within society. The broad effect of this upheaval in literature "means that the student comes to class less and less to learn the 'truth' of literature as interpreted by the teacher and more and more to learn how to perform in various ways, both as a reader and a human being."[5]

In addition to stressing the importance of the sociological and psychological content of literature, *Responding to Literature* extends categories and goals to include the ideological (beliefs and ideas), the ethical (e.g., poetic justice), the epistemological (the nature, extent, and limitations of ways of knowing), the ontological (reality in the work), and the structural

3. Lester S. Golub, "The New American Revolution: Multi-Cultural Literature in the English Program," *English Journal*, September, 1975, Vol. 64, No. 6, p. 23.
4. R. W. Lid & Philip Handler, *Protokollon*. Northridge: California State University Foundation, 1975, p. 5.
5. *Ibid.*, p. 11.

(diction, style, convention, authorial voice). This approach, like the Golub approach, focuses on student response as having as much or more significance than the work itself.

Both of these approaches derive from the work of Louise Rosenblatt, who, in *Literature as Exploration*, first published in 1938, wrote the following:

> The demand that the teaching of literature have some relation to the pupil's immediate human concerns has usually been countered by pointing to the horrors of the didactic, moralistic approach to literature. Wise teachers have opposed any tendency to make of literature a mere handmaiden of the social studies or a body of documents illustrating moral points. . . .
>
> Yet when the literary experience is fully understood, it becomes apparent that teachers of literature have indeed been somewhat shortsighted. They have not always realized that, willy-nilly, they affect the student's sense of human personality and human society. More directly than most teachers they foster general ideas or theories about human nature and conduct, definite moral attitudes, and habitual responses to people and situations. Preoccupied with the special aims of their field, they are often not conscious of dealing, in the liveliest terms, with subjects and problems usually thought of as the province of the sociologist, psychologist, philosopher, or historian. Moreover, these attitudes and theories are proffered in their most easily assimilable form, as they emerge from personal and intimate experience of specific human situations, presented with all the sharpness and intensity of art.[6]

The humanistic approach to adolescent literature attempts to remind teachers that they are dealing with subjects usually thought of as the province of the sociologist, psychologist, philosopher, or historian.

The primarily contemporary setting of adolescent literature, its focus on adolescent problems and behavior, its clarity of language and allusion, its lack of ambiguity in relation to questions of right and wrong, its emphasis on straightforward plot and character presentation, its highlighting of ethical dilemmas, and its relation to social and political events of the contemporary world mean that the student reading a young adult novel is learning about more than what is in the novel. The work provides a jumping-off place for his examination of self and world.

Why a Methods Text for Adolescent Literature?

It is possible to become a teacher having had little or no experience with the real world of secondary literature. The classics that are read in college are rarely the works that the new teacher will be using, and the college methods used to teach them are rarely useful in the secondary school.

I have had future English teachers come into my undergraduate methods classes and practicing teachers come into my classes on adolescent literature who have read no works about the American Indian,

---

6. Louise M. Rosenblatt, *Literature as Exploration*. New York: Noble and Noble, Publishers, Inc., 1968, pp. 4–5.

Black, Jew, etc. Some students, when first exposed to *Return to Manzanar*, a book about the internment of Japanese Americans during World War II, had never heard of this shameful event in our national history. They know more about eighteenth-century England than they do about the ethnic and socioeconomic groups within their own country.

In addition, many of these teachers have never been in a situation in which they could confront, discuss, and begin to understand their own feelings about such aspects of contemporary life as homosexuality, alcoholism, drug addiction, the repression of institutions, child abuse. To illustrate, one of my adolescent literature classes was reading *Good Times, Bad Times* (James Kirkwood), which deals with boys at a boarding school who are suspected of being homosexual and with their mistreatment by a sadistic headmaster who *is* a closet homosexual. One of the major points of the book is that the headmaster is so distorted that he is unable to recognize the pure friendship of the boys.

One English teacher in my class had never before read a book about real or implied homosexuality. He kept insisting that the "pure" friendship between the two boys, was, in reality, a homosexual one. "I know kids like that," he said, furiously, "and they're not fooling me. If Jordan hadn't died you can bet they would have turned into practicing homosexuals."

In the heated discussion that followed he had the opportunity for the first time to see some of his own attitudes toward and fears about homosexuality. In addition, he was forced to use the text rather than his own feelings about homosexuality. Then some class members brought in newspaper articles about the persecution of homosexuals and about the laws intended to lessen this persecution. The movement, during the three hours that we discussed this book, swung back and forth constantly from book to self to the world to the book. Through the medium of literature he was forced to confront his own value structure, apart from and in relation to the dominant one in society.

We then read another book about homosexuality, Scoppetone's *Trying Hard to Hear You*, which carries the message that homosexuality is a proclivity of a private nature and should not be perceived as a criminal offense. A lively class discussion followed that referred to the recent Supreme Court ruling that this private matter is still a public crime. This is exactly the kind of class discussion we would espouse for teenagers. Exposure to a problem through literature enables the reader to express himself in relation to the literature and thus to escape possible embarrassment and vulnerability.

Many adults go through their lives without ever having the opportunity to discuss such matters in constructive and controlled circumstances. The college classroom gives us this opportunity which we may then, later, extend to our own secondary school students.

Another example of student growth through adolescent literature occurred in relation to Ray Bradbury's *The Martian Chronicles*. One self-assured, veteran teacher immediately volunteered an answer to the following question: "If you went to Mars, and were in charge of the country, what three values would you immediately establish?" She stood up and proudly informed the class, "The first value I'd establish is respect for the one, true God."

Repressing amusement, the class was firm but insistent. "Who is the one *true* God?" they asked her. Was it Jesus, Jehovah, Buddha? Hadn't the world gone through enough suffering because of each group's insistence on the one, true God? Wasn't Ireland still living through daily agony because of religious divisions?

The class referred her to another adolescent literature book, Judy Blume's *Are You There God? It's Me, Margaret*, in which Margaret, who is half Jewish and half Christian, talks directly to the one true God, for her. She says, "You know, God, my new friends all belong to the Y or the Jewish Community Center." The class showed her how the insistence on one, true religion or God could even cause problems in this pleasant little book. Margaret asks, "Which way am I supposed to go? I don't know what you want me to do about that." (p. 37)

Members of the class stated that this was the first time they had ever dealt with their feelings about religion in a college classroom. One class member even felt that this book should not be used in the public schools. He viewed it as religious indoctrination because of its firm belief in the existence of God. He regarded this as a breach of the separation between church and state. "How come," he asked, "there are no books about happy atheists?" He stated that atheism was one of the first values he'd establish on Mars.

Valuable class controversy also arose in response to the following topics:

1. The use of dialect (*His Own Where*, Jordan; *A Hero Ain't Nothin' But a Sandwich*, Childress; *A Day No Pigs Would Die*, Peck)
2. Teenage pregnancy and sexuality (*For All the Wrong Reasons*, Neufeld; *My Darling, My Hamburger*, Zindel; *First Person, Singular*, Demas)
3. Treatment of prisoners (*Soledad Brother*, Jackson; *Soul on Ice*, Cleaver; *Hatter Fox*, Harris; *Run, Shelley, Run*, Samuels)
4. Racial and religious prejudice (*Summer of My German Soldier*, Greene; *My Last Butterfly*, Jacot; *The Bluest Eye*, Morrison)

A college methods course in adolescent literature is essential to acquaint teachers with a variety of books in this genre, to explore methods and materials for teaching these works, and to give teachers the opportunity to examine their own feelings about the controversial episodes and ideas contained in so many of these works.

Jerzy Kosinski, the noted author of *The Painted Bird* and other contemporary novels, described the schools as "among the few remaining institutions that can help tomorrow's adults become thinking individuals, able to judge and function in a world of pressures, conflicting values, and moral ambiguities."[7] Kosinski sees the vital function of education in our society as its ability to help students cope with life by exploring with them

---

7. Interview, *Media & Methods*. January 1976.

the realities and ambiguities encountered in literary works. To Kosinski, "the school offers one of the few structured forums for analyzing . . . [life] situations . . . and . . . [the] opportunity to critically evaluate the human condition within the guidelines of literary value and human interchange."[8]

Teachers need this experience as much as their students do, and in the course of exploring adolescent literature in methods classes, they, too, can analyze life situations "within the guidelines of literary value and human interchange."

Which Adolescent Literature?

Good adolescent literature tells the truth, mainly. Bad adolescent literature pretends to tell the truth but confuses sentimentality with sentiment, panders to the cheap triumph, and sacrifices the universal for the topical. It attempts to feed on the youth culture, to espouse values it thinks young people will respond to, and to pretend closeness, interest, and sincerity, only in order to sell.

Poor adolescent literature is remarkably like advertising. It sells spurious products to the reader (viewer) by appealing to the basest emotions (fear, greed, the desire for conformity) rather than by making the reader think. This kind of literature uses current slang, current values, current trends, and, fortunately, is generally as transitory as most popular songs. Teachers must be particularly wary of this kind of book because it is often flashy and appealing—as interesting, involving, and tempting as a cheap or violent television show. The medium is so impressive to the reader that he is overwhelmed by it and does not have time to think about the lack of message.[9]

1. Good adolescent literature meets adequate literary standards.
2. Good adolescent literature helps young people become more in touch with themselves by establishing a common bond with the rest of humanity.
3. Good adolescent literature shows young people that they are not the only ones to suffer their problems.
4. Good adolescent literature makes the world knowable by telling the truth.
5. Without being didactic, good adolescent literature affirms and reaffirms those values that keep people hoping, that give young people the strength to continue to grow.
6. Good adolescent literature helps combat the values and events that result in apathy, disillusionment, and retreat.
7. Good adolescent literature has a humanistic base of respect for human beings.
8. Good adolescent literature deals with eternal problems rather than with the transitory, commercialized, manufactured mores of the youth culture.
9. Good adolescent literature reflects the affirmative, hopeful vision of the

---

8. *Ibid.*
9. For a discussion of poor adolescent literature, see Appendix, page 199.

twenty-first century embodied in the *Humanist Manifesto,* which says, in part:

> Humanity, to survive, requires bold and daring measures. We need to extend the uses of scientific method, not renounce them, to fuse reason with compassion in order to build constructive social and moral values. The ultimate goal should be the fulfillment of the potential for growth in each human personality — not for the favored few, but for all of humankind. Only a shared world and global measures will suffice.
>
> A humanist outlook will tap the creativity of each human being and provide the vision and courage for us to work together. This outlook emphasizes the role human beings can play in their own spheres of action. . . . Humanism can provide the purpose and inspiration that so many seek; it can give personal meaning and significance to human life. . . . Humanism is an ethical process through which we all can move, above and beyond the divisive particulars, heroic personalities, dogmatic creeds, and ritual customs of past religions or their mere negation . . . for us, it is a vision of hope, a direction for satisfying survival.[10]

Method in Adolescent Literature

1. The classroom is viewed primarily as an arena for the exchange of ideas. Therefore, the major teaching technique will be the use of small groups within the classroom. The purposes for the division into small groups are the following:
   a. Students who are inhibited in front of a larger group will more readily participate.
   b. More students can be simultaneously involved.
   c. Peer teaching is inescapable.
   d. Discipline problems are diminished, since talking, the present cardinal sin, is expected and is a necessity rather than a crime.
   e. The class atmosphere relaxes, thus freeing students to focus on content rather than on form.
   f. The teacher is freed to move around the classroom and is thus able to have individual contact with many more students per period.
   g. Dialogue and the exchange of ideas, essential for the teaching of adolescent literature, are increased.
2. Ways of devising small groups vary. Some variations follow:
   a. Random grouping, "All right, divide into groups of three with the two students sitting near you."
   b. Purposeful grouping, devised before the class period. In this case, names of group members can either be dittoed or posted before the class begins, in order to minimize confusion.
3. Kinds of purposeful grouping:
   a. One leader per group to make sure the group functions.
   b. No leaders per group (all leaders put together in one group, to ensure additional participation).
   c. Socialization group to help young people make friends.

---

10. *Humanist Manifestos I and II*. Prometheus Books, 923 Kensington Avenue, Buffalo, New York 14215, 1973.

   d. Grouping for peer teaching.
   e. Grouping for special skills and abilities.
   f. Remedial grouping.
4. Group activities:
   a. All groups doing the same work based on LAPs.
   b. Each group working on a different book.
   c. One or more small groups going to the library.
   d. One group preparing a creative dramatics assignment.
   e. One or more research groups going to the library, interviewing someone, going on a field trip.
   f. One group preparing a debate.
   g. One group working on an art experience (mural, music, crafts, etc.).
5. Class organization:
   a. Groups for one day.
   b. Groups for longer periods of time, depending on the task.
   c. Groups to remain constant throughout the reading of a book.
6. Structure of one period:
   a. Groups work throughout.
   b. Groups work for part of the period, then assemble as an entire class.
   c. Groups work for an entire period, then go into individual follow-up tasks for homework.
   d. Groups work on special problems while remainder of class works individually or as a whole.
7. Written work for adolescent literature. The heart of the teaching of adolescent literature is the Learning Activity Packet (LAP), which is prepared in advance by the teacher. The values of the LAP are the following:
   a. The students see the entire course of study laid out before them instead of going from day to day, in fragmented fashion, with the teacher the only one who understands the total plan.
   b. The students have the responsibility for fulfilling the total plan.
   c. There is ample time throughout the study for students to ask the teacher about aspects of it that aren't clear.
   d. The LAP is like a roadmap. It provides for individual, group, and class work. All materials can be used for any one of these three arrangements.
   e. The LAP encourages a student-centered approach to curriculum building.
   f. Using a LAP frees the teacher during class time to circulate, work with small groups or individuals, handle any problems that might arise. Instead of performing in front of the class as chief actor, the teacher is freed to act as guide, consultant, and facilitator.
   g. Once a LAP has been prepared, it provides for maximum flexibility in grouping, because the same LAP can be used by individuals, small groups, and the entire class.
   h. The students know exactly what to do even if the teacher is absent.
   i. The LAPs provide an excellent, concrete body of work on which to base student evaluation. Record keeping is simplified.
   j. Once the teacher has done the initial work of preparing a LAP, he or

she can amend it each time the literary work on which it is based is used.

The chapters that follow are concerned with topics, trends, and ideas in contemporary society that seem to be the focus of current adolescent literature. In many cases, books that are not contemporary (that is, from the 1960s or 1970s) are included because of their popularity in the secondary school classroom.[11]

The basic ideas that determine the selection and organization of these chapters are the following: I have attempted to define the subjects, topics, concerns, or ideas that have a direct and pervasive relevance to human values in general and to American values in particular, and then to suggest the ramifications of these topics—the kinds of questions they raise, insights they insist on, understandings they require. I am working from the conviction that the purposes of the study of adolescent literature are, among others:

1. To focus on ideas or concerns that underlie and find expression in human behavior.
2. To bring to consciousness and examine open-mindedly the mores, beliefs, values, convictions, and ambiguities of a society or individual.
3. To raise issues that are central to personal behavior.
4. To clarify and deepen students' understandings about human beliefs, feelings, and behavior.
5. To help students understand more clearly why they are what they are, why they believe what they believe, and why they do what they do, in order that they may behave toward themselves and others more intelligently, thoughtfully, and compassionately.

Two methods for working with adolescent literature follow. One is a Teaching Guide (TG), designed for teacher use. It is the total resource from which individual lessons for students are drawn. The other is a Learning Activity Packet (LAP), a series of activities that constitute the complete program for the weeks the students spend on a particular book. Goals, instructions, evaluation are all addressed to the student. The examples reproduced here in extracted form were put together by two students in my graduate adolescent literature course for teachers.

TGs or LAPs are not intended to demonstrate the only ways to teach adolescent literature. They are merely suggestions, ways of proceeding that I have found useful in the classroom. The main concern is not the particular form but rather the experience for the students, the experience that helps make the world more comprehensible to them.

---

11. Since as many books had to be omitted as could be included, lists of additional works have been placed at the end of each chapter.

TEACHING GUIDE (TG)
Janet C. Eckert

(I Never Promised You a Rose Garden, by
Joanne Greenberg [Hannah Green, pseud.])

I. Biographical Sketch of the Author; etc.

II. Critic's Corner:

"In a quiet way [the story] creates a vivid tableaux
of life in a mental institution, and of the characters who come and go, some helplessly sliding toward
destruction, a few recovering. Mainly though, the
book focuses on one girl and her agonizing fight to
re-enter the actual world. The novel is written
under a pseudonym and the reader suspects that the
author knows first-hand whereof she speaks. If this
speculation is wrong, she has one of the most powerful imaginations now going. Though the book deals
with infinite sorrows and terrors, the total effect
is heartening."

Chad Walsh, Book Week, p. 14, May 3, 1964.

etc.

III. Synopsis of Plot (Student Introduction); etc.

IV. Factual Questions and Answers

A. Below are words and phrases which the central
character, Debby, uses. Explain the meaning each
has in this book. Page numbers are given so that
you can note the context from which the item is
taken.

1. Honeymoon phase, p. 47: initial phase spent in
a mental hospital. Three-month period during
which patient becomes used to routine. Most
patients submit to authority at this time.

2. Ward A and Ward B: places in hospital where
less seriously ill (neurotic) patients live.
Patients feel they must appear and act normal.

3. Ward D, the disturbed ward, pp. 47, 53–54, 72:
   place in hospital where seriously ill (psychotic)
   patients live. This ward has a severe atmosphere
   (the chairs are not upholstered, the windows are
   barred, and the personnel are tough physically)
   but it offers several advantages: (1) patients do
   not have to keep up the false pretense of being
   well and acting normally; (2) there is no worse
   place to worry about. Being crazy is not as
   terrifying as being afraid of becoming crazy.

4. Pencil doctor, pp. 15–16, 21: doctor whose function seems to stress administration over medical
   treatment. The patient is seen as a statistic on
   a form; he is seen as an object.

5. Great Deceits, pp. 96–97: illusions maintained
   despite reality. They include all the lies and
   hypocrisy which had contributed to Debby's illness: (1) society's hypocrisy, (2) Grandfather
   Blau's pretensions, (3) Debby's dependence on
   precocity despite rejection by her own age group.

   etc.

V. Convergent Questions

A. Many incidents in Debby's life and during her stay at
   the institution appear to be setbacks in her progress
   toward sanity. Discuss the meaning of each of the
   following quotes and explain how each incident cited
   actually shows Debby's progress.

   1. "Puberty normal physically, but at age 16 patient
      attempted suicide," p. 19.

      The attempt was made to call attention to her
      illness and her need for help. It was this inci-
      dent which led Debby's parents to commit her to a
      mental hospital. (See pages 16, 40 for Esther's
      explanation; p. 24 for Debby's explanation.)

   2. "Oh, they moved her up to Disturbed," p. 51.

      Debby's self-mutilation, a symptom of her illness,
      seems terrifying to normal people because it is
      senseless. By being moved to D Ward, however,
      she was going to live in the only ward where she

could be completely honest in her emotions. (See
pp. 47, 54, 72 for an explanation of this
paradox.)

3. "I'm sorry for what I said. I did it for me and
not against you. I didn't want to hurt you--to
make you sicker," p. 76.

Debby is admitting here that she has hurt Carla
to protect herself. It is the first time she has
taken responsibility for the effect of her
actions.

etc.

B. 1. Debby has noticed that the best hospital personnel
(attendants, nurses and doctors) are not attacked
by the patients while the worst are regularly
attacked (pp. 65-66). Choose any character from
the book except Hobbs or McPherson. Explain why
Debby would think this character makes a good or
bad hospital staff member.

Good hospital staff members treat the patients as
equals. They look for qualities in the patients
that they have in themselves. The worst are
afraid of the patients. They see similarities
between themselves and the patients as threats to
their own sanity.

Dr. Royson is a bad member. He cannot treat Debby
as an equal and shows little compassion toward
her. His medical concern is treating her symtoms,
not curing her illness. Dr. Royson cannot help
her because he sees her illness as an intellectual puzzle which he cannot solve. He correctly
admires Dr. Fried, but his admiration is mis-
placed. Dr. Royson values intellect over compassion. (See pp. 159-160, 169, 188 for discussion
of Dr. Royson.)

etc.

VI. Divergent Questions

　　A. Answer the following questions in your own words.
　　　　There are no right or wrong answers. Your work
　　　　will be judged by how you back up your answers.

　　　　1. Compare Joanne Greenberg's conceptions of the
　　　　　　treatment patients receive in a mental institu-
　　　　　　tion with Ken Kesey's conception.

　　　　　　I Never Promised You a Rose Garden

　　　　　　Part of the trials of every patient is the cold,
　　　　　　impersonal treatment he receives from some
　　　　　　attendants, nurses, and doctors. Ward doctors
　　　　　　are more concerned with administration than
　　　　　　medicine. "Pencil doctors" see patients as
　　　　　　statistics on forms; a nurse prefers to fill
　　　　　　out a report rather than call a doctor about
　　　　　　Sylvia's speaking; too many staff members use
　　　　　　"Treatment No. Three" to avoid making any
　　　　　　changes in the hospital system or putting them-
　　　　　　selves out for the patient.

　　　　　　Greenberg does describe indifferent, bureau-
　　　　　　cratic behavior on the part of staff members in
　　　　　　the mental institution, but for the most part
　　　　　　her characters are described realistically with
　　　　　　all the virtues and faults of real people.
　　　　　　Emphasis is placed on the individual, not the
　　　　　　structure or power of the institution. No
　　　　　　character is seen as evil. Student nurses, at-
　　　　　　tendants, and conscientious objectors are seen
　　　　　　as people who treat the patients poorly because
　　　　　　they are fearful. What they do is not excused,
　　　　　　but it is understood. Even good staff members
　　　　　　have faults. Dr. Fried has to struggle with an
　　　　　　overburdening number of cases and she does not
　　　　　　choose to take on the administration when Debby
　　　　　　reports Ellis's hitting Helene while she was in
　　　　　　a cold pack. What Greenberg portrays is a
　　　　　　realistic view of life with all its joys and
　　　　　　hardships.

　　　　　　One Flew over the Cuckoo's Nest

　　　　　　Kesey seems interested mainly in how society,
　　　　　　or an institution which is part of that society,
　　　　　　can force the individual into submission. He

accurately portrays the petty bureaucratic rules
enforced in a mental institution, the perversion
of democratic practices, and the false claim
that everything is done in the patient's best
interest. He is more interested in showing how
people are made dupes of a system than in
showing that they are individuals with all the
strengths and weaknesses of typical human
beings. Women and Blacks are presented as
stereotypes. Big Nurse and the doctor are caricatures. RPM stands out as a tragic hero
because he is an individual and a rebel.

etc.

VII. Conceptual Questions

1. After reading <u>Rose Garden</u>, discuss Joanne
   Greenberg's philosophy of life. Is it one you
   could accept?

   Greenberg's conception of life is revealed in her
   title, <u>I Never Promised You a Rose Garden</u>. The
   rose is the symbol of love and romance. To see
   through rose-colored glasses is to see life with a
   romantic, Pollyanna viewpoint. Gardens are places
   of beauty, where experiences of relaxation and
   pleasure can be expected. <u>I Never Promised You a
   Rose Garden</u> means that people should not take a
   romantic view of life. Life should be viewed as
   being comprised of hardships, ambiguities, and
   disappointments as well as rewards. The title
   conveys the book's theme: no person or situation
   is perfect; man must expect and tolerate failures
   within himself and others.

   The theme is explained and expanded in two passages on pp. 105-106 and pp. 173-174. In the first
   passage, Dr. Fried acknowledges that injustices
   occur in the world, but stresses the value of accepting these injustices as challenges rather than
   rejecting the world because of them. In the second
   passage, Dr. Fried counsels Debby to accept her
   failure in not comforting Sylvia. Mistakes are
   part of life. It is more important to work for im-
   provement than to dwell on past mistakes.

   etc.

2. After reading <u>Rose Garden</u>, define sanity. In
    your opinion is Greenberg's definition a good
    one? If not, why not?

    Dr. Fried gives a good definition of sanity on
    several occasions. She observes that Esther
    Blau is sane, "she accepted the heavy penalties
    of reality and enjoyed its gifts also," p. 33.
    Dr. Fried attempts to convince Debby that sanity
    can be reached only when she accepts reality
    (pages 106 and 174) with all of its joys and
    betrayals. Sanity begins when people stop
    looking for perfection in the world. It begins
    when they tolerate the imperfections in others
    and themselves.

    etc.

VIII. Creative Activities

A. Improvised Scenes (Drama)

1. Have your students act out the scene in which
    Debby tells her mother and father that she
    has earned her high school equivalency
    diploma, p. 251. The scene could be changed
    to take place in the Blau home instead of
    over the telephone. Susan, Grandfather Blau,
    and other relatives could take part in the
    reactions to Debby's announcement.

2. Have Debby, Jacob, and Esther Blau discuss
    with their family physician sending Debby to
    a mental hospital.

3. Have Doris Rivera, Debby, and Carla discuss
    with staff members of this institution (Dr.
    Fried, Dr. Halle, Dr. Oster, Dr. Royson, Dr.
    Venner, Quentin Dobshansky, Mr. Ellis, Mr.
    McPherson, etc.) the problems of living out-
    side a mental institution.

B. Interviews

1. Have students interview leaders in their
    community to discover how mentally ill stu-
    dents are discovered and what treatment is

available for them. Students in the Sullivan
County area could interview their high school,
junior high school, or grade school principal
to find out whether medical assistance is
available within the school system or outside
the school system. They could also interview
the following people: a staff member of the
State-County Mental Health Association in
Monticello; Tybee Oesterreicher, Acting Team
Leader and Psychiatric Social Worker, Rockland
Children's Psychiatric Center; John Hoss,
Center for Independent Living, Psychiatric
Day Treatment Center for Adolescents.

LEARNING ACTIVITY PACKET (LAP)
Mrs. Lesley Hurd

(<u>Shane</u> by Jack Schaefer)

Directions:

1. You will be given a copy of the novel <u>Shane</u> at the end
   of this period.

2. You must read the novel over the next two weeks, and
   then continue with the activities given to you in this
   LAP.

3. Other than actual reading of the book, you will not do
   any work at home. Each activity is designed to be completed within one class period. This allows enough
   time to discuss any part that may be confusing.

4. All activities, when completed, must be placed in a
   folder which I will give you.

5. Follow the directions carefully as there are times when
   group work is required, and others when it is not.

6. <u>Important</u>: All written work is to be done on the pages,
   and in the spaces provided, and then placed in your
   folder.

7. Should there be any questions please see me and I will
   help you out.

Now you are ready to do activity 1. This is to be done
today, part one on your own, and then part two as a group.
Upon completion, place these pages in your folder and begin
reading. Each day, you will have at least fifteen minutes
to discuss your reading. At times I will read with you.

ACTIVITY 1:

On Your Own: In the following spaces write five words,
phrases, or things that come to your mind when you think of
the "old West." An example is given.

Example: ____cowboy____

1. _____

2. _____

3. _____

4. _____

5. _____

Group: When you have your five choices written down, get
into the group and read your choices to the others. Discuss how you came to this idea of the West. Put all your
ideas together, then write down where you got them from.

Example: T.V. westerns

1. _____

2. _____

3. _____

4. _____

Now you are to begin reading the novel. You may choose to
read individually or as a group; however, please continue
reading at home, and bring your book to class each day.

ACTIVITY 2:

On Your Own: Vocabulary: Read the sentence from the book
and note the underlined word. Choose from the meanings
below each quote whichever one would best fit the word's
meaning. Circle the correct letter. The page from which
the quote was taken is given at the end of each quote. This
is for your convenience, should you wish to read the quote
in context, as it applied to the story.

1. "She was an <u>unpredictable</u> woman." page 5

    a. hard to figure out
    b. good
    c. unlucky

2. "Not another separate <u>discernible</u> movement did he
    make . . ."   page 25

    a. quick
    b. noticeable
    c. noisy

3. "Father sent me once for the <u>hone</u>, so they chould
    sharpen the blades . . ."   page 21

    a. whetstone (grinding stone)
    b. plow
    c. knife

etc.

Group: Go over your choices from the vocabulary exercise
above, and discuss any differences you may have. Use a
dictionary, if necessary, and correct your work. Write
sentences using each of the underlined words.

ACTIVITY 3:

Crossword Puzzle: Complete the following puzzle by filling
in the name of the person in the story who said the quote
listed. Work alone. You will be given an opportunity to
compare answers after you are done.

Across: 2. "Joe Starrett, don't you dare touch a one of
              these apples."

          4. "A man is what he is, Bob, and there's no
              breaking the mold."

          6. "I'll be out money on the deal anyway, so I'll
              shave it to a hundred if that'll make you feel
              any better."

          7. "My little lean-to room was added back of the
              kitchen."

          9. "That's a lie!... My mother wasn't no Indian!"

Down: 1. "That's the millstone around my neck. That's
             the one fool thing about this place I haven't
             licked yet."

          3. "I bought that for Bob. I'm a poor substitute,
             Starrett. But as soon as this arm's healed,
             I'm asking you to let me work for you."

          5. "I've no quarrel with you," he said flatly,
             "even if you are Starrett's man."

          8. "Even without that, I can't let a bunch of
             nesters keep coming in here and choke me off
             from my water rights.

         10. "We're riding you out of this valley on a rail,
             Shane. We're going to rough you a bit and ride
             you out and you'll stay out."

HINT: Use a pencil when filling in your answers. This will
be easier to erase and keep neat looking. You may also wish
to change to someone else's choice after the discussion.

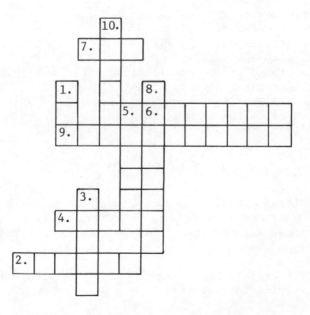

ACTIVITY 4:

Plot: Group: <u>Shane</u> is a compact novel. There are no
unnecessary scenes, no wasted words. Three incidents set
the background. Then the action soars to a climax and
suddenly concludes. We could diagram the plot this way,
with each square representing an important scene that carries the action forward. Beside each letter in the diagram,
write the number of the phrase below that best fits in that
space.

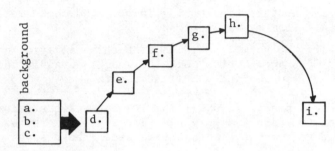

1.   Shane whips Chris
2.   The stump scene
3.   Fletcher makes his offer
4.   Shane strikes Joe
5.   Scene with the peddler
6.   Shane fights Wilson and Fletcher
7.   The Starretts decide to stay
8.   Shane and Joe fight Fletcher's men
9.   Wilson kills the farmer

ACTIVITY 5:

Group: Discuss possible answers to these questions, then
write down agreed upon answers. Be sure to express your
own opinions. If each one contributes, you are more likely
to arrive at good answers.

1.   In what ways is Shane similar to television heroes? In
     what ways is he different?

2. In a run-of-the-mill Western, the conflict is easy to understand: hero against villain, cowboy against Indian, man against nature. These are all physical conflicts. In Shane there are a lot of physical conflicts, but there is also the kind that goes on in a person's mind. These are called psychological conflicts. What psychological conflicts affect the Starretts?

What is the conflict within Shane?

3. One source of conflict in Shane is the historical struggle between the ranchers and the homesteaders. The author is careful to show good and bad, strong and weak on both sides of the struggle. Tell (with your reasons) which side you agree with.

etc.

ACTIVITY 6:

Group: Library Research: Hint: As a group, decide who will look up what and in what source. This way you will be able to cover more material. If each one takes notes on his own topic, the facts may be shared at the end of class.

Shane deals with a historical conflict. The problems between the homesteaders and the ranchers grew out of our westward expansion. You are to go to the library and look up material on this period of American history. Take notes on what you find, then write a short composition dealing with the historical facts of this period and the people involved.

The following is a list of possible sources of information.
Some are books, some are encyclopedias, some are magazines.
The notes can be written on looseleaf paper, but please
write your composition on the blank page provided.

Sources:

Sea of Grass by Conrad Richter. Jim Brewton, an old
Indian fighter turned cattleman, rules his empire of grass
with self-willed justice and battles the "nesters" who want
to plow up his land. Using as background the same historical conflict that Shane does, this story is told from the
rancher's point of view.

If you choose to look in an encyclopedia, look under the
following headings or any others you may find:
A.   Westward Movement, The   E.   Homestead
B.   Ranching   F.   Homestead Act, 1862
C.   Range Movement   G.   Guns
D.   Cowboy

ACTIVITY 7:

Theme and Values

Group: Discuss possible answers to the questions given.
Think about each question before writing, then put down the
answer you feel best explains what is needed.

1.   A novelist can have many reasons for writing a book.
     Probably, Jack Schaefer's main reason was to tell an
     exciting story, but he also tells us something about
     life. Shane is not only a major character in the story
     but also a symbol. "He was the symbol of all the dim,
     formless imaginings of danger and terror in the un-
     tested realm of human potentialities beyond my under-
     standing." When Bob sees Shane in this way, he is
     afraid. What frightens him? Is Shane a symbol of good
     or of evil? Of both? Explain your answer.

2. There is another symbol that is referred to in the last few chapters. Marian is the one who recognizes it as such and calls Joe's attention to it. What is the symbol and what does it stand for?

3. "Ideal friendship is a characteristic theme in stories of the old West." Why is this sort of friendship so important in this story? How does Shane's friendship with the Starretts display this "ideal" friendship? (Think about how this relationship helped both sides.)

4. Bob thinks of Shane as a hero. Pick out a couple of scenes from the book that point this out to the reader. There is also an instance when Bob is not so sure of his idol Shane. Find this instance and briefly explain what had happened.

etc.

ACTIVITY 8:

Creative Writing

On Your Own: Choose either of the following and write about it. Be sure and put yourself into the role asked for.

1. You are Shane. It is now many years since you left the Starretts' homestead, and you want to write them a letter telling them what has become of you. Write the letter, putting down what could have happened to Shane.

2. Write a "chapter" that would come before Chapter One.
    In this "chapter" you could put down what you think had
    happened to Shane before his arrival in town. Remember
    to write in character with the story.

ACTIVITY 9:

Group: Now that you have finished the novel and almost all
of the LAP, go back to your folders and take out Activity 1.
Re-read the activity and your answers. Below, write five
words, phrases, or ideas that explain your idea of the old
West now. Consider what you have read, looked up, and discussed. Some or all of your answers may differ, others may
not. Share your ideas with the group and compare answers.

                 Example: __hard work__

1. _____

2. _____

3. _____

4. _____

5. _____

ACTIVITY 10:

Final Test

On Your Own:

1. When an author makes one of his characters narrate the
    story, he limits it to what that character sees and
    hears and understands. What scenes could not be in-
    cluded because Bob could not have witnessed them? What
    could the author not tell you about Shane?

2. In a novel there are many characters. Some of the
   characters seem to play such minor roles that you
   wonder why they have been included. However, these
   characters do play a part in the novel. Pick out some
   of these "vague" characters from <u>Shane</u> and give some
   reasons why these background figures are needed.

3. List, on the lines below, three things that could
   possibly have happened to Shane after the gunfight.
   Put your favored choice first, etc.

   1. _____

      _____

   2. _____

      _____

   3. _____

      _____

4. Had Shane not met the Starretts when he did, do you
   think he could just as easily have joined up with
   Fletcher? If so, explain how this might have changed
   the end of the story. If not, explain what there was
   in Shane that would prevent this possibility.

etc.

Both the TG and the LAP reproduced here are based on the following hierarchy of thinking skills:

1. *Factual.* Under this heading come yes-no questions, factual questions, multiple choice, fill-ins, definitions, etc. This category contains questions essentially lacking in ambiguity.

2. *Convergent.* These are questions that draw together a number of facts and require analysis of those facts. Convergent questions stay within the confines of the particular work under study. They are the literary analysis questions we are familiar with in dealing with such matters as plot, character and setting. They require the reader to read between the lines, to draw conclusions, to interpret.

3. *Divergent.* These are questions that go outside the individual work. They require knowledge and understanding of more than one work. Comparison and contrast questions fit into this category. "Compare the treatment of the mentally ill in *One Flew over the Cuckoo's Nest* and *I Never Promised You a Rose Garden.*" Divergent questions also relate the literary work to society and to the life of the reader. A student reading Karl Shapiro's "Auto Wreck" may be asked to use that as a springboard for writing about an automobile accident he has witnessed or experienced.

4. *Conceptual.* This is the highest category of thinking skills. Here, students are asked to arrive at categories, at generalizations, at concept development, at evaluation techniques. "After reading *Typee*, *Benito Cereno*, and *Bartleby the Scrivener*, describe and evaluate Melville's world view."

Books Discussed in the Introduction

I Never Promised You a Rose Garden, Joanne Greenberg (Hannah Green, pseud.), Signet, 1964.
Shane, Jack Schaefer, Bantam, 1963.

I
the outsider/
the other

Why, in a society that has prided itself on its openness, its egalitarianism, its generosity, its welcoming the stranger, its sense of caring and sharing, are there so many people who see themselves as strangers in a strange land? Who makes it in this country? Who doesn't make it and why? Are there unspoken and unwritten expectations for success or for fitting in that make it impossible for some people to live with themselves and others with contentment or self-respect? What happens to the aged? the mentally ill? the physically handicapped? the slow learner? the drug or alcohol addict? the deviant?

The Mentally Ill

One out of every ten Americans is destined for a bed in a mental institution. Mental illness is on the rise, and this traditionally taboo subject can now be studied in the secondary school classroom through the adolescent novel.

But before we examine this novel, let's look at the attitudes toward mental illness that predominate in the contemporary world. In her article "TV's Cop Shows Are Crazy About Psychotics" (*The New York Times*, February 1, 1976), Caryl Rivers points out that the old genre of "cops and robbers" has been superseded by a new genre of "cops and crazies," a phenomenon she describes as the "Psycho of the Week Syndrome." She explains this phenomenon as follows:

1. "There is a need for action and violence in this medium which must somehow be satisfied week after week."
2. "Viewers find it reassuring to see a killer who is outright crazy—not at all like themselves."

3. "The stable of once-acceptable bad guys available to scriptwriters has dwindled considerably during this era of concern for minorities. Use of the old stereotypes—the menacing Black, the swarthy cunning Mexican, the castrating woman, the devious Oriental—is now taboo. The mental patient has become TV's latest scapegoat."

Apparently, it's all right to depict mentally ill people as villains, because they are not organized into a voting or protest group.

The implicit values beamed to watchers of such programs are that violence is needed to attract attention, that violence helps to sell products, that people need scapegoats and stereotypes, and that it is best to pick on those deviants who are not organized for legal action. Such programs also suggest that the supposedly healthy and functioning citizens of our society need not concern themselves with their oppressed, depressed, and downtrodden brothers and sisters because if they are crazy, it's probably their own fault; if they suffer and die, they probably deserve it.

All of the above ideas are directly opposed to the humanistic values needed by young people. They create fear rather than empathy, increase alienation and anomie by emphasizing the idea of the different, and permit society to escape any involvement in the fate of its less fortunate citizens. The result is denial of humanity rather than affirmation of life.

Traditional literature in its caricatures of "crazy people," such as the mad wife, the mad doctor, and the mad scientist, reflects society's unsympathetic attitude toward the mentally disturbed. The only mentally ill person I read about in high school was Mr. Rochester's wife in Charlotte Brontë's *Jane Eyre*, and my sympathies were all with Mr. Rochester and Jane. Poor Mr. Rochester, duped into a marriage with a mad girl of black ancestry, forced to live a hounded, haunted life because his innate nobility would not permit him to desert a madwoman, and, finally, blinded in his vain attempts to save her. And poor Jane, deprived of so much for so long and then thwarted at the altar by this same inconvenient madwoman.

One hundred years later, in her novel *Wide, Sargasso Sea*, Jean Rhys tells the story of *Jane Eyre* from the point of view of Mr. Rochester's mad wife, Bertha. While in the West Indies, Mr. Rochester marries Bertha only for her dowry, neglects and mistreats her, drives her mad, and then returns with her to England to claim his inheritance. Accustomed to a lush, warm, free climate, Bertha is unable to adjust to life on an English estate and is locked away in a frigid attic room. She is guarded by Grace Poole, a brutal woman who is alcoholic and totally unsympathetic.

The treatment given to Mr. Rochester's wife exemplifies one way that the mentally ill are treated, even today. Constant revelations in the newspapers of places such as Willowbrook or the Suffolk County Mental Institution (in February 1977, a doctor and social worker there filed suit because of the mistreatment and sexual abuse of young inmates) tell us that this way of dealing with the mentally ill is not just a thing of the Victorian Age.

What makes Rhys's book a particularly valuable humanistic statement is that we see mental illness from the point of view of the victim:

In this room I wake up early and lie shivering, for it is very cold. At last Grace Poole, the woman who looks after me, lights a fire with paper and sticks and lumps of coal . . . the flames shoot up and they are beautiful. I get out of bed and go close to watch them and to wonder why I have been brought here. For what reason? There must be a reason. . . . When I first came I thought it would be for a day, two days, a week perhaps. I thought that when I saw him and spoke to him I would be as wise as serpents, harmless as doves. "I give you all I have freely," I would say, "and I will not trouble you again if you will let me go." But he never came. . . .

There is one window high up—you cannot see out of it. . . . There is no looking-glass here and I don't know what I am like now. I remember watching myself brush my hair and how my eyes looked back at me. The girl I saw was myself, yet not quite myself. Long ago when I was a child and very lonely I tried to kiss her. But the glass was between us—hard, cold and misted over with my breath. Now they have taken everything away. What am I doing in this place and who am I? (pp. 179–180)

We no longer perceive Bertha merely as an obstacle to the happiness of Mr. Rochester and Jane. She is an imprisoned human being, so traumatized by her circumstances that she has slipped into madness, and so desperate that she must burn down her prison to escape.

The first contemporary, popular fictional work written from the point of view of the mad patient appeared in 1946, and because it was about one of those topics that nice people didn't talk about, it created a great stir. The book was Mary Jane Ward's *The Snake Pit*, the story of Virginia Cunningham, a beautiful, happily married writer who has a breakdown and is committed to Juniper Hill, an overcrowded, coldly efficient mental hospital. The book begins with her breakdown and recounts her slow recovery.

An important concept for young readers is the wide gap between what the mentally ill comprehend and what their warders perceive. Sometimes patients are scolded as if they are being recalcitrant about doing something when, instead, they are struggling to make sense of their confusion, which is heightened by poor living conditions, shock treatment, and constant medication. It seems as if they are not given the time or place for their heads to clear. Everything done to them after the initial commitment only intensifies the original breakdown that brought them to the hospital. Here, for example, is a description about the demoralizing bathing facilities:

You bathed twice a week. You lined up for the showers. There were two stalls for the forty or fifty women who lived in Ward Three and in order to speed things up you were told to soap yourself before you got under the water. You reached a hand into the spray and caught enough moisture for a lather and in that way you could spend your bath time in rinsing. You might even get completely rinsed before the nurse would tell you to get out. (p. 49)

Ward also wants the reader to think about the arbitrariness of the hospital committee that decides whether the inmates are sane and ready to leave. This committee lacks humor, tolerance, and the ability to accept creative and divergent responses to their questions. At one point in an interview, Virginia's flippancy with them prevents her discharge. What is significant for the reader is that in her exchanges she sounds as sane as the interview board.

Students should also note the primitive techniques used to shock disturbed patients back into health: cold packs for long periods of time, straitjackets, endless electric shocks, and long hours in tubs. Virginia thinks of the techniques that were used in primitive times for the mentally ill. They were lowered into snake pits on the theory that if snakes could make a sane person insane, they might drive an insane person back to sanity. This seems to be the dominant technique of this hospital. Patients have to be shocked back into sanity or remain ill forever. They are "shocked" rather than helped.

Juniper Hill Hospital is not an evil institution; it is an inadequate, inefficient one:

> There wasn't enough of anything at Juniper Hill. Not enough doctors, not enough nurses, not enough toilet paper, not enough food, not enough covers for cold nights. When the laundry did not get around to the wards in time there were not enough sheets and not enough pillow cases . . . there were not even enough beds. There wasn't enough of anything but patients.
>
> "There's no middle ground," Robert had said recently. "I fought this. I investigated private places all over. . . . I couldn't find a single private sanitarium that charged as little as my entire salary. . . ." (p. 175)

Miss Somerville's change from nurse to patient illustrates how thin the line is between sanity and insanity. Discussion of this change should help students to understand that the insane are not a different breed but people in many ways like themselves. As Miss Somerville's friend explains it:

> "She felt things too much. She tried to get some changes made. It was like beating her head against a stone wall. . . . A good nurse can't be a reformer. . . . A good nurse has to take orders and get along with what she has at hand." (p. 179)

Another work that makes a special plea for the mentally ill is Ken Kesey's *One Flew over the Cuckoo's Nest*, which has achieved popularity with the American public through the 1975 film starring Jack Nicholson. This work belongs to that category of adolescent novel which was written for the general public, has no teenage characters, and yet has been appropriated by the teenage audience as a meaningful book that speaks for them.

In the uncomplicated plot of this work, Randall P. McMurphy, a swaggering, humorous, zesty, freewheeling, unemployed itinerant laborer has himself transferred from the work farm to the local mental institution because he thinks he will not have to work so hard there for his food and board. As in classical tragedy, the hero himself sets in motion the events that lead to his demise.

In the mental institution McMurphy finds a group of demoralized men whose original illnesses have been exacerbated under the rule of Big Nurse, an unfeeling tyrant who rules over her charges with destructive authority. McMurphy rallies the ward and brings love, sex, life, and laughter into it. He is able to bring hope and salvation to some of the men—most notably to Chief Bromden, an Indian whose mental illness has been caused by two things: the treatment of the Indian by white America and a destructive mother who, in common with Big Nurse, was able to make men shrink in size while she could swell to monstrous proportions. A Christlike figure, McMurphy refuses to escape from the hospital when he has the chance and consequently is crucified through lobotomy.

Although the plot is simple enough, the symbolic nature of the book and the point of view require reader discussion. The narrator is Chief Bromden, a schizophrenic, and students may need help in understanding the unique nature of his subjective perceptions. Chief Bromden perceives the facts of his situation but not in a purely objective way; his terror gives figures such as Big Nurse and his mother mythic proportions. For example, Big Nurse is seen as an evil machine, cold and functional, capable of swelling to twice her size when angry. Therefore, the machine metaphor must be examined in relation to Big Nurse. Readers should look at statements such as: "She's got a bag full of—wheels and gears, cogs polished to a hard glitter, tiny pills that gleam like porcelain, needles, forceps, watchmaker's pliers, rolls of copper wire. . . ." (p. 42)

Racial questions, too, must be examined. Big Nurse has two black orderlies who do her dirty work. She has chosen them because they are consumed with hate which can be used to control the inmates. Critics have asked why these orderlies must be Black. One explanation is that Kesey, who is certainly not a racist, is dealing with what hate does to people; he assumes that people who are mistreated by society will, in turn, mistreat others. This idea need not be accepted as an absolute. The manifesto of the Attica Prison uprising and the contributions that survivors of the Jewish Holocaust made to society counter the theory that being hated automatically turns one into a hater.

The male-female relationships in Kesey's book need to be discussed because it is primarily women who are responsible for the mental illness of the men. Big Nurse is never explained clearly. Seemingly, her hatred of men is caused because of her anger at looking like a woman. "A mistake was made somehow in the manufacturing, putting those big, womanly breasts on what would of otherwise been a perfect work, and you can see how bitter she is about it." (p. 11).

Chief Bromden's mother destroyed his father; Harding's wife is unfaithful and diminishing (Harding says that the matriarchal society destroys men by castration); and Billy commits suicide out of fear that his mother will discover his sexuality. The only women who possess any humanity are the whores. Many readers today, influenced perhaps by the Women's Liberation Movement, feel that Kesey's depiction of women as either monsters or whores is sexist and outmoded. This is an important idea to discuss in class.

Another subject to explore is the treatment given to the mental patients in the cuckoo's nest. Both shock treatment and lobotomy must be defined and discussed, as well as contemporary use of oral medication and neurosurgery. Are these techniques evil, weapons to be used against patients, as Kesey perceives them? Mark Vonnegut, in *The Eden Express*, recounts his own schizophrenic episode and credits shock treatments with helping him to return to normality.

Students should also be helped to see that Kesey is using the mental institution as a metaphor for all of society, which imprisons and destroys those who will not conform. Students may have some knowledge of the fact that the Soviet Union uses mental institutions to imprison dissidents and nonconformers.

The cuckoo's nest is only one institution presided over by the Combine, a symbolic, inescapable controlling organization whose aim is to adjust the world to its specifications. Chief Bromden speculates that the Combine has invisible wires attached to people to control their behavior, and he thinks that whenever people start to see the truth of its operation, the Combine turns on the fog machine, which makes everything murky again. Students must be helped to see these perceptions as symbolic, representing a universal truth about the human condition, and as realistic, being the actual thoughts of a mentally ill person.

McMurphy, the hero, is set up by Kesey as the opposite of conforming man, who, as Chief Bromden puts it, are like eggs laid by commuter trains, living in identical row houses with identical wives and children. The Chief speculates that McMurphy escaped the Combine because he grew up wild, like a contemporary Huck Finn, never settled down in one place, and thus never gave institutions like schools the chance to condition him. Students should discuss Kesey's view of the socialization function of the school.

Students should discuss Kesey's belief that those in control of the institution are more disturbed and dangerous than the men they imprison. Consider the questions Kesey poses: What kind of "normal" person can prescribe and administer electric shock and lobotomy to another person? Which is more sane: to retreat from a hostile society (as Chief Bromden did), or to use hostility as a method of control (as Big Nurse does)? Is it more sane to be a lusty lover like McMurphy or to be filled with hate like Big Nurse and her orderlies? Students should note that, ultimately, the book examines the nature of societal control and makes a plea for laughter and sex, as the antidotes to sterility and hate.

In *I Never Promised You a Rose Garden* the reader gets a completely different view of mental illness and of the functioning and purpose of a mental institution. Teenaged Debby comes to the institution from a middle-class family that is genuinely concerned about the bizarre symptoms of her mental illness. They see the hospital not as a place of imprisonment but as a place for healing.

Students should note that the most positive people in this book are the women. Greenberg sees mental illness as a mystery, caused in part, but not completely, by family and society. There is no Big Nurse in this novel. Dr. Fried, Debby's analyst, is an extraordinary woman—a loving, intelligent, constructive guide to sanity. It is Dr. Fried who utters the title to Debby: "I never promised you a rose garden." Students should discuss the meaning of this statement, as well as how Dr. Fried is different from Big Nurse, who wants to keep her patients perpetually dependent.

Dr. Fried cannot promise Debby an easy, simple reality devoid of the pain and anxieties of normal life; she keeps reminding Debby of the difficulties and ugliness of life, and it is this insistence on reality that finally restores her to health. Students should compare Greenberg's geniune therapeutic community with the phony one in the Kesey work.

Particularly significant for students is the fact that Debby, no matter how demented her behavior, still has some degree of free will. It is the very exercise and acceptance of this quality of the human personality that are necessary for her recovery.

Students who are particularly interested in the subject of mental illness might be directed to the non-fiction work *Autobiography of a Schizophrenic Girl,* Anonymous, which bears a remarkable similarity to the Greenberg book. Frank Conroy in his foreword notes that he obtained the kind of experience from the diary which we would want young people to get from such works. He writes about the heroine:

Renee's courage inspired me. . . . She wrote her book very soon after her cure, imaginatively re-entering a world of which she had been terribly afraid. My own fears of reliving what had been a chaotic, frightening and confusing childhood seemed, after her example, fears I could not allow myself. She had faced her large demons; I would face my small ones. During four-and-a-half years of work on *Stop-Time* [Conroy's autobiography], years in which there were many violent and unexplained emotional storms battering me about, arising presumably from the . . . rediscovery of my childhood, I invoked Renee often, holding her in mind as a nervous traveler might hold a St. Christopher medal in his hand.

Conroy points to this book as an affirmation of the meaning of literature: one person writing something down to communicate with others of his/her kind—calling, like the Saroyan character, "hello out there" to other human beings who might also have the need for connection. He says:

. . . the book moved me because it was so clearly a triumph of faith, of faith in the act of writing. Beset by all sorts of difficulties . . . she nonetheless went on to write the book, giving us the sensations of schizophrenia more vividly and I suspect more honestly than anything I've read. As a human document Renee's book is without doubt inspirational. . . . She had faith in words, believing in their ability to carry inexpressible messages, trusting that what cannot be said can somehow be borne aloft by what is said. . . .

Conroy's remarks apply to much of good adolescent literature and to its value for young people: It says in writing what cannot be said aloud.

John Neufeld's *Lisa, Bright and Dark* deals with mental illness on a reading level appropriate for the junior high school.

When sixteen-year-old Lisa Shilling feels she is losing her mind, her parents refuse to believe that a child of theirs could be mentally ill. This kind of stigma is for other families, not theirs. They think that if they deny it, it will go away.

Lisa's classmates recognize her dangerous state of mind and decide to help her. The narrator, one of Lisa's friends, writes:

. . . most of Lisa's classmates were sympathetic. The word was out. People were as careful as they could be around her. We tried our best to adjust to her so as not to jar her any more than was necessary. We ignored her when she seemed to want this, and when she wanted friends, we were available. We didn't need to know why it was happening. It *was* happening and it needn't have happened to Lisa alone. It could have happened to any of us. (p. 36)

This statement, "it could have happened to any of us," is the ethical essence of Neufeld's book, the core of a worthwhile value system for young people, and therefore, the focus for class discussion. Lisa's friends try to understand her and to demonstrate their awareness of the arbitrary workings of fate.

One day, Lisa attacks a friend, and when she calms down, she tells her friend to call the police if this ever happens again. The narrator says:

But while I had promised Lisa I'd call the police if she ever went berserk again, I didn't want to. I kept hoping that when it came, if it came, it would be no worse than before. Something we could handle ourselves. . . . I hated the thought of showing Lisa off to outsiders. It seemed cruel and mean, and the very idea made me depressed. (p. 108)

This compassion is the kind of value young people should get from adolescent literature.

M. E. Kerr is a highly acclaimed writer of adolescent literature. In her book *Dinky Hocker Shoots Smack*, she writes about fifteen-year-old Tucker Wolff, who falls in love with fifteen-year-old Natalia Line, a girl who has been in a mental institution. "I'm not ashamed of it," Natalia tells Tucker, "but sometimes it's harder when everyone's looking at you for signs of something." (p. 40)

Like Lisa in the well-known work *David and Lisa*, Natalia rhymes when she gets nervous, and, like David and Lisa, Natalia and Tucker are able to help each other. Tucker's mother and Natalia's aunt exemplify the anti-humanistic attitude toward mental illness that we do not want young people to develop. Tucker's mother warns him:

"Tucker, Mrs. Hocker thinks you're a little too involved with the girl."
"So what?"
"You know the girl's background."
"Some of it. She's been in a special school," Tucker said.
"She's from a very, very bad background," his mother said. "It wasn't easy for Helen Hocker to tell me about it. It's her sister's child, you know."
"I'm not planning to marry her yet."
"Tucker, don't be flip! Natalia Line isn't your ordinary high-school girl. Her mother was a mental case and her father killed himself."
"Oh." Tucker let that information digest.
"Yes. She's been through a great deal in her fifteen years."
Tucker took a bite of his hamburger. He finally said, "Well, what's that got to do with what we do together?" (pp. 91–92)

Because of Mrs. Hocker's interference, Natalia is forced to return to her special school for a while. When she gets out, as a result of Tucker's friendship, she is finally able to reach a stage of self-acceptance that frees her to face the past. She tells Tucker:

"After my father killed himself, I couldn't talk for a long time. Then I could only talk if I rhymed."

"I guess you've been through a lot," Tucker said.

"He went through a lot, too," Natalia said. "That's the thing." (p. 156)

That really is the thing; Natalia has finally come of age through her acceptance and understanding of her father's suffering, as well as of her own.

The Boy Who Could Make Himself Disappear, by Kin Platt, is a particularly painful book about thirteen-year-old Roger, whose mother is so cruel to him that he can literally make himself disappear into schizophrenia. An important aspect of this book is its depiction of the antidotal effect of good influences on evil ones; in each chapter, the evil people are counterbalanced by good ones. As Roger retreats further and further into himself in response to his mother's cruelties, he also meets people who love and care about him: a beautiful model who lives in his apartment building, her fiancé, a hero of the French Resistance, a speech therapist, and a deformed little girl who gives the neglected boy her scarf. All of these people are on the side of life, constructive and compassionate, and the reader is left with the feeling that their love will restore Roger to health. Teenagers reading this book exclaim, "I just hate that mother," and it is through the contrast between her and the loving people that a value structure emerges that emphasizes the redemptive powers of love.

At the end of the book, Roger's mother has been imprisoned for her mistreatment of him, and Roger lies in a hospital in a schizophrenic state. His father visits him and offers only a check; Roger Tunnell, the fiancé of the model, comes and holds Roger in his arms. He holds him and talks to him, and finally a tear escapes from the boy's eye. The author leaves the reader with the feeling that the older Roger, true to his last name, will be the boy's tunnel back to mental health.

Another important work about mental illness is Mary McCracken's *A Circle of Children*, included on the American Library Association's list of "Best Books for Young Adults, 1974." It is the true story of a suburban woman who left her husband after her children had grown up and found new meaning in her life through teaching emotionally disturbed children. She describes how these children are helped by a constructive, therapeutic school situation, and young people like this story for the same reason they like the Kin Platt book: It emphasizes the healing power of love and the necessity for acceptance of diversity. Although these truths may seem like clichés to teachers, they are not clichés to adolescents, who need to have these ideas affirmed and reaffirmed.

In Sylvia Plath's *The Bell Jar*, the reader sees the horror and fear induced by incarceration and shock treatment. In *One Flew over the Cuckoo's Nest*, mental illness is attributed to all of the combined, repressive forces in society, including self-righteous, domineering females. But in *The Bell Jar*, Esther, the victim, *is* a female, and her problems are caused by *both* the men and women of her society because there is no room in it for the diversity of the artist. Esther's breakdown results from her feelings of being different, of being an outsider, of being unable to function as an individual woman in the clichéd feminine role assigned her by society, and of having the intellectual avenues she wishes to take closed to her.

Even though the collective position of women in American society has changed somewhat since Plath's book was written, there are still parental and societal pressures to conform. Students may note that many social dropouts of the 1960s such as those depicted in Mark Vonnegut's *The Eden Express*, were attempting to escape from predetermined roles when they went to live on communal farms in remote parts of America.

The feeling of being an outsider is common during adolescence, and students should discuss this feeling in terms of Esther's experiences in *The Bell Jar.* To the outside world, Esther is a winner. She is a prize-winning Smith College student who is awarded a guest editorship on *Mademoiselle* magazine, but none of these honors changes her negative feelings about herself and the world in which she feels trapped. The analyst to whom her mother takes her succeeds only in making her feel more alienated. This is how she describes him:

> Doctor Gordon's features were so perfect he was almost pretty.
> I hated him the minute I walked in through the door.
> I had imagined a kind, ugly, intuitive man looking up and saying "Ah!" in an encouraging way, as if he could see something I couldn't, and then I would find words to tell him how I was so scared, as if I were being stuffed farther and farther into a black, airless sack with no way out. . . .
> And then, I thought, he would help me, step by step, to be myself again.
> But Doctor Gordon wasn't like that at all. He was young and good-looking, and I could see right away he was conceited. (p. 105)

Esther looks at a picture of his family and thinks:

> . . . how could this Doctor Gordon help me anyway, with a beautiful wife and beautiful children and a beautiful dog haloing him like the angels on a Christmas card. (p. 106)

Doctor Gordon takes the easy way out and gives Esther shock treatments, which deepen her feelings of alienation and lead to her suicide attempt. She is sent to a mental institution and is seemingly cured. She returns to college, but her feelings of alienation continue because of society's attitude toward the mentally ill:

> Doctor Nolan had said, quite bluntly, that a lot of people would treat me gingerly, or even avoid me, like a leper with a warning bell. My mother's face floated to mind, a pale, reproachful moon, at her last and first visit to the asylum since my twentieth birthday. A daughter in an asylum! I had done that to her. Still, she had obviously decided to forgive me. (p. 193)

Students should discuss the ideas in this last quote, particularly Esther's guilt about what she has done to her mother by getting ill; whether or not Esther should feel guilty; and why the statement, "she had obviously decided to forgive me," is ironic.

Students also should discuss the character of Buddy, Esther's old boy friend, who, when he visits her at the asylum says, "I wonder who you'll marry now, Esther. Now you've been . . ." (p. 197)

The ending of Plath's novel also has an important message for young people. At the funeral of her friend and fellow inmate Joan, who hanged herself, Esther says: "I took a deep breath and listened to the old brag of my heart. I am, I am, I am."[1] (p. 199) No more wonderful message than this can be given to young people.

The Dying

Until recently, death was one of the taboos of public education and when dealt with, usually was approached on the rarefied, spiritual plane of John Donne's "Death Be Not Proud" or Dylan Thomas's "Do Not Go Gentle into that Good Night." Death was looked at from the outside but never from the point of view of the person who was dying. Other than in wars and automobile accidents, the possibility that death might occur to secondary school students was carefully avoided. Since 1970, a number of books have appeared that describe the feelings of the dying person and deal with death honestly, compassionately, and realistically (even, at times, to the point of being too clinical). These books have enabled young readers to empathize with the problems of the person facing death, to understand what it means to suddenly be thrust into the outsider role, to face the gulf between those who are continuing and those who are ending.

Gunnel Beckman's *Admission to the Feast* does exactly what adolescent literature should do for young people: it reaffirms the beauty of being human even while it details the tragedy of human finiteness. In this short novel, an entire world is depicted with poetic economy by a nineteen-year-old girl who is dying of leukemia. The book takes the form of a letter that she, Annika, writes to a friend to keep herself from falling apart as she tries to understand what has happened to her and why. She describes the shock of aloneness—the immediate feeling of being outside society, the terrible loneliness of the outsider. When she leaves the hospital, immediately after receiving the news, she finds, to her amazement, that everything but herself seems to be the same:

. . . my marble eyes saw again. And I saw and saw and saw . . . the street the park the buses the insurance company sign the clock the church tower the quays the tomatoes in the grocer's shop the sky the airplane drawing white smoke words above the station building . . .

People . . . people walking quickly and people walking slowly . . . old people young people . . . two policemen wearing fur caps walking together with their hands behind their backs . . . people carrying bags briefcases school satchels sticks children . . .

Just as it had been an hour ago. . . .

I was sick in the gutter, but no one took any notice, except an errand boy on a bicycle who grinned slightly. He probably thought I was pregnant. (pp. 25–27)

Annika flees to a cottage in the country, and there, she tries to come to terms with the past. She thinks about her boyfriend, Jacob, with whom she

---

1. The biographical essay about the life of Sylvia Plath at the end of the Bantam edition is an important aid to students in understanding the societal pressures leading to her own and her heroine's breakdowns.

has had many intellectual quarrels about politics. As she thinks about death, these squabbles seem unimportant, and all she can write to her friend is, "I do love him." Students should discuss the irony of how imminent death puts quarrels and petty problems into perspective.

Annika also begins to think about the meaning of "identity." Because she has always admired and wanted to be like her independent, physician mother, everyone has always taken it for granted that she would become a doctor. Now, she asks herself, "But what did I want myself—did I want to be a doctor? Was I suited to that? How could I know that?" (p. 59)

As she ponders the experiences of her short life, she comes to realize, gratefully, that the people closest to her have been good people and that she has been loved. Gradually, she attains a remarkable maturity, and as she waits for Jacob to come for her she writes:

> I was terribly scared as well as fearfully anxious to hear his voice. Now my solitude was over. And I probably wouldn't have managed much longer. But at the same time, I had reached a kind of calm during these last few days, had scrambled up out of a dark hole full of insane despair and had begun to function almost normally. And now, everything was to begin again, but much worse. For now, it wasn't only my own despair, but theirs too. (p. 112)

What can young people learn from this book? They can learn about the need to reflect, which, unfortunately, Annika does only in the face of death; about the need to appreciate those who love us; about the need to fulfill ourselves in our own terms while life still remains.

Norma Klein's *Sunshine* is a moving book about a young person who, paradoxically, discovers that she is dying at the moment when she feels that she has finally begun to live. An outsider long before death marks her, Kathryn Hayden marries at sixteen to escape from a mother who doesn't love her. Pregnant, she leaves her husband and meets Sam, the fine young man with whom she spends the last years of her life. After having the baby and knowing for the first time in her life the joy of a beautiful family relationship, she finds that she has cancer.

Klein does not sentimentalize the sadness of this situation, which is based on an actual case:

> Am I not going to see my baby grow up? I never thought of that before this second. No, why would God do that? He doesn't need me, why should he bother? I remember this poem we learned in school by Edgar Allan Poe about this girl, Annabel Lee. She dies and he said the gods were jealous of them. Are you jealous of us, God? Don't be. We fight, we have problems, we don't have much money. Sam doesn't even have a job. You don't have to be jealous of us. (p. 54)

Like Annika, Kathryn feels she must protect those she loves from the full, horrible knowledge of her illness for as long as she can. When her sister visits and looks at her new crutches, Kathryn says, "I can see all those questions in Pat's eyes, the way she looks at my crutches. She wants to know, but doesn't. I don't think I'll tell her. It would just be putting a burden on her and she's too young for that." (p. 102)

Kathryn finds after a while that the attempt to participate in normal activities as if nothing were wrong makes her feel self-conscious and more alone. The description of the dance she goes to with Sam and her sister gives students an excellent picture of what it means to be an outsider:

> Of course I can't dance! It isn't that I thought I could, but sitting here for three hours watching is more depressing than I thought it would be. It's not just jealousy. I like Sam to dance, I like watching him. I know he loves me, but I know he likes women and he's appealing to them. He ought to dance, it's good for him. And I like watching Pat too. But at the same time it really makes me hurt, makes me want to cry. I don't think that's silly. I love to dance and I think it's a shame that I can't. . . . (p. 105)

As the illness progresses, Kathryn gets moody, depressed, and irritable, and Sam, too, goes through unpleasant mood swings. Finally, she refuses to take any more medication and Sam, not understanding, leaves her. Kathryn writes:

> Night time is overtaking me
> as daylight falls behind.
> My life is slowly losing
> the sparkle and shine.
> A life filled with promises
> and empty bottles of wine.
> This loneliness is beginning to
> encloak me,
> I've lost all sense of time.
> Self-pity overwhelms me,
> I've begun to lose my mind.
> White death is overtaking me
> and daylight falls behind. (p. 108)

Is this unnecessarily morbid stuff? Shouldn't the schools be a refuge from the negative aspects of life? Maybe they should be, but they certainly are not. Life inside the school is inescapably connected to the outside world. Teachers can adopt one of two positions: either the "don't-look-and-it-won't-hurt" position, or the one espoused by Stein in Joseph Conrad's *Lord Jim* — that in order to survive you must immerse yourself in the destructive element. Ignorance is not bliss; it is dangerous. The only way to live is through understanding and confrontation.

Sunshine depicts not only human misery but also the extraordinary heights of love and joy of which people are capable. Rather than depressing the reader, the book leaves him/her with a euphoric sense of the beauty of the human spirit.

Marcia Friedman in *The Story of Josh* has written a non-fiction account of her twenty-one-year-old son's death from cancer. By placing his death in the framework of classical tragedy, she offers secondary-school students a valuable way of viewing contemporary ordeals. Teachers and students are accustomed to thinking of the deaths of such figures as Oedipus, Antigone, Hamlet, and Macbeth as tragic, but Friedman shows that the death of a contemporary young man can also be seen this way. She writes:

> In classical drama, a tragedy was a story of a seemingly most fortunate protagonist who suffered a frightful end as the result of a single flaw. Whatever

the flaw, it set in motion a series of events that, once initiated, led inexorably and irreversibly to the destruction of the central figure of the drama. The purpose of the tragedies was two-fold; they were cathartic, as the viewers identified and empathized with the figure in the play. And they were educational in that they revealed some of the complex interrelationships between action and its consequences, and how the people caught up in them rose to the challenges and were destroyed but not defeated by them. Not every sad story of death is a tragedy. To qualify for that status it must have universality and grandeur; the protagonist must rise above mere extinction and, in losing, somehow win. I do believe my son Josh was such a figure. (p. 5)

Students should discuss the above definition of tragedy, particularly the idea that the "protagonist must rise above mere extinction and, in losing, somehow win," which is at the core of every inspiring story, whether it be that of Anne Frank, Kathryn Hayden, Josh Friedman, or Helen Keller. The paradox of "winning in losing" needs to be explained—what is lost contrasted with what is won.

In this work, the parents express resentment against "medical evaluations" versus "human evaluations." They plead for humane treatment of Josh as an individual rather than as a case or as a mass of symptoms. Friedman writes: "Death is the only recognized enemy. But we—Josh, Leib, and I—learned bitterly what most of us instinctively know is the real truth: that dying is the real terror and death can be a welcome friend." (p. 13)

Friedman's depiction of Josh's growing alienation from his peers takes the reader into the world of the outsider:

. . . Josh felt surprisingly good that day, but the boys were simply unable, as I had noticed with so many other young people throughout the development of Josh's illness, to make natural contact with him. The short conversations were awkward and stilted. Oh, they were polite. They spoke a few meaningless sentences with him, but basically they avoided him. I had seen this so many times before; it was as though the ill person had become in some way ritually impure and was almost taboo. Whether it is out of embarrassment or fear or guilt, I do not know. There is, however, a pervasive pattern of treating terminally ill people almost as though they don't exist. They become, in effect, nonpersons. Perhaps this avoidance makes the healthy feel less personally threatened by death. (p. 234)

Understanding how the outsider's world looks from the inside can help students to become less afraid of this world and more humane in their responses to it. Josh's way of living in the face of death also offers students meaningful definitions of such abstractions as courage, love, and dignity. Friedman writes: "My son was courage, love, and dignity. . . . He taught those of us willing to learn how to die." (p. 279)

Paige Dixon's *May I Cross Your Golden River?* is another excellent adolescent novel about the subject of teenage death. Eighteen-year-old Jordan Phillips seems to have everything to live for: a loving family, a girl friend, scholastic and athletic ability. Suddenly, strange symptoms start to appear when he plays tennis; his wrists seem weak and his knee buckles. He discovers that he has the same rare muscular-vascular disease that killed baseball star Lou Gehrig.

After his family finds out about his condition, Jordan has his first intimations of how it feels to be an outsider. When his mother looks at him, he thinks, "She'll always be looking at me like that now, with the anxiety not quite hidden." For the first time he feels like crying. Jordan and his brothers also become uncomfortable with each other. They don't know how to proceed, and Jordan tells them, "Don't hover around waiting for me to collapse, okay?"

Students should discuss the guilt that the victim seems to feel. Seeing new lines on his mother's face, Jordan is angry that he is responsible for this family crisis. He thinks: "It was bad enough to face it himself, without making everybody else suffer." All of their kindnesses are particularly difficult to bear.

Jordan's separation from society proceeds quickly. He can no longer do any of the things that he loves, like skiing and playing tennis. He goes to a dance and finds that he cannot dance; he loses his girl friend; he drops out of college. He contemplates suicide, but cannot do it. Students should discuss Jordan's feelings about suicide, described in the following passage:

> For some reason that he couldn't quite define, he knew he could not do it. It wasn't fear; it seemed preferable to die a quick, self-chosen death than to wait around for his body to run down and give out. It would have more dignity, more an element of choice. One of the things he hated most about his disease was the helpless feeling that he was being kicked around by something entirely out of his control. And yet, he couldn't bear to cut life short before he had to. The doctors had said he might live several years. In several years he could see Terry's child get started as a person. He could see how Alex's marriage went. He could read a lot, and with any luck, ride around, see things, maybe even travel if he could get somebody to go with him. Grimly he saw himself in a wheelchair being pushed up a plane ramp, . . . It would be lousy and he'd hate it, but he didn't hate the idea enough yet to kill himself. Once you pressed that trigger, you couldn't change your mind. (pp. 123–124)

Even under circumstances as extreme as Jordan's, life is good and can be sweet. Jordan dies in the midst of his loving family—not isolated in a ward somewhere but in his own bed; and somehow, the presence of so much love makes this tragic death bearable.

Dr. Elizabeth Kübler-Ross has written: "Dealing with death at an early age means opportunity to evaluate one's character, courage, values, and willingness to face the hurt that comes with growth."[2] Through the study of adolescent literature that deals with death, young people will be better able to face this "hurt".

The Physically Different

Good adolescent literature dealing with the subject of physical disability or difference teaches young people that the physically different

---

2. Charles S. Adler, Gene Sanford, Sheila Morrissey Adler, *We Are But a Moment's Sunlight*. Pocket Books, 1976, 249 pp., Intro.

have feelings that are not necessarily different from their own and, further, that there are helpful and harmful ways to treat physically different people. President Carter's appointment of a legless Vietnam War veteran to head the Veterans' Administration demonstrates dramatically to the public that a disabled person can still play a significant role in society. We want young people to share this humanistic perception of the so-called outsider—to perceive difference as an asset to society rather than a liability.

In Mildred Lee's *The Skating Rink*, fifteen-year-old Tucker Faraday stammers so badly that he has almost given up talking and is referred to by his family and the kids in his school as The Dummy. The very day Tuck decides to quit school because of his speech problems, he meets Pete Degley, who is building a roller-skating rink near Tuck's home. Degley sees in Tuck something that nobody has seen before: a fine athletic body plus the capacity for hard work. Degley trains Tuck to perform on skates with Degley's wife, Lily, and, on opening night, Tuck comes into his own:

There was not a sound from the audience till Tuck lifted Lily and swung her at the level of his outstretched arms, unconsciously counting the bars, gradually lowering her till her feet touched the floor and she was skating beside him. Howls, cheers, stamping, and madly crackling palms brought Tuck to himself.

When the overhead lights sprang on and he saw the faces his numbness continued for a second, then feeling poured through him. He felt like God. As if nothing ever again would be beyond his grasp. They were pounding and screaming for more—those who had ridiculed him year after dreary year. His awareness sharpened to an ecstasy that was almost pain. He had done it. He, Tucker Holland Faraday. He had made Mr. Degley's dream come true. (pp. 116–117)[3]

This book, with its hopeful fairy-tale ending, teaches students that an outsider need not stay an outsider, that the ugly duckling can turn into a swan. It also shows that there are many different ways of belonging and contributing to society. If one does not do well in school, this does not mean that one is destined to a life of failure and rejection. Young people need to understand that book-learning is just one way of knowing and that there are other kinds of abilities—such as art, music, athletics, construction—that are equally significant and necessary in our society. The academic outsider can achieve vitally needed community recognition and acceptance through numerous non-intellectual activities.

In Kin Platt's *Hey Dummy*, the Dummy of the title can say only one sound, "Ahhhh." Because he is different, his peers delight in persecuting him by taking away his hat, tripping him, making fun of him. When a little girl is assaulted in the park, the Dummy is automatically blamed. A lynch mob forms, and Neil, a seemingly normal boy with a big conscience, tries to hide the Dummy.

During the flight from mob, family, and authorities, Neil suddenly remembers something that happened when he was only one year old. His parents were talking about their firstborn child who had died:

---

3. *The Skating Rink* has been made into a fine film by Learning Corporation of America.

"If only the other one had lived," I heard my father say. "Danny would have been a fine boy."

"Well, we've got this one now," my mother answered. "Maybe the Lord is punishing us for our sins."

I couldn't believe it! I couldn't have been more than a year old at the time, and I swear I was in my crib when they were talking. It cleared up the mystery anyway. They hated me because I wasn't the firstborn. They never forgave me for living in place of my older brother who died when he was five! (pp. 162–163)

This sudden recognition plus the trauma of the flight turns Neil into a dummy. Neil realizes that his empathy for the Dummy that he helped to escape is based on his always being treated like an outsider in his family. This somber book ends with Neil's thoughts:

The more I thought about everything, the more it seemed to make sense to be like *him*. No reason why there couldn't be two Dummies, is there? No brains, no feelings. I'm going to try that. Instead of turning on, I'm turning off.

I found out whatever I got it's not neurological. I heard one of the smiling people tell that to another smiley. I'm not even mentally retarded, for Pete's sake. I got some kind of altered personality due to an existing anxiety state from unknown, psychogenic, I think, causes. (p. 169)

Physical appearance that deviates from the norm is another cause of alienation and isolation from society. Obesity, in particular, is a problem for adolescents. Paula Danziger in *The Cat Ate My Gymsuit* writes about thirteen-year-old Marcy Lewis, who hates her appearance. She says: "All my life I've thought that I looked like a baby blimp with wire-frame glasses and mousy brown hair. Everyone always said that I'd grow out of it, but I was convinced that I'd become an adolescent blimp with wire-frame glasses, mousy brown hair, and acne." (p. 7)

The problems of her physical appearance are increased by an insensitive father who says: "Why do I have to have a daughter who is stupid and so fat? I'll never get you married off." (p. 26)

Marcy has only one friend, a popular pretty girl, and so Marcy refers to the two of them as "Beauty and the Blimp." The title of the book refers to one of the excuses Marcy gives the gym teacher to avoid changing into her gymsuit in front of the other girls.

A new, progressive teacher comes to school and each of her methods helps Marcy. On the first day, she asks the students to write a paper about what communication means to them. Marcy thinks:

Dumb teacher. . . . What does a blimp know about communication? How could she know what it feels like to be so fat and ugly that you're ashamed to get into a gymsuit or to talk to skinny people? Who wants to say, "This is my friend, the Blimp?"

But the teacher, Ms. Finney, persists in her quest for communication. She helps her students get over embarrassment by openly discussing herself. She forms a club named Smedly in which the students really start to talk to each other and to communicate. When they have to introduce other students, Joel Anderson says about Marcy: "She has a nice smile." Marcy thinks:

I couldn't believe it. I'd been sure he was going to say something like "This is Marcy Lewis. She's a real creep and doesn't know how to talk." Or "This is Marcy. She might even look human if she didn't look like a Mack truck." I wasn't used to anyone saying anything nice, except Nancy and my mother because they had to. (p. 23)

Ms. Finney is fired because of her progressive techniques, and Marcy and Joel lead the fight for her reinstatement. Things haven't changed dramatically by the end of the book, but Marcy is now able to perceive herself, not as a blimp, but as a soaring, flying helium balloon. Involvement in a worthwhile cause has helped her to see beyond her physical appearance. The important message for teenagers is that a fat person can still be perceived as a valuable human being.

Dinky Hocker Shoots Smack, discussed in Section 1 of this chapter, also deals with teenagers who are outsiders because of being overweight. Dinky is a girl who envelops herself in layers of fat and constantly eats herself into a state of lethargy. She hides behind ugly, bizarre clothing, and her philosophy of life is summed up in the statement: "The meek inherit the shaft." (p. 145) She sees that those who do not speak up are ignored, as she is ignored by her mother, whose major interest in life is working to rehabilitate drug addicts.

Finally, in order to force her parents to see her needs, Dinky writes "Dinky Hocker Shoots Smack" all over the sidewalks and buildings outside of the civic auditorium where her mother is being honored for service to the community. By the end of the book, the reader feels that Dinky's parents are going to help their daughter to become a healthy, normal, functioning teenager.

This book emphasizes the fact that fat outsiders are not to blame for their plight and pleads for compassion on the part of those who view such outsiders with scorn.

A real-life example of somebody who was mocked and reviled because of her appearance can be found in Myra Friedman's biography of the singer, Janis Joplin, *Buried Alive*. Average-looking as a child, Joplin's change in appearance during adolescence caused her to be treated as an outsider:

As a blight on an adolescence that was already rocky enough, Janis lost what prettiness she had in those ways so judged by children. Her chubbiness bloated to a hefty bigness; she developed a terrible skin condition, far beyond anything that could be termed a teen-ager's siege of acne. It was severe enough to require sanding. Jack Smith . . . was certain that her skin condition did not really affect her popularity, but that Janis herself withdrew, self-conscious and ashamed. Depression and conflict can themselves contribute to physical change. . . . Janis would have needed a charm of incalculable dimensions to compensate and a granite-strong inner security. She had neither. Moreover, her assets—her intelligence and talent—were handicaps in the mindless monochrome of Port Arthur. (pp. 20–21)

Because she couldn't look like one of the "proper ladies" of Port Arthur, Janis became loud, crude, and boisterous. She began to hang around with a group of five boys who were more adventurous and less conforming than most of her peers. Because she couldn't become the little doll figure admired by the town culture, she made herself into a freak. She dressed peculiarly, would yell out, "well, fuck you baby," embarrassing even the boys in the group, and would go out of her way to "freak out" people.

Her persecution in high school was horrendous, actually worse than any such incidents in adolescent fiction:

> Janis became as hated as an epidemic of horse fever. The students threw things at her, they mocked her, they called her names, of which "pig" was the favorite. "Janis would laugh," Karleen told me, "you know, playing along to get along. But she'd go home and cry."
>
> Just why the assault was so savage is complex. Karleen intimated that Janis appeared to draw the hatred to her, behaving as if she didn't care what people thought, although it was obvious to Karleen that she cared a great deal. . . .
>
> "She dressed sloppy," Terry Owens agreed, "she was overweight, she didn't wear makeup, just refused to do anything to compromise . . . like anybody who's different—or an *oddball*—or a *freak*—or a *creep*—she was persecuted. (p. 23)

In every high school there are kids who are ridiculed as creeps. Discussion of passages such as the above may result in more humane treatment of such people and in hope for them to turn into swans.

John Neufeld's *Twink* deals with another kind of physical disability, cerebral palsy. Sixteen-year-old Harry Walsh's new stepsister, Twink, has cerebral palsy. Harry finds himself thinking about things that never occurred to him before: When did Twink first realize "she was different from other kids, and what about being a girl and being different?" (p. 33)

Twink is sent to a special school and makes her first real visit home at the age of eight, "a tiny, undernourished-looking kid huddled in steel and leather, or standing surrounded by shiny metal that was cruel to the eye." (p. 88)

One night the family decides to take Twink to a restaurant. The family puts her into a pretty dress, wheels her into a restaurant, and takes a corner table because of the fear that people might be upset by seeing them feed Twink. (p. 89) Here is an excellent description of how the entire family are made to feel like outsiders:

> The maître d' appeared from nowhere. Had we finished? Would we mind hurrying a little? We were making it difficult for other members and guests to dine comfortably.
>
> We had been so intense in our corner we hadn't noticed how many people there were around us, sitting in silence, staring. I looked around and nearly died from embarrassment. Then I got mad. . . .
>
> But then, of course, we couldn't just slip out. We had to weave through all the tables, pushing Twink's chair. I'll never forget the look on Mother's face as she threaded her way through members and guests, memorizing every face in the room, drawing up lists of whole families never to see or speak with again. ((pp. 89–90)

The family has to send Twink to a variety of schools. Some of them close for lack of funds; others give her poor care. Finally they find a good school where the emphasis is on developing "that part of the child not damaged: his brain."

But Twink's condition continues to deteriorate, and Harry finds himself becoming more of an outsider, too. Twink's disease forces him to constantly reevaluate his own ways of perceiving the universe. He says, about God: "For myself, looking at Twink, it's impossible to believe in Him at all. He must be so cruel, if He exists, to do this to her. . . . If there is a God, I say He's a rotten one. . . ." (pp. 105–106)

There is no happy ending here. Twink goes through a series of torturing operations, which don't help her but leave her blind. But her family is held together by love and admiration for her courage. In common with all of the already mentioned books on physical disability, this book makes a plea for us to empathize with the unfortunate outsider.

The Incarcerated

Another important category of outsider described in contemporary adolescent literature is the incarcerated. Many young people are institutionalized for no other crime than running away from destructive families or playing truant from school.

Run, Shelley, Run is the story of a girl who comes under the category of "Person in Need of Supervision" (PINS). The book is based on the research of Gertrude Samuels, a staff writer and photographer for *The New York Times,* who has covered the subject of juvenile justice (or the lack of it) in courts throughout the United States.

When a young person is categorized PINS, he automatically becomes an outsider to mainstream society. Shelley is institutionalized because her alcoholic mother has remarried a brutal man who doesn't want Shelley in his home after she informs her mother of his sexual advances to her. Each time Shelley is imprisoned she runs away, and each time she runs, time is added to her sentence until she is sentenced to endure mistreatment and incarceration until she reaches the age of eighteen for no other crime than running.

Shelley's history reads like a classic set of directions on how to produce an outsider:

> Shelley never knew her own father. She was, by the age of ten, left to play on the street after school, till Mama got home from work. Late at night very often, too. The cops and Welfare investigator reported that Mama was an alcoholic. They warned Mama, in front of Shelley, to give up the bottle if she didn't want to give up Shelley. (pp. 23–24)

Readers should note the beauty and wonderful possibilities of Shelley as a young child, and how these possibilities are eventually almost destroyed through the systematic brutalization by society:

> At ten, Shelley wanted desperately to do four things: to write a book, because she wasn't named for a great poet for nothing; to become a nurse; to grow a tree in the back yard of their house on West Eighty-Fourth Street; to wean Mama from the bottle. Of the four, the tree seemed the easiest to realize. (p. 24)

By the end of the book, Shelley has been gang-raped, forced to endure lesbian advances in prison, shackled and placed for long periods in solitary confinement because of her attempts to escape. The judge who finally has Shelley released finds her, at the age of sixteen, in solitary confinement:

Wall was what the five-by-eight-foot rectangular, barred cell, stripped of furniture and adornments, had plenty of. It was made of grayish cinder block; the floor was bare; there was not even a bed or cot. A pinewood platform extending from a wide wall served as bed and desk and chair. The platform had no mattress or blankets, and no pillow (to preclude destruction) during the day; two blankets were provided at night. No books or reading matter allowed. No writing allowed. No clothes—other than the pajamas in which she was transferred. Nothing to hear or listen to, except perhaps the sound of a girl's voice—her own. (p. 124)

Shelley continues to be an outsider even after her release from prison. Her peers treat her like a freak, and she finds that during her years of incarceration she "had fallen so far behind her peers that she had to go into remedial classes for all ages." (p. 148) Despite her sadness at being an outcast, Shelley seems to grow, and the book ends on a note of optimism about her chances of becoming a happy and constructive member of society.

Hatter Fox, by Marilyn Harris, has a heroine who, like Shelley, has been turned by a hostile society into a seemingly wild and vicious girl who has declared war on the world. An Indian, she is treated like a contemptible outcast by both the whites and Indians of Santa Fe.

Hatter has always been an outsider. She has no memory of her parents. Her first memories are of living with a strange old Indian woman in a hogan. When the woman dies, Hatter wanders until she finds an Indian family that takes her in. They unjustly blame her when one of their children falls off a cliff, and as punishment they abandon her, tied down beside the corpse.

Finally "rescued," Hatter is sent to a missionary school, where the white man's religion becomes a new source of torture and where punishment for any infraction of the unfathomable rules is to be hung naked from a tree by the wrists and ankles, beaten, and left suspended there. Hatter escapes from the school and makes her way to town, where she lives by prostitution, escapes through drugs, and eventually ends up in prison.

In *Run, Shelley, Run*, it is a compassionate woman judge who rescues the victimized young person; in *Hatter Fox*, it is a young white doctor, favored by society with everything, who uses the advantages of his position to help a less fortunate human being. When Hatter stabs the doctor at their first encounter in prison, he cannot ignore the desperation inherent in this irrational act; he interprets her attack as a plea for help or death. He traces Hatter to a prison for girls in Santa Fe, where he discovers that for "rehabilitative purposes," she is kept doubled up in dog cages in the snow, restrained for hours in solitary confinement, force-fed to prevent her from dying, and repeatedly raped by the brutal attendants. The doctor, a secure, middle-class New Englander, is so horrified by this world beyond his experience that he stays at the prison to help her. Unfortunately, in his determination to make Hatter an "insider," a person with his own values, the doctor fails to comprehend her unique identity; and his insistence on a certain form of behavior eventually results in her death.

Teachers must help students understand the ironic ending of Harris's book and the meaning of responsibility—responsibility for the awesome power for life and death, good and evil, that all people have over someone else. Students should discuss why people who are unaffected go out of their ways to help the less fortunate. In both *Run, Shelley, Run* and *Hatter Fox*, it is the responsible "insider" who has the power and desire to help the outsider—to reclaim a seemingly hopeless victim of social abuse through love, understanding, and humane treatment. It is the person who, like Marlow in Conrad's *Lord Jim*, cannot turn his eyes away from human misery and who comprehends the relationship that exists between the haves and the have-nots.

Another book dealing with the incarceration of a young person is David Elliott's *Listen to the Silence*. Timmy is sent for observation to a mental hospital by his foster family because he masturbates. He was supposed to stay only overnight for a mental examination, but he is forgotten there and so his sentence becomes open-ended.

Darrell, one of the older boys there, explains to Timmy that most of the incarcerated boys are not crazy. Describing succinctly the fate of the American outsider he says:

> You see, Timmy, most of the rest of the kids here are just confused, lonely, or afraid. They've been in orphanages, homes, and observation centers all their lives and will continue to be until they're old enough for jail or until they crack completely and have to spend forever in a K building somewhere. . . . The ones in here are the professionally rejected. No one wants them and no one ever will. (p. 125)

This book does not end on an optimistic note. Timmy leaves with a new set of foster parents, but the author implies that no one will love him enough to save him.

The Addicted

Another category of outsider we find in adolescent literature is the addict. The dimension of this problem in the United States is especially severe and it seems to be increasing. Note the excerpt below from a news story:

School Study Calls 28% of Teen-Agers 'Problem' Drinkers

RALEIGH, N.C. Nov. 20 (AP)—A national study has found that 28 percent of the nation's teen-agers are problem drinkers.

The survey of 13,000 youths in 450 schools around the country found that 28 percent reported that they were drunk at least four times in the last year or that their drinking got them in trouble with peers or superiors at least twice in the last year.

The study said that this behavior constituted a drinking problem. . . . *The New York Times*, 11/21/75.

A recent report on the 19th International Conference of Young People in Alcoholics Anonymous (which drew almost 1,000 recovered alcoholics from the United States and Canada) stated: "Their ages ranged from 17 to 40, they came from small towns and large and every conceivable economic and educational background. The middle class predominated, as it does in A.A. and in the nation."[4]

A good, non-fictional background book written for teenagers is Jim Haskins's *Teen-Age Alcoholism.* Haskins writes:

> By the early 1970s, teen-age alcoholism was a serious problem and society recognized it. But by the time people had thoroughly digested the idea of a teen-age drinking epidemic, studies were beginning to show a sizable number of problem drinkers among adolescents and even younger kids. Nine-year-olds are missing school because they are too hung over to attend. Ten-year-olds are sneaking bottles from their parents' liquor closets. Eleven-year-olds take thermoses of vodka and orange juice or scotch and milk for lunch. Twelve-year-olds are admitted to hospital emergency rooms vomiting blood. Today, there are some 500,000 alcoholics between the ages of ten and nineteen, and it is estimated that one out of every fifteen young people today will eventually become an alcoholic. (p. 42)

Sarah T., by Robin S. Wagner, is the first adolescent novel to deal specifically with teenage addiction. Although it is not a particularly well-written book, being a somewhat shallow adaptation of a TV play, it illuminates the contemporary drinking problems described by Haskins, and raises psychological and sociological questions that are worth classroom discussion.

Sandra Scoppetone's *The Late Great Me* is the best book yet on the subject of teenage alcoholism. Seventeen-year-old Geri Peters never feels comfortable with either herself or her school achievements until a handsome new boy in school introduces her to liquor, which opens an entire new social world for her: the world of the "juicers," those teenagers who keep liquor in their school lockers, get smashed every weekend, black out, forget what has happened.

Geri's problem is particularly acute. She discovers that she is an alcoholic, a person allergic to liquor who is incapable of handling it. While Geri gradually sinks into Skid-Row status, her problem-ridden parents seem incapable of helping her. Finally, a compassionate teacher at her school, Kate, reveals that she herself is an ex-alcoholic. She is willing to endanger her job to keep Geri from total destruction.

Geri is finally forced to admit that she is alcoholic, the first of Alcoholics Anonymous's twelve steps to sobriety. "We admitted we were powerless over alcohol—that our lives had become unmanageable." (p. 231) Geri learns to get through one day at a time and to accept some of the slogans of A.A., which had originally seemed so square, so corny to her. She starts to believe Kate's words, "You're not a bad person, Geri . . .

---

4. Nan Robertson: "The Young of A.A.: When Euphoria of Wine and Drugs Is Gone," *The New York Times,* Monday, August 2, 1976.

you're a sick person." She learns a lesson that is useful for all young people trying to find themselves: "It didn't matter what had happened in the past and I couldn't do anything about tomorrow. Now. That's all I had. That's all anyone ever had." (p. 235)

Students should discuss all of the issues raised in Scoppetone's book, particularly why people drink. Haskins tells us that teenagers drink for the same reasons that adults drink. They should also discuss the words of one young member of Alcoholics Anonymous:

> I want to grow now. I was scared, immature, unequipped to deal with a sober life. I drank rather than grow, rather than feel. I feel safe when I'm with A.A. people. To open up to them—that's where I want to go. That's where I want to be.

Two valuable, recent adolescent novels, *First Step* and *An American Girl,* deal with the addiction of the teenagers' parents to alcohol. In Anne Snyder's *First Step*, a mother's drinking is ruining her teenage daughter's life. Cindy lives in constant terror of her mother's embarrassing her in school; she is unable to have friends at the house; and the car pool to her school refuses to let her mother participate any longer.

Finally, through a boy she meets in high school, Cindy joins Alateen, the spin-off organization for children of alcoholics. The things she learns there help her to grow and to deal constructively with her home situation. She learns that she has a choice: "I can allow my mother to ruin my life, or I can let her go . . . release her. I can concentrate on her or on me, it's my decision." (p. 126)

The terrible feelings of being an outsider that assail Cindy are probably common to every young person who is ashamed of his/her parents. Cindy becomes stronger when she is able to face her mother's alcoholism and perceive herself as a separate and different person. She tells her younger brother:

> We can't do anything about her drinking itself. We have to let her drink all she wants. But when she *is* drinking we can keep out of her way . . . keep out of any arguments; then when she's okay, we can tell her how we feel about it, ask her to talk to the doctor or the minister or go to A.A. And we can show her we care, that we love her. . . . We have to learn to be stronger ourselves. We can learn how to live from the Alateen kids—other kids who have the same problem. . . . We're not alone. There are twenty million other kids like us . . . living in alcoholic homes. (p. 130)

First Step ends more optimistically than Patricia Dizenzo's *An American Girl*, in which the narrator's mother is an all-day alcoholic, and her father starts to drink when he gets home from work. The family is upper middle-class, but the teenage daughter suffers from the same fears, embarrassments, and anxieties that afflict Cindy. One additional fear she has is her mother's driving. Because they live in a suburban community she must be driven around by her mother, and each time she gets into the car she does so in fear and anxiety. Unlike Cindy, the heroine of *An American Girl* is left isolated in her predicament, without help from peers or adults.

In Theodore Weesner's *The Car Thief*, the protagonist is a teenage boy who is rejected by his divorced mother and lives with his alcoholic father, with whom he has no communication. Unable to make friends, Alex spends much of his time in movie theaters and the rest of it stealing cars and fellow students' wallets.

Alex is arrested in school in front of the other students and is sent to a reformatory on an indeterminate sentence. When finally released, he attempts to go back to school but is not able to make contact there with either teachers or students. Throughout every moment of the day, he aches with loneliness. The reader keeps feeling that Alex has possibilities if only someone would talk to him, relate to him, show him what it means to be human.

Alex finally joins the army, where he begins to experience his own manhood emerging. The reader is glad that Alex has at last reached safe harbor, that he will find some community in the army; but, at the same time, the reader regrets that the better parts of Alex have been defeated in civilian society and that he can find social identity and companionship only among soldiers. Readers should discuss the army as a community of outsiders, Alex's fate, and the ambience of loneliness that pervades this book.

Drug addiction also creates outsiders. In Vida Demas's *First Person, Singular*, the only person to whom Pam, a loner, can relate is Greg, a kind, sensitive, wonderful boy who uses drugs to make life bearable. Greg's feelings of alienation are caused by his perennially drunk father.

Without parental supervision, moral code, or direction, and without money to go to college, Greg flounders and finds refuge in drugs. Looking for communion through drugs, Greg only increases his alienation. He takes off on a cross-country trip to look for some meaning for his life and writes to Pam:

> I've been all over the place, I went down south first. Bad scene. I got out of there fast. You're not safe with long hair anywhere past West Virginia. You could get busted just for hitching a ride. I went out west from there . . . and ended up somehow up above the Grand Canyon. . . . I went up north after that where the mountains were all blue and into clouds and fuzzy with spruce trees but up close were more bare and made me feel about two inches tall and lonely as hell. I didn't dig that too much, so I circled around and went into Kansas. . . .
>
> You won't know me when you see me. I shaved off my hair. Except for a little ponytail at the top, I'm bald. What happened is I got into the Hare Krishna thing . . . sometimes when I'm all wiped out and I think everybody's after me . . . I chant this mantra. That's a prayer. It seems to help. . . . (pp. 87–88)

Finally, Greg becomes a drug dealer. Pam gives him money to leave town, and she knows that he is forever lost both to her and to himself. In this book, as in *The Car Thief*, students should discuss the making of an outsider, the waste, and how things could have been different.

A good contrast to Demas's and Weesner's books is Alice Childress's *A Hero Ain't Nothin' But a Sandwich*, in which Benjie, a thirteen-year-old drug addict, is saved from destruction by a caring stepfather who refuses to let him go.

Benjie's world is quite different from Greg's. Benjie becomes hooked on heroin in order to fit into his world; Greg becomes hooked in order to escape from his. Both boys initially find their way to drugs because they want to be in harmony with society, to establish contact with it somehow. Benjie describes his world as follows:

My block ain't no place to be a chile in peace. Somebody gonna cop your money and might knock you down cause you walking with short bread and didn't even make it worth their while to stop and frisk you over. Ain't no letrit light bulb in my hallway for two or three floors and we be living up next to the top floor. You best get over bein seven or eight, right soon, cause seven and eight is too big for relatives to be holdin your hand like when you was three, four, and five. No, Jack, you on your own and they got they thing to do, like workin, or goin to court, or seeing after they gas and letrit bills, and they dispossess—or final notice, bout on-time payments—walking like that, you dig? (pp. 9–10)

Benjie can't see why his family gets upset about his taking drugs. In his world, everybody takes drugs. At first, he takes drugs only on weekends because he doesn't want the isolation that he understands must come *even* in a society where so many are hooked.

He tells us casually (and the reader must remember that this is a thirteen-year-old child talking): "Fact is, I used to skin-pop only on weekends cause I wanted to keep my mind on school and wasn't near ready to give up on the society." (p. 11). But soon he starts to take drugs more for his nerves. What child wouldn't be nervous in conditions such as these:

Walkin through dark, stinky hallways can be hard on anybody, man or child, but a child can get snatch in the dark and get his behind parts messed up by some weirdo; I'm talking bout them sexuals. Soon's you get up to leven, twelve, and so—they might cool it cause they scared you know where to land a good up-punch, dig? I say alla this cause it's a fact. (p. 10)

When Benjie, becoming more and more enmeshed in drugs, tries to kill himself, his stepfather grabs his arms and won't let go. His love helps to straighten Benjie out:

"Dammit, Benjie," he say, "you gotta do it [stay clean] even if *nobody* believe in you, gotta be your own man, the supervisor of your veins, the night watchman and day shift foreman in charge—a your own affairs."
Butler pull me over to the window and we lookin down in the courtyard what's mixed up from people who throw garbage.
"Straighten up, Benjie," he say. "Do it even living on the edge of ugly, cause we got nowhere else to go right now." (pp. 120–121)

It is these words of Butler's plus his love for Benjie that should provide the focus for class discussion of this fine novel.

Another popular novel about teenage drug addiction is *Go Ask Alice*, Anonymous, based on the actual diary of a fifteen-year-old drug user. The title is taken from the lyrics of the Jefferson Airplane's song "White Rabbit," which deals with distorted perceptions produced by a drug high. Although, as the editors note, the book "is not a definitive statement on the middle-class, teenage drug world" and "does not offer any solutions," it is "a highly personal and specific chronicle" that provides "insights into the increasingly complicated world in which we live." (p. 5)

Alice's problems begin when her professor father changes positions and the family moves to a new town. She writes:

. . . I'm not too sure I'm going to make it in a new town. I barely made it in our old town where I knew everybody and they knew me. I've never even allowed myself to think about it before, but I really haven't much to offer in a new situation. Oh dear God, help me adjust, help me be accepted, help me belong, don't let me be a social outcast and a drag on my family. (p. 19)

Alice's fears prove to be rooted in reality. She writes:

Oh Diary it was miserable! It was the loneliest, coldest place in the world. Not one single person spoke to me during the whole endlessly long day. During lunch period I fled to the nurse's office and said I had a headache. Then I cut my last class and went by the drugstore and had a chocolate malt, a double order of french fried potatoes, and a giant Hershey Bar. . . . All the time I ate, I hated myself for being childish. Hurt as I am when I think about it I have probably done the same thing to every new person that came to my schools, either ignored them completely or stared back at them out of curiosity. (p. 21)

Passages such as the above can be used to stimulate class discussion of what it feels like to be an outsider—a feeling common to most teenagers at some point during adolescence.

As her alienation increases, Alice makes her way to drugs, leaves home, goes to San Francisco with a friend, experiences a variety of degradations, and calls her parents to come for her. For a while everything seems fine, then she goes back to drugs, leaves home, and again finally calls her parents. At this point, Alice is ready to go straight but finds that she is more of an outsider at school than before. The "drug kids" resent her because she is trying to go straight, and the straight kids view the ones on drugs as "social lepers." At the end of the book she dies from an overdose of drugs.

As with the other books, the important questions to be discussed with students are those dealing with how Alice might have been saved from becoming an outsider, from feeling so alienated that she had to turn to drugs.

Books Discussed in Chapter I

Wide, Sargasso Sea, Jean Rhys, Popular Library, 1966.
The Snake Pit, Mary Jane Ward, Signet, 1946.
One Flew over the Cuckoo's Nest, Ken Kesey, Bantam, 1975.
The Eden Express, Mark Vonnegut, Bantam, 1976.
I Never Promised You a Rose Garden, Joanne Greenberg (Hannah Green, pseud.), Signet, 1964.
Autobiography of a Schizophrenic Girl, Anonymous, NAL, 1960.
Lisa, Bright and Dark, John Neufeld, Signet, 1970.
Dinky Hocker Shoots Smack, M. E. Kerr, Dell, 1972.
Buried Alive, Myra Friedman, Bantam, 1974.
The Boy Who Could Make Himself Disappear, Kin Platt, Dell, 1974.

A Circle of Children, Mary McCracken, Signet, 1974.
The Bell Jar, Sylvia Plath, Bantam, 1972.
Admission to the Feast, Gunnel Beckman, Dell, 1973.
Sunshine, Norma Klein, Avon, 1974.
The Story of Josh, Marcia Friedman, Ballantine, 1974.
May I Cross Your Golden River?, Paige Dixon, Atheneum, 1976.
The Skating Rink, Mildred Lee, Dell, 1969.
Hey Dummy, Kin Platt, Dell, 1971.
The Cat Ate My Gymsuit, Paula Danziger, Dell, 1974.
Twink, John Neufeld, Signet, 1970.
Run, Shelley, Run, Gertrude Samuels, Signet, 1974.
Hatter Fox, Marilyn Harris, Bantam, 1974.
Listen to the Silence, David Elliott, Signet, 1969.
Teen-Age Alcoholism, Jim Haskins, Hawthorne, 1976.
Sarah T., Robin S. Wagner, Ballantine, 1975.
The Late Great Me, Sandra Scoppetone, Bantam, 1977.
First Step, Anne Snyder, Signet, 1976.
An American Girl, Patricia Dizenzo, Avon, 1976.
The Car Thief, Theodore Weesner, Dell, 1974.
First Person, Singular, Vida Demas, Dell, 1974.
A Hero Ain't Nothin' But a Sandwich, Alice Childress, Avon, 1973.
Go Ask Alice, Anonymous, Avon, 1971.

Other Related Books

Eric, Doris Lund, Dell, 1975. (Death of a seventeen-year-old)
Deenie, Judy Blume, Dell, 1974. (Teenager has to wear back brace from
     neck to hips for four years or longer)
Gift of Gold, Beverly Butler, Pocket Books, 1973. (Blind girl wants to
     become a speech therapist)
The Summer of the Swans, Betsy Byars, Viking, 1970. (Sara's dull life is
enlivened by the disappearance of and frantic search for her retarded
brother)

II
minorities

How can individuals come to terms with their own group identity? What are the problems of extolling or denying, ignoring or being ignorant of, one's cultural past as seen through family and/or group (Black, Chicano, Jew, American Indian, etc.)? How have minorities been helped and hurt in the United States? How have the positions of minorities improved or remained the same in this last quarter of the twentieth century? Why is the mosaic or pluralistic image of Americans a better and more realistic one than the melting-pot metaphor of the past? What are the present and future for deprived ethnic minorities? How does an understanding of these circumstances benefit all Americans?

Introduction

When I was a secondary school student, Blacks were depicted as happy slaves on plantations, and school literature about American Indians, Chicanos, Puerto Ricans, or Oriental people (except for Pearl Buck's *The Good Earth*) was nonexistent. Contemporary adolescent literature that depicts minorities from a humanistic point of view can give students insight into many ethnic groups.

Those pessimists who say that racial and religious prejudice will never die must remember that traditionally there has been little information given to American youngsters to counteract generations of stereotypes, and this remains the situation in many parts of the United States today. Prejudice feeds on lack of knowledge. As recently as 1975, in San Diego, when the Japanese-American author of *Farewell to Manzanar* spoke about the internment of Japanese citizens during World War II, there were people in the audience who did not know that this had ever occurred.

I would not recommend all ethnic literature for the secondary school. I would prefer the well-written works that bring people closer together rather than those that highlight the exotic, brutal, and freakish. (I would not use Herbert Selby's *Last Exit to Brooklyn*, in which the Blacks and Puerto Ricans in a housing project amuse themselves with gang rapes and with betting on whether or not a baby will fall out of a window. I would prefer to use a work such as *Anne Frank: The Diary of a Young Girl,* which focuses on the unconquerable human spirit rather than a book that details the grisly experiments of concentration camp doctors.) The books discussed in this chapter are all honest books, worth reading and important in the fight against prejudice. Daniel J. Dieterich, in an article entitled "Teaching Cultural Appreciation Through Literature," puts it this way:

The barriers which separate [people] are still great. The tendency to exalt one's own accomplishments and ignore or underplay the accomplishments of others is quite natural at every level of human society. But the dangers which have resulted from this attitude on the national level have increased to such a critical stage that nearly everyone now recognizes the need to reduce or eliminate it. Provincialism, chauvinism, and ethnocentrism are luxuries mankind can no longer afford.

What can the teacher of English do to improve his students' appreciation of other races and cultures? Nancy Arnex points out that there are three ways to know what it means to be a Negro: "1) Be a Negro, 2) Interact with him day-by-day, or 3) Read literature in which the Negro authors expressed themselves in such a way that we can identify with them and live their experiences vicariously." *(English Journal,* January 1969) The same obviously holds true for all races and cultures.[1]

Most of the space in this chapter is devoted to books about Blacks and American Indians, because more adolescent literature is being written about those two groups. I have also included comments on adolescent literature about Chicanos, Japanese Americans, and Puerto Ricans but have, for space reasons, omitted references to other ethnic groups (Irish, Italian, etc.). That does not mean that books about such groups would not be valuable in classrooms.

Blacks

Good black adolescent literature does not depict Blacks as simpletons or as superhuman beings. For a long time the Black in American literature was a stereotyped character: Uncle Remus, Uncle Tom, and the everloving Mammy. Paule Marshall describes the image of black women in literature in the following way:

. . . the Negro woman has been until recent times almost nonexistent in the prose literature of the country.

This is not to say that some creature which has been passed off as the Negro woman hasn't appeared in stories and novels written by both white and Negro writers since the earliest beginnings of the country's literary history; but I contend that, by and large, the figure which emerges, even upon the most cursory examination of these works, is a myth, a stereotype, a fantasy figure, which has very little to do with the Negro woman in reality.

In other words, the black woman as portrayed has suffered the same unhappy fate as the black man. She has in a sense been strung up on two poles and left

---

1. Daniel J. Dieterich, "Teaching Cultural Appreciation Through Literature," NCTE/ERIC, Summaries & Sources.

hanging. At one end of the pole, there is the "nigger wench"—sensual, primitive, pleasure-seeking, immoral, the siren, the sinner. Her type was perhaps best summed up by Gertrude Stein in her description of Rose in the story "Melanctha." "Rose," Miss Stein wrote, "a real black, well-built, sullen, stupid, child-like, good-looking Negress," who had, in Miss Stein's words, "the simple, promiscuous immorality of the black people."

At the other end of the pole, we find that larger than life figure, the Negro matriarch, who dominates so much of fiction—strong, but humble, devoted, devoutly religious, patient—a paragon of patience, if you will—wise beyond all wisdom, the saint, the mammy, the great wet nurse of the society . . . (pp. 33–34)[2]

Good adolescent literature adopts neither of the above extremes. It presents honest pictures of black people; it shows them as both good and bad, and emphasizes the humanity in its characters, which causes the reader to identify with them. In this way, such literature helps to dispel stereotypical ideas about Blacks. Clichés disintegrate as the reader feels emotionally moved by the transcendent human condition.

When I read a book like James Baldwin's *If Beale Street Could Talk*, I think of one of my graduate students who recently protested, "but what will happen if they miss Keats, Byron, and Shelley in high school?" I would prefer to apply this question to Baldwin's book. What will happen to our students if all of their education fails to acquaint them with the possibilities of love, hate, beauty, ugliness, hope, and despair, which are the basic content of this book? What will happen to them if they continue to fail to understand and acknowledge the fate of most Blacks in the United States in the last quarter of the twentieth century?

Baldwin's book, listed by the American Library Association as one of 1974's *Best Books for Young Adults,* is set in the Harlem ghetto. It deals with the love between nineteen-year-old Tish and twenty-two-year-old Fonny, who has been imprisoned for a crime he did not commit. The book begins with Tish's telling Fonny, through the glass partition of the jail, that she is pregnant; and it ends with their certain understanding that he will not be out of jail when the baby is born.

Baldwin has developed an extraordinary range of individual black people, similar only in the social and geographical limitations placed on them by white society, but, within those limitations, inspiring in their individuality, vitality, tenacity, and determination to love and not be destroyed. Perhaps their vitality (and this is a trait shared by minority characters in many other books) is based on their inescapable necessity to be in touch with reality. They understand what's happening to them; nevertheless, they struggle, conscious at every moment that their chances of success are slim and that the two most probable choices open to them in a white society are apathy (i.e., drugs, withdrawal) or the minimal level of consciousness that permits them to survive without seeming rebellious or aware enough to threaten white existence.

---

2. Pat Crutchfield Exum, *Keeping the Faith: Writings by Contemporary Black American Women*, Fawcett, 1974, 288 pp.

Students studying minority literature might do well to read Albert Camus's *The Myth of Sisyphus*, for minority people are the true existential heroes who roll the rock to the top of the mountain each day despite their agonizing understanding that it is all in vain. Baldwin's characters never doubt the precariousness of their lives. After Fonny's arrest, Tish says: "I admit, I'm scared . . . because nobody can take the shit they throw on us forever," (p. 8) and Baldwin, describing conditions in the ghetto, writes: "the kids had been told they weren't worth shit and everything they saw around them proved it. They struggled, they struggled, but they fell, like flies, and they congregated on the garbage heaps of their lives, like flies." (p. 45)

It is important for students to discuss the sociological trap in which minority people find themselves. One or more students might do some research into the employment history of Blacks, who have always been the last hired and the first fired. When they do have jobs, the jobs pay them a bare subsistence wage, so low that even when every member of a family is employed, they all have to live together and endure degrading physical conditions daily.

Minority people also live in constant daily fear that they can be picked up, arrested, and given long jail sentences even if they are completely innocent. The injustice of cases such as those against Dreyfus, Sacco and Vanzetti, and Tom Mooney are reenacted every day in this country against poor, helpless, and ignorant dark-skinned people. Fonny's friend, Daniel, unemployed and sitting apathetically on his front steps, is arrested and jailed for two years for allegedly stealing a car. If all Blacks are presumed guilty of something, what difference does it make which one is arrested? When Daniel is told that he can make one phone call—when he is told, in addition, that if he pleads guilty, he'll receive a more lenient sentence—he has no one to call, no lawyer, no middle-class relatives, nobody with any meaningful power. Frightened and confused by the concept of plea bargaining, he goes quietly.

When Daniel, broken in spirit, gets out of jail, he says: "Maybe I'd feel different if I had done something and got caught. But I didn't do nothing. They were just playing with me, man, because they could. And I'm lucky it was only two years, you dig? Because they can do with you whatever they want. *Whatever they want*." (p. 127)

Baldwin's point, of course, is that this omnipresent fear that "they" can do whatever they want is a realistic fear. Fonny's future imprisonment is inexorably determined when a "bad" cop who wants to arrest him unjustly for assault and battery is deterred by the intercession of the white store owner. After that, it is only a matter of time.

After being imprisoned, Fonny goes through psychological stages that are similar to those endured by the central character in Bernard Malamud's *The Fixer*. He derives the strength to endure his imprisonment only when he realizes that it really has nothing to do with innocence or guilt. He is a *political* prisoner, imprisoned not for what he has done but for what he is:

Now, Fonny knows why he is here—why he is where he is; now, he dares to look around him. He is not here for anything he has done. He has always known that, but now he knows it with a difference. . . . he looks to the others, he listens: what have *they* done? Not much. To do much is to have the power to place these people where they are, to keep them where they are. These captive men are the hidden price for the hidden lie: the righteous must be able to locate the damned. To do much is to have the power and the necessity to dictate to the damned. (p. 235)

This is the kind of book that should be read and discussed in English, social studies, and humanities classes, for it cannot fail to evoke and extend compassion and brotherhood; it can aid in the understanding of any society in which racism diminishes an entire group of people. Like all good literature, it stimulates the intellect and imagination, and enables readers to comprehend vicariously what cannot be experienced personally.

Rosa Guy's *The Friends* is another good book set in Harlem. It is told in first person by fourteen-year-old Phyllisia Cathay, who has just come to New York from the West Indies. She is an outsider, hated by the children in the ghetto, who resent her superior education, fine clothes, and slightly better economic status. She is beaten and insulted daily by her classmates until fifteen-year-old Edith Jackson becomes her protector. Edith tells the hostile mob:

I hear tell that some of you been messing with a good friend of mine. Well, let me tell you one thing. If anybody in this room feel like messing with a monkey chaser, I got your monkey and I got your chaser. So come on and try me. . . .
That girl, Phyllisia, is my friend. My best friend. If anybody hits on her, they hitting on me . . . (pp. 37–38)

But Phyllisia is ungrateful. She looks down on Edith for being poor and ragged. Gradually, her better side emerges—the side that admires Edith for her unfailing good humor, for the loving care she gives the many children in her motherless family, for her perseverance. It is the friendship of Edith, a lost soul at the lowest end of the social ladder, that eventually helps Phyllisia become mature and compassionate enough to return love and friendship.

The interesting psychological dimensions of the many relationships in this book should be examined: The terror of being a new girl in school; the conflicts between Phyllisia and her sister, Ruby; the hostility between the girls and their irrational and authoritarian father, Calvin. But, as is the case in most ethnic literature, the sociological content of the work is overpowering and more significant than the psychological. The psychological problems are exacerbated by the condition of belonging to an ethnic minority. Someone once said that in science fiction, setting becomes the major character. The same might be said about ethnic literature.

The Harlem of *The Friends* is similar to *Beale Street*'s. It is a steaming, chaotic jungle in which violence is omnipresent, waiting to explode. Encountering a riot on the way home from school is not at all unusual. Poverty and poor living conditions are major elements of setting in every work about ethnic minorities. Edith and her family live in one large shabby room that serves as a kitchen, bedroom, and dining room. Their pot-bellied stove reminds Phyllisia of poor people's outdoor stoves in the West Indies.

The police are enemies to these poor ghetto inhabitants, and when Edith's father disappears, the children are afraid to go to the police to find out about him. Edith says: "If he's sick and in some hospital, he'll be back when he get well. If he ain't . . ." she paused, ". . . ain't nothing anybody can do about it, and bringing cops to *this* house sure ain't gonna help." (p. 80) Edith's father doesn't come back, and she has to drop out of school and get work as a maid to support the smaller children.

Death comes casually and often to the family. Edith's brother Randy is shot in the back by a policeman for absolutely no reason. One of Edith's little sisters dies, two are taken to an orphanage, and Edith is forced to go to the orphanage until she is eighteen.

In Guy's book, as in Baldwin's, people exist on varying levels of good and evil. Calvin, the girls' father, is more destructive and authoritarian than any white person in the book. The white teacher is also a destructive figure. Exasperated one morning by the difficulties these tormented ghetto children have comprehending the irrelevant facts she is teaching, she tells them: "Perhaps it is because you greased your hair so well this morning that things keep slipping your mind." (p. 42)

In the Baldwin and Guy novels there is no escape, and sadness and pessimism are the dominant tones. In *The Soul Brothers and Sister Lou* by Kristin Hunter, the inhabitants of the Southside ghetto also live in a state of poverty and cold war, but musical talent provides a way to escape. This is a particularly good book for adolescents, because at the same time it depicts all of the problems, terrors, persecutions, and divisions within the ghetto, it shows that human dignity and hope can emerge from the ugliness.

Hunter presents a large canvas to the reader, a total panorama of many different kinds of Blacks within the ghetto: sincere hard-working ones, police informers, fanatic black militants, junkies, unemployed musicians, teachers, parents, teenagers.

Sister Lou and the Soul Brothers are a struggling singing group that succeeds in spite of the endless obstacles indigenous to life in the ghetto. The first of their problems is the pervasive poverty that prevents them from getting a piano and finding a place to practice. The second major obstacle is the white policeman in the ghetto. Sister Lou says:

They knew that all policemen were not *their* friends, even if they might be the friends of children on the other side of town, and that some policemen, like Officer Lafferty, were their worst enemies. Officer Lafferty's favorite sport was to catch groups of Southside boys in out-of-the-way places like vacant buildings and alleys, where there would be no witnesses to what he did. He would call them names and accuse them of committing crimes, just to provoke them into saying something back or hitting him or running away. If they ran away he would shoot them. If they did anything else, he would beat them up with his club and take them to the police station and charge them with resisting arrest and assaulting an officer. You couldn't win with a bully like Officer Lafferty. (p. 11)

But not all of the whites are enemies: Mr. Lucitanno, the school music teacher, tries to help the young musicians and ends up learning from them. And not all of the Blacks are friends. Fess, the young black revolutionary, cares more about politics than people and is willing to sacrifice the musicians and their families to achieve his dreams of political power.

Finally, the group is successful; they cut a record and change "from shy, awkward, amateurs to poised professionals, accustomed to singing before audiences and even able to speak to groups about their experiences." (p. 190) But it is not a conventional, happy ending. Sister Lou discovers that life is never really free of problems and that success and sophistication also mean losing something:

> The joy of discovering inspiring poetry and exciting historic heroes at school was gone, because she would never quite believe in those mottoes and heroes again. . . . The excitement of improvising the first songs and making the first recording had become the hard work of rehearsing and perfecting numbers for the second. It got tougher, not easier; the Jewel Records people and the agent the four had inevitably acquired kept urging them to achieve a unique style and stick to it, and to beware of their competition, lest they become has-beens at seventeen. Music had been a childhood pleasure to Louretta, but now it was work. (p. 190)

Alice Childress's *A Hero Ain't Nothin' But a Sandwich* focuses on drugs and also shows the horrors of ghetto life, but ends on a note of hope. (See discussion of this book in Chapter I.)

Drugs also cast a shadow over the lives of the entire Brooke family in Sharon Bell Mathis's *Teacup Full of Roses*. Pop is a weak semi-invalid who spends his days watching television. The family is supported by Momma and by Joe, the middle son, who has spent eight years going to high school at night so that he could work during the day. The book opens just after Paul, the oldest son, a gifted artist who turned to drugs when he couldn't get started as an artist, has been released after seven months in a drug rehabilitation hospital. A tragic chain of events is set in motion when Paul takes the money that Davey, the youngest brother, was to use for college.

The psychological complexities of the Brooke family are interesting and the characterizations worth discussing. Especially moving is the figure of Joe, who takes on his shoulders all of the family responsibility after his father gets sick. The things that seem so simple to middle-class America become exceptionally difficult or unattainable for people like the Brookes. Completing high school is almost impossible, and going to college is a dream for all but a very few.

Life in the ghetto is hard and dangerous. The criminals, drug dealers, and payoff men socialize with their victims, who are their own people. Crime seems to be just about the only way that a Black can survive in style, and its omnipresence is accepted and understood by all. Ironically, life outside the ghetto is no safer or better for Blacks like Joe. One of the few legitimate careers open to him is military service, so he joins the Navy while the Vietnam War is raging. When he asks the black recruiting officer how the Navy treats Blacks, the officer replies: "Like the rest of America. Can you deal with that?" (p. 81)

Mathis's book is most useful for giving students insight into a black family. (Other such works are *Raisin in the Sun* and *Ceremonies in Dark Old Men*.)

In Maya Angelou's *Gather Together in My Name* (listed by the ALA as one of the *Best Books for Young Adults* of 1974), the heroine engages in a number of activities that are not socially acceptable (i.e., running a house of prostitution, engaging in prostitution, having an illegitimate child); but she emerges from these experiences as a fine, intelligent, and admirable woman. What the teacher of adolescent literature would want students reading this book to understand is the nature of gallantry, the wonder of the human spirit that can keep trying despite terrible obstacles. In this work, the second volume of Angelou's autobiography, she begins with the post-World-War-II period when Blacks who had helped fight the evils of totalitarianism in Europe and Asia returned home believing that finally life would be better for dark-skinned people in the United States. Of course, their hopes were dashed, as were Angelou's time and time again as she attempted to enter the economic mainstream of American life and to find a career that would employ some of her marvelous intelligence and creativity. This is how she describes the end of the war:

It was triumph and brotherhood. Everybody was a hero. Hadn't we all joined together to kick the hell out of *de Gruber*, and that fat Italian, and put that little rice-eating Tojo in his place?

Black men from the South who had held no tools more complicated than plows had learned to use lathes and borers and welding guns, and had brought in their quotas of war-making machines. Women who had only known maid's uniforms and mammy-made dresses donned the awkward men's pants and steel helmets, and made the shipfitting sheds hum some buddy. . . .

Soldiers and sailors, and the few black Marines fresh from having buried death on a sandy South Pacific beach, stood around looking proud out of war-wise eyes. . . . All the sacrifices had won us victory and now the good times were coming. . . . There was no need to discuss racial prejudice. . . . Hadn't we all, black and white, just snatched the remaining Jews from the hell of concentration camps? Race prejudice was dead. . . .

Two months after V-Day, war plants began to shut down, to cut back, to lay off employees. Some workers were offered tickets back to their Southern homes. Back to the mules they had left tied to the tree on ole Mistah Doo Hickup farm. No good. . . . Those military heroes of a few months earlier, who were discharged from the Army in the city which knows how, began to be seen hanging on the ghetto corners like forgotten laundry left on a backyard fence. . . . Thus we lived through a major war. The question in the ghettos was, Can we make it through a minor peace? (pp. 1–3)

Angelou is left an unwed mother, with a small son to support. Her attempts to find the kind of work she is fitted for by temperament and intelligence remind the reader of Sisyphus. The telephone company hires only white operators, but gives her a job as a bus girl in the kitchen; she works for a while as a Creole cook, as a waitress in a night club, as a madam of a small house of prostitution employing two lesbians, as a dancer, and as a prostitute. Throughout her experiences she never loses her dignity, her belief in herself, her celebration of life. The book resembles a picaresque novel as she confronts a variety of situations and, in the process, attempts to find and to define herself.

It is important for adolescents to understand that every experience, both bad and good, should be viewed as a learning situation. Angelou never curses her color, never wants to be otherwise, never lapses into hopelessness because of her experiences. For a while she returns to the South, where despite the omnipresent fear, she can still find beauty in the surroundings and in the behavior patterns of her people:

I had seen the formality of black adult equals all my youth but had never considered that a time would come when I, too, could participate. The customs are as formalized as an eighteenth-century minuet, and a child at the race's knee learns the moves and twirls by osmosis and observation.

Values among South rural blacks are not quite the same as those existing elsewhere. Age has more worth than wealth, and religious piety more value than beauty. (p. 65)

In Angelou's work, the teenager can find a portrait of a life-affirming, creative person, who can say no to the values of the black and white society that degrade her and yes to the values of the black society that ennoble her.

Another compelling picture of black society is Sharon Bell Mathis's *Listen for the Fig Tree*. The heroine, Muffin, is a blind girl of remarkable beauty, spirit, and self-reliance, whose mother has been destructively drinking ever since her husband's death. The existence of love—love between the parents and love between Muffin and her mother and various neighbors, despite their poverty and problems—makes the book a moving experience for young readers.

Leola, the mother, loved her husband so much that she wears his thin jacket, even in the coldest weather, and spends hours sitting in the cab company where he worked. She drinks to still her pain of loss and loneliness. Neighbors of all types try to help the mother and daughter despite Leola's abusiveness when she's drunk. Through all of her problems, Muffin keeps learning about life and about what it means to be black:

Most of all she liked Ernie's market because her father had liked shopping at the small Black grocery. In fact, as much as he could, she remembered, he went to Black stores for everything. The cleaners, the fish market, the drugstore. He was always saying, "Give the money to the Black stores, give it to our own people, then you know you helping and you know you not giving your money to the white all the time."

But her father had been killed, beaten to death by two Black men. His head crushed by lead pipes held by Black men and nobody had found them yet, and people said if it had been a white cabdriver they would have found the killers right away. But finding the killers wouldn't make her father alive. . . . (p. 30)

When Muffin is attacked in the hall of her tenement, it is a poor old black man who saves her, but her attacker is also black. She tells Ernie:

. . . I felt so pretty and the dress turned out and I didn't make any mistakes and I was going upstairs to show Mr. Dale how I looked and when the man said, "Little yellow riding hood," at first I smiled—I smiled a little and I was getting ready to tell him I made the dress and—I knew he was Black. Remember before when it happened to Queenie and the man was white—but the man wasn't white this time. . . .

He was Black. And poor Mr. Thomas, he's so old and he kept hitting the man with a strap and the man hit him so bad and he had a knife and cut him too . . . (p. 121)

It is important for young people to understand that there are black rapists and white rapists, good and bad in both black and white, victims and rapists in both colors.[3]

Another excellent book, which deals with the history of Blacks in America but is actually fiction, is Ernest Gaines's *The Autobiography of Miss Jane Pittman.* In the guise of a tape-recorded recollection of a 110-year-old black woman, Gaines traces the history of Blacks in America from slavery to the militancy of the 1960s. The book provides students with an inspiring account of the endurance of the human spirit.

Jane first tells about the early days of slavery, of her first meeting with the Yankees when she was only ten or eleven. At first she was afraid to talk, but when one pressed her for information, she admitted that she was beaten with a cat-o'-nine-tails, especially if she fell asleep when looking after the young mistress's children. When Corporal Brown, the Yankee, asked her what she was going to do after freedom, she said, symbolically, "just sleep." Corporal Brown gave her her new name, Jane Brown. One hundred years later, in a moving and memorable concluding scene, Jane Brown Pittman, with her walking stick, is leading a freedom march. The time of freedom has been a time of waking up rather than sleeping.

Gaines's work humanizes history and gives the reader insight into the terrible problems following the Emancipation Proclamation. Some slaves want to stay and "see if old Master go'n act different when it's freedom." (p. 13) But Jane has a hunger to go North. They ask her, "before y'all start out here heading anywhere, what y'all go'n eat? . . . Where y'all go'n sleep? Who go'n protect you from the patrollers? . . . They ain't go'n just beat you if they catch you, they kill you if they catch you now. . . . Before now they didn't kill you because you was somebody's chattel. Now you ain't owned by nobody but fate. Nobody to protect you now. . . ." (p. 13)

With no map and no compass, following the North Star, Jane goes with a group of others. With nothing but some apples, potatoes, and a few clothes, they start out. The patrollers, "poor white trash that used to find the runaway slaves for the masters," the ones who later become the founders of the Klan with the "Secesh soldiers," find the little group and beat most of them to death; but Jane escapes with Ned, a little boy. Stopping to ask for water from a white woman, they are at first refused; but she finally pours some into their hands and says:

"You think I'm go'n let you put your black mouth on this cup?" she said. "Hold out your hands." . . .

---

3. Some students may wish to do some research in Susan Brownmiller's book, *Against Our Will*, in which she documents the fact that most rape victims are poor, young, black girls.

"Don't think I love niggers just because I'm giving y'all water," she was saying. "I hate y'all. Hate y'all with all my heart. Doing it because I'm a God-fearing Christian. I hate niggers with all my heart. Y'all cause of all this trouble, all this ravishing. Yankee and nigger soldiers all over the place stealing my hogs and chickens. Y'all cause of it all. I hope the good white people round here kill y'all off. Hope they kill y'all before the night over. I'm go'n tell them which way y'all went, and I'm go'n tell them go kill y'all. Now, get away from here before I kill y'all myself. If I wasn't a God-fearing Christian I'd kill y'all myself." (pp. 40–41)

If the teacher reminds readers that this woman is speaking to an eleven-year-old girl and five-year-old boy, nothing much more has to be said about this passage. Students might note the irony in the God-fearing Christian who wants someone else to do her killing.

Space does not permit extensive discussion of the wealth of significant material in this book, but one element of particular interest is the way the Blacks are always looking for the One—for their Messiah who will improve their lives. Jane says:

People's always looking for somebody to come lead them. Go to the Old Testament; go to the New. They did it in slavery; after the war they did it; they did it in the hard times that people want call Reconstruction; they did it in the Depression—another hard times; and they doing it now. They have always done it—and the Lord has always obliged in some way or another. Anytime a child is born, the old people look in his face and ask him if he's the One? (p. 199)

How beautiful it is at the end of the book to find out that the One is not a child but Miss Jane, at 110, leading a freedom march.

An interesting book that shows the legacy of slavery is Grace Halsell's *Soul Sister.* In 1969, Grace Halsell, a researcher for President Johnson, decided to repeat John Howard Griffin's experiment, described in 1959 in his landmark book *Black Like Me.* (I have seen this book used in high school classrooms during the past decade more than any other about Blacks.) Griffin, a white Texan, dyed his skin black and made an odyssey through the South to find out from within a black man's skin just how searing life was for Blacks. Halsell wanted to see how life had changed for Blacks since Griffin's book was written. Black friends warn her that she will not be able to endure it. One tells her, "when you're *born* black, you get prepared for shame." (p. 19) Halsell comes to understand, particularly, the shame of being a black woman:

I'm trying to imagine . . . what it is to be born a black girl, and all of my life have the people around me accept the idea that being beautiful is to have white skin and long straight hair, good hair. . . .

I'm a black girl and I have to spend endless hours of agony having hot combs put on my curly hair to straighten it, and rubbing bleach cream on my skin to lighten it, in order to achieve that national, *white* ideal. And all the while knowing that black men . . . think that a white girl is more attractive. . . . What does this do to me? To my morale? (pp. 37–38)

At first, black Grace Halsell goes to live in Harlem. A world traveler, she writes:

I can't imagine how I could see Harlem unless I had also seen New Delhi . . . the slums of Lima . . . Rio . . . Hong Kong. Here in Harlem is a special kind of "poverty," poverty amid affluence. In *our* slums the poor drink *diet* colas. And they go to the "poorhouse" in an automobile. Poorness here is of a different, more dismal, more poignant and paradoxical texture. (p. 63)

It is difficult for her to find a room, and when she finally does, it is as dreadful as the ones Griffin was forced to stay in. She finds that in the ghetto, garbage is never collected; food costs more than outside; there is a shortage of good food, such as fresh fruit; but that there are "sudden kindnesses" to her and to others that keep the ghetto moving.

They understand me, they are my fellow sufferers. We recognize that the ghetto is hell but that we're in it together. And the spirit is plain: for four hundred years we've smiled, licked boots, played prostitute, told the lies the white man wanted to hear. We put our best selves forward, giving the white man not only our physical energies as field and house slaves, but our best music and religious devotion. Now it's time for us to help ourselves, the niggers. (pp. 81–82)

Life only becomes dangerous when Halsell insists on leaving the security of the Northern ghetto to go to Mississippi. The only jobs she can get are as a domestic, and white housewives there still pay $5 a day for eight hours, despite the passage of the national minimum wage law. Her mistreatment moves her to the kind of thinking we found in the Angelou book. After several housework jobs, in which she is given ten minutes to eat a poor sandwich off a paper plate, prostitution appears less degrading than this kind of work:

. . . if I feel cheap and degraded, very much like a prostitute (except that a prostitute could make far more per hour without any more humiliation than mine), then I wonder what must a woman feel whose entire life stretches out before her with no other prospect? Selling oneself all day long for five dollars! (p. 158)

Halsell travels to Greenwood, Mississippi, where, in freezing weather, the bus clerk refuses to let her wait for her friends in the waiting room. When she insists, the clerk sends for the police. She is saved from arrest by the intervention of a white priest, but the experience has shaken her. She has found that a Black can be arrested for nothing more than asking to use the phone.

Someone warned Halsell that if she went through with her adventure, she would learn to hate her own people. Her discoveries are particularly important for class discussion. Her findings are hard, heavy, ugly, evil, but it is only through the recognition of what racism really is that our country can hope to improve:

. . . as a black woman, I found the devils of Harlem less menacing, craven, dishonest, cruel, ruthless, than the "superior" Caucasians of the South. The black devils of Harlem did not attempt to assault me and made no claims that compromised their dignity or mine. I hold no brief for their weaknesses and justify none of their delinquencies. I met them on their terms, as men and women whose color in no way deprived them of the complexes, hopes, fears, strivings, of the desire to make something of value and perhaps beauty out of the squalid and limited alternatives bequested them by white America.

Then I went South and was reminded again that nature is no match for man in his wayward ability to inflict pain. Nature can kill and maim, but lacks the capacity for psychic malice, for scarring the mind and spirit, that humans have.

Nothing in all my travels over the past two decades, nothing in my experiences, prepared me for going to the South as a black woman. The emotions I harbored belonged to two persons: a black woman and a white woman. I was cast in a twin, paradoxical role of oppressor and oppressed. (p. 220)

There are myriad books dealing with the black experience that are useful for the teenager. I have omitted some of these books because of space limitations; others (like Ralph Ellison's superb *Invisible Man*) because they are difficult to read; and still others because they are badly written. Books like James Cain's *Blueschild Baby* were omitted because of the language and excessive detailing of drug addiction.

American Indians

In 1964, for the first time, I visited the Canyon de Chelly, near Window Rock, Arizona. Until then, as an adult and mother of three children, as a university professor, I had never read any books dealing with the condition of the native Indian in America. The films I had seen always depicted Indians as drunken, irrational murderers and the only good Indians I had encountered were in the Leatherstocking Tales by James Fenimore Cooper and on the radio program, "The Lone Ranger." Although the condition of the American Indian has not improved notably since then, adolescent literature has erupted with books about the American Indian. Books written for adults, such as Berger's *Little Big Man*, have been made into films. Other films depicting the Indian as a sympathetic figure include *Billy Jack*, *Tell Them Willie Boy Is Here*, and *One Flew over the Cuckoo's Nest*. Landmark books such as Dee Brown's *Bury My Heart at Wounded Knee* and the writings of Vine Deloria, Jr., have been best sellers and have filtered down into adolescent literature. The Indians themselves, forming the militant American Indian Movement (AIM), have reached the news with events such as the takeovers of Alcatraz and Wounded Knee. Public figures such as Marlon Brando and Jane Fonda, continuing their fight for human rights, have demonstrated for and contributed to the Indian struggle.

Still, as with Blacks, the fate of the American Indian continues to be a sad and depressing one, and the need for young people to read and learn about the lives of their Indian brothers and sisters is of great importance. The following situation still exists:

1. Twelve thousand American Indian children are suffering because they cannot afford surgery.
2. The average American Indian child can expect to die before he reaches 48 years of age. Compare that with the average national life expectancy of over 70 years.
3. The average Indian family lives on less than $7.00 a day.

4. The suicide rate of the American Indians is 10 times the national average.
5. Fifty thousand American Indian children are living in filth and danger because of substandard housing.
6. The unemployment rate of the American Indian is 12 times the national average. And the average education level is 5th grade. (Statistics from the Native American Development Foundation.)

Good contemporary adolescent literature helps dramatize facts like those above and gives readers the information that has been hidden far too long. One of the best new novels is Mel Ellis's *Sidewalk Indian*, the story of Charlie Nightwind, a city (sidewalk) Indian who, during an Indian demonstration to protest inadequate and substandard housing, is accused of killing a policeman with a rock. He escapes from the police and returns to the land of his fathers—the Lost Nation Indian Reservation.

His mother had hated the reservation and called it a place of exile, "a trap, because that is what it was meant to be: a place to die, but no place to live." (p. 11) Charlie sees beauty in the reservation, even though his mother had told him only stories about the hardships of living there. She had told him "of unbelievable blizzards. Of snow for cauterizing the flow of blood at childbirth. Days in bed just to keep from freezing. Desperate men numb for weeks with whiskey. Rice and more rice, until it congealed, lumped in the throat." (p. 11)

The police come looking for Charlie, and the reservation Indians try to help him. When Betty Sands, one of the girls, asks him why he doesn't give himself up if he is innocent, he tells her with sad wisdom, "No. Someone is going to prison. They've decided it's going to be me. I'd rather be dead than locked up." (pp. 29–30) Students reading this book will find a parallel between the Indian and the black attitude toward white justice.

Together Charlie and Betty dream of what the reservation was like in the past, before the white man flooded it to make a dam. Betty tells him:

. . . it was as beautiful as it was bountiful. You must remember that when the water backed away from the dam, it covered the richest, probably the only rich soil in all this vast forest. The water drowned out 20,000 acres of the finest crop land anywhere. It was all bottom land. . . .

Everybody farmed, and in the river sloughs there were wild rice beds like you'd never believe. And on the slopes there was wood enough for everything and everyone. And with all this bottom land riches there was plenty left over for the deer, for all the animals and birds, and sometimes the partridges were so thick the people packed them in barrels and preserved them, nobody was ever hungry. An Indian could live like an Indian, and the old ways were observed. . . . (p. 55)

In those days, Betty tells him, the reservation was out-of-bounds to white men. "They were not permitted to fish or hunt here, and it was even illegal for a white man to buy game or fish from an Indian." (p. 56) They talk about how wonderful it would be to live again in the old way of their people. Betty says:

. . . and when that someday comes, the Indians will not have to dance for the tourists. They will not have to buy trinkets from Japan and blot out the message "made in Japan" so they can pawn them off as Indian handiwork. Maybe then the roads will not be lined with beer cans and whiskey bottles, because maybe then the Indian will have hope. (p. 56)

But for the present, while the dam covers the good land, the reservation is a prison on which the Indians starve. The land the government has given to them has no possibility of industry. And the government only gives them a pittance which saps their pride. Betty tells him, "I don't want the life of a revolutionary. Indians don't make good revolutionaries. They're idealistic but they have difficulty organizing and they have no stomach for brutality. I'm not asking for much. I only want enough to raise my children in dignity. As it is, it would be criminal to have children." (p. 135)

Charlie Nightwind helps his people dynamite the dam and dies in the attempt. But toward the end, he thinks:

Right or wrong, Charlie knew that at last he had come back to his people, that now he had earned the right to be proud of his ancestry. He had taken up the cause, fought the good fight with every ounce of his strength, his courage. And, he had found love, something he had not dared to hope for after the death of his mother. He felt he was an Indian. (p. 195)

This beautiful book is good for adolescents because it reveals not only the truth about the Indian condition but also the nobility, loyalty, and love that men are capable of under even the most terrible conditions.

The best books about American Indians are more than sociological exposés of the mistreatment of a minority group; their focus is not only on the need for acceptance in the white man's world and escape from poverty but also, and most importantly, on the necessity for every Indian as he/she matures to somehow remain *both* Indian and American—to honor the old Indian gods, ways, and traditions, while simultaneously adjusting to the new ways necessary for survival in American society. The need for this dual identity is a major topic for class discussion. Students must also consider and evaluate the old ways. How were they valuable, and what can they teach white America?

Hal Borland's *When the Legends Die* is a novel of the extraordinary strength and courage of a young Indian boy who is torn between the ancestral ways of his youth and the new ways of the white man. When his father takes young Thomas Black Bull and his mother into the wilderness in order to escape punishment for a murder, he is forced to take up life as it was in the old days, hunting and fishing. But an accident kills the father, and the grieving mother dies shortly afterward. The young Indian boy, despite his efforts not to enter the white man's world, is slowly and relentlessly drawn into it; and the book depicts his journey through life and his search for his own identity.

This book should be studied in both sociological and psychological terms. Indian psychology is intimately connected with nature: Everything springs from and returns to nature, and to live in harmony with nature and within yourself is the Ideal. Borland, a great nature writer, describes how Indian culture is expressed through nature. The Indian perceives life in terms of "roundness." Everywhere he looks he sees the roundness of things — the grass stems, the sun, the days, the nature cycles. These are all seen and experienced by the Indian as good, as part of his religion. Songs are perceived as the human way of expressing emotion. Women sing to their babies; men sing for the joy of the hunt; and there are songs of thanksgiving and mourning. The songs become the Indian prayers.

The reader should analyze and discuss the sociological aspects of the white man's world and their effect on the Indian. Tom is taken from the "real" and purposeful world of nature, alienated from it, and given "fake" work in the reservation in school. He has no interest in the reservation class in carpentry, and he is not a willing hand in the cow barns. He has more skill in the cobbler's shop and in the basketry shop where, using the old ways, he produces works of art. Students should do research into the Bureau of Indian Affairs' deliberate effort to destroy Indian culture by forcing the Indian children to leave their families and go to the reservation schools. This gratuitous act of cruelty, perpetrated against an already destroyed people, has the tragic implications of the Greek destruction of the last of the Trojan princes or of the Sicilian Don's desire, in the film *Godfather II*, to wipe out the Godfather as a child, to destroy the last of his line. Without didacticism, students may be encouraged to investigate these parallels.

The world of the white rodeo can be seen as a microcosm of white society. When Tom leaves the reservation school to live and work with Red Dillon, without any qualms Red turns Tom into a criminal, a con man who leads people to bet against him through trickery. Red teaches Tom, who has revered animals as part of Indian culture and considered even the bear as his brother, to ride his horse into the ground.

Red also teaches Tom another aspect of white morality: never trust anybody. To drive this lesson home, Red cuts the cinches on Tom's saddle and lets him take his fall. When Tom attempts to beat Red and is himself beaten, Red teaches him that he should never jump anyone bigger than he is unless he has an "evener," such as a club or gun. Red's philosophy, reflecting the values of white society, should be contrasted with the teachings of Tom's parents.

The exploitation of the Indian should be discussed. The Indians are offered silver for working in the saw mill, but most of their salaries are taken from them in order to pay for the furniture and supplies bought at the company store. They sign papers saying that they cannot quit and go away while they owe money for these things. In this way the Indians become serfs like the black sharecroppers after the Civil War. ("My soul belongs to the company store.")

I have heard students say that Red Dillon was not a bad man, because he gave Tom a trade through which he could achieve some fame and make a living. This is a shortsighted view, for although Red is no more evil than the rest of society, the fact remains that he turns a young boy, with so much capacity for good, into an animal killer.

The psychology of Tom and the people around him should be discussed. How has society changed Tom from a whole person in harmony with nature into a violent man, a killer of animals? What kind of people can give such enthusiastic receptions to Tom Black's devilishly violent rides?

The crowd didn't recognize him at first, then remembered his ride of the day before and began to applaud. Then it fell silent, awed at the cold viciousness and superb skill Tom showed. The horn blew and the crowd exploded in a roar of cheers. The horse was snorting bloody foam as the pickup men rode up and Tom pivoted out of the saddle . . . the crowd still roaring . . . (p. 124)

Tom becomes a living legend, and one of the fantastic stories about him says that Tom and the Devil were first cousins but that, in a fight, the Devil chopped off Tom's tail, and Tom was so enraged that the Devil had to turn himself into a bronc to get away. And so, the story goes, Tom Black became a bronc rider and tried to kill or maim every bronc he rode, just to be sure he got the right one. Tom's furious rides can be seen by students as his means of suppressing his Indian identity, of riding out his hatred of the white man and of himself.

The beauty of Borland's conception of the human soul is that it is never too late for regeneration. Tom sees time as similar to an onion, and when he returns to his ancestral home, he finds that he is able to let the layers of time slip off. "Time, he thought, was like the onions he had just peeled. Layer on layer, and to get down to the heart of things you let the layers peel off, one by one." (p. 18) Searching for himself, Tom reaches back to his beginnings and gradually begins hunting down all the painful things of the past, in order to kill them. In an ultimate, symbolic journey up a mountain, he kills Tom Black, the vengeful demon who rides horses to death; he finds and understands his own proud inheritance; and he again becomes Tom Black Bull, Indian. This is the significance of the novel's title: "When the legends die, the past dies, the dreams end, and then there is no future and no past greatness." Individuals must see their lives as both individual and collective. In order to have a future, an individual must recognize, accept, and be proud of his past. Borland shows the reader the terrible anguish that human beings must endure when society condemns the legends that have given their lives meaning and direction.

Hatter Fox, by Marilyn Harris, also depicts a young Indian's coming of age (see discussion in Chapter 1, pp. 53-54), and is particularly good for adolescents because it shows so clearly the different fates for whites and Indians in our society. The young white doctor's successful, middle-class existence, which began with "a morbidly normal, slightly indulged childhood, safe in an all-white world," contrasts sharply with Hatter's history of early and repeated abandonment and abuse, culminating in imprisonment and despair.

It should be noted that in both Borland's and Harris's books, violence is perpetrated against the protagonist by both white *and* Indian society, and it is this avoidance of black and white absolutes that gives the works both complexity and depth. However, it should also be noted that often the behavior of Indian society is caused indirectly by the effects of white society. Poverty, contempt, cruelty, and deprivation can cause people to see their own survival as the only goal, unrelated to the well-being of their brothers. *Sidewalk Indian* is the only one of these three books in which all of the Indians are good and treat each other as brothers. In *When the Legends Die*, Blue Elk is the Judas who assists the white man in degrading the ignorant and illiterate Indians; and in *Hatter Fox*, a superstitious Indian family falsely blames the child Hatter for the death of one of their children, torments and abandons her:

... The woman said I was a witch, said people died when I came around. I tried to tell them, but they wouldn't listen to me. They had a Sing then, and they all took me out to that canyon at the bottom of the cliff where the kid's body was and tied me up and made me lie down next to her. Her head was broken open, and they made me lie down in the blood, and they said her ghost would come back and kill me, and then she could be alive again. And they just left me there. (pp. 202-203)

But, as with Tom Black, the most terrible of Hatter's childhood experiences is at the white mission school, where kids are tortured, beaten, and humiliated.

The sympathetic young doctor describes his frustration over the continuing condition of the American Indian:

But the fate of the American Indian wasn't my fault. The melting pot or poverty were not my alternatives for them. Others had learned to adjust. "Adapt or perish"—that applied to all of us. Since I'd been in Santa Fe, I'd been rather impressed with our attempts to apologize to them. We fed them when they couldn't or wouldn't feed themselves. We provided them with free medical services and made concerted attempts to enlighten them, to destroy their myths and taboos. We made pets out of them, mascots for our football teams. We studied them, made graphs and statistics out of them, wrote anthropological tracts on them—a technological society's way of saying, "I'm sorry." Who said, "When a Democracy that advertises trust in God practices genocide, whom can you point a finger at and call villain?" ... (p. 61)

The young doctor in *Hatter Fox* cannot sweep away the facts, cannot mend the aftereffects of genocide, and ultimately can do nothing to help the doomed Indian. This same point is made in *Forever Island* by Patrick D. Smith, a story about how the Indian is doomed by what the white man considers progress. This novel is set in the Big Cypress Swamp, where Charlie Jumper, an eighty-six-year-old Seminole Indian, lives with his wife in the old Indian way. The Indian respect for nature pervades the book. Charlie tells his grandson who strikes out at a swarm of dragonflies, "Do not kill the creatures unless you have need of them. When you kill them without need you destroy a part of yourself." (p. 91) When his grandson replies that they are nothing but pesky dragonflies, Charlie gives him a lesson on ecology that trained ecologists are belatedly trying to explain to contemporary American society:

They are eating the mosquito. ... Then the bird will eat the dragonfly, and the bird will help spread the seeds of the plants and trees. The deer will eat the plants, and then we will eat the deer. We all have need of each other, and I have told you this before. ... The minnow will eat the mosquito also. ... The bass and the turtle will eat the minnow, and we will eat both of them. The snake will also eat the fish, and the alligator will eat the snake. Many years ago we used the hide of the alligator to make our war shields, and we ate the flesh of its tail. All things in the swamp are important, Timmy, and you should not kill without need." (pp. 91-92)

When the swamp is bought by a development company, Charlie and his wife, like so many Indians before them, are told that they must leave. The Indians are offered five hundred dollars for their houses, sheds, fences, and everything. Charlie's son's agonizing examination of options is a prototype of what so many dispossessed Indians have experienced:

His first inclination was to retreat further into the swamp, but he knew instantly that he must not do this for Timmy's sake. If he ran, like many of his people had run in the past, there would be no future life for Timmy. And he knew that he could not live along the Tamiami Trail. He had driven that highway many times, and he had seen many of his people reduced to the status of freaks in a circus, not by choice but by necessity to live. He closed his eyes and he could see the signs, Visit Joe Osceola's Indian Village, stop five miles ahead and see John Tiger Tail's Indian Village, the group of chickees behind the board fence, the souvenir shop in front, pay fifty cents and go through this door into the village, watch the Seminole wash his clothes, watch the Seminole cook, watch the Seminole eat, pay an extra quarter and watch the Seminole brave wrestle the alligator.

He knew also that he could not live in the labor camps to the north. He had once been to Pahokee, and he had seen the shacks one on top of another, stacked together like cordwood, the cheap whitewash gone and the roofs sagging, the bare dirt yards, the shacks so close together that they seemed to touch, crushing the life out of a man. . . .

There would also be no place for him on the reservation, where most of the land was either under water or so poor that it would grow only wiregrass and scrub cattle, and would not sustain even those who lived there now in scattered clusters of chickees and block houses (pp. 66–67)

The developers kill Charlie Jumper's old white friend who refuses to relinquish his one corner of the swamp. They poison the water and kill off the fish and wild life; and they make it impossible for Charlie and his family to continue to be self-sufficient with food taken from the swamp and surrounding brush. At the end of this book, Charlie Jumper's son, grandson, and wife make ready for the sad move to town, but Charlie will not go with them. He takes some food and goes off in his dugout to die in the heart of the swamp which has nurtured him for so many years. He says he is going to look for Forever Island, a legendary place where the original Seminoles hid when they had to flee from the white soldiers.

Forever Island is simple enough for junior high school students to read and deals with the same significant ideas (genocide and the rape of the land) presented in more complex books about the American Indian. The question should be raised: Are the Indians the only ones who have suffered from white society's greed, from the rape of the land? I would also hope that the teacher of adolescent literature would not merely expose readers to situations such as the terrible dislocation of people described in *Forever Island* but would also feel and convey to students moral indignation at such atrocities. The teacher, as a humanist, must help students make connections and develop a moral code that says, "this is wrong," whether the dislocation applies to displaced Europeans, displaced American Indians, or displaced American Japanese.

As in the study of black culture, it is necessary to go back in history to find out how the Indian got to his present position in society. No teacher can take it for granted that students know this history, or know it from the

Indian's point of view. Most Americans had never even heard of Wounded Knee until the publication of Dee Brown's book *Bury My Heart at Wounded Knee: An Indian History of the American West* and the contemporary occupation of Wounded Knee by members of the American Indian Movement. There are many good adolescent books that truthfully depict the plight of the American Indian, and it is important that these be studied because treaties between the U.S. Government and Indian tribes continue to be broken, and there is still some attempt being made to re-write American history. To illustrate, in 1975, the government attempted to charge that the original Wounded Knee massacre was not a massacre but a legitimate army skirmish in which the Indians fought back. Here is a description of this supposedly "legitimate skirmish":

The end of the 19th century Indian wars of the West occurred at Wounded Knee, South Dakota in 1890. After being relocated throughout the western states, the Indians realized that they could not win, that the warpath did not lead to victory. They turned more and more to messianic religious leaders who promised the return of the buffalo, or who called out against the farming of land. The use of peyote, a drug prepared from certain cactus, became part of their religious celebrations. The Ghost Dance was performed to hasten the mythic "Second Coming of the Buffalo" and the return of a way of life long gone.

Federal response was quick; the military and the government agents, concerned about these tribal rites, decided to put an end to them. Indians who did not comply with orders to cease the Ghost Dance were killed. (Sitting Bull and several of his Sioux braves died in such an encounter.) But at Wounded Knee, a group of Dakota Sioux continued their dance and used their peyote. The authorities ordered them to stop. The Indians continued their ritual. A new weapon, the Hotchkiss, a rapid-fire, mortar-like gun, was finally tested on Indians. When the smoke had cleared, three hundred Sioux had died.[4]

The Dee Brown book presents the settling of the West from 1860–1890, from the Indian point of view. Brown says about his book:

This is not a cheerful book, but history has a way of intruding upon the present, and perhaps those who read it will have a clearer understanding of what the American Indian is, by knowing what he was. They may be surprised to hear words of gentle reasonableness coming from the mouths of Indians stereotyped in the American myth as ruthless savages. They may learn something about their own relationship to the earth from a people who were true conservationists. The Indians knew that life was equated with the earth and its resources, that America was a paradise, and they could not comprehend why the intruders from the East were determined to destroy all that was Indian as well as America itself.

And if the readers of this book should ever chance to see the poverty, the hopelessness, and the squalor of a modern Indian reservation, they may find it possible to truly understand the reasons why. (p. xiii)

---

4. Gerald Messner, "Our Indian Heritage: An Instructor's Manual to *Rabbit Boss, The Lost Universe, Indian Oratory, The Way to Rainy Mountain, Geronimo: His Own Story.*" Ballantine, 1974. This brief instructor's manual is free and provides a concise, simple introduction to the history of the American Indian. *Rabbit Boss,* the novel with which most of this guide is concerned, is an outstanding novel, but is too long and complex for most secondary school students.

"To truly understand the reasons why" is at the heart of a study of adolescent literature dealing with minorities.

Each chapter in the Brown work deals with the history and destruction of a different tribe—a destruction paralleling the Nazis' extermination of the Jews. In both cases—the Nazis against the Jews, the whites against the American Indians—the end goal was total genocide. There never was any hope for the American Indian. Genocide was the goal, and in between the conception and the realization, the Indian was just being toyed with. It is painful to read of the gratuitous cruelty of the whites. In addition to lies, broken treaties, torture, rape, and robbery, we read of episodes such as the following:

I saw the American flag waving and heard Black Kettle tell the Indians to stand around the flag, and there they were huddled—men, women, and children. This was when we were within fifty yards of the Indians. I also saw a white flag raised. These flags were in so conspicuous a position that they must have been seen. When the troops fired, the Indians ran, some of the men into their lodges, probably to get their arms . . . I think there were 600 Indians in all. I think there were thirty-five braves and some old men, about sixty in all . . . the rest of the men were away from camp, hunting. . . . After the firing the warriors put the squaws and children together, and surrounded them to protect them. I saw five squaws under a bank for shelter. When the troops came up to them they ran out and showed their persons to let the soldiers know they were squaws and begged for mercy, but the soldiers shot them all. I saw one squaw lying on the bank whose leg had been broken by a shell; a soldier came up to her with a drawn saber; she raised her arms to protect herself, when he struck, breaking her arm; she rolled over and raised her other arm, when he struck, breaking it, and then left her without killing her. There seemed to be indiscriminate slaughter of men, women, and children. There were some thirty or forty squaws collected in a hole for protection; they sent out a little girl about six years old with a white flag on a stick; she had not proceeded but a few steps where she was shot and killed. All the squaws in that hole were afterwards killed, and four or five bucks outside. The squaws offered no resistance. Every one I saw dead was scalped. I saw one squaw cut open with an unborn child, as I thought, lying by her side. . . . I saw the body of White Antelope with the privates cut off, and I heard a soldier say he was going to make a tobacco pouch out of them. I saw one squaw whose privates had been cut out. . . . I saw a little girl about five years of age who had been hid in the sand; two soldiers discovered her, drew their pistols and shot her, and then pulled her out of the sand by the arm. I saw quite a number of infants in arms killed with their mothers. (p. 88)

These terrible, sickening, heartrending episodes, as reported by both whites and Indians, go on and on. And painful as it is for students and teachers to know, it is even more dangerous not to know. The following are three important topics for student discussion: 1) The parallels between American attitudes toward all dark-skinned people. (Arthur Kopit wrote his play, *Indians*, during the Vietnam War, and the centerfold of the published play contains photographs of American actions in Vietnam.) 2) The beauty of Indian religious philosophy—the oneness with nature, the desire for freedom, the simple kindness of the original Indians who believed in sharing, in giving, in friendship and trust; in essence, the Indian value system contrasted with the greed of the white settlers. 3) The results of genocide, greed, and lack of respect for the earth—the destroyed and debased Indian nation, the continued poverty and mistreatment of the Indian, and ecological problems, such as pollution and depleted natural resources.

Brown ends with the words of Black Elk after Wounded Knee:

I did not know then how much was ended. When I look back now from this high hill of my old age, I can still see the butchered women and children lying heaped and scattered all along the crooked gulch as plain as when I saw them with eyes still young. And I can see that something else died there in the bloody mud, and was buried in the blizzard. A people's dream died there. It was a beautiful dream . . . the nation's hoop is broken and scattered. There is no center any longer, and the sacred tree is dead. (p. 419)

A book that complements Brown's is *The Road to Wounded Knee* by Robert Burnette and John Koster. This book deals with the 1973 second war at Wounded Knee. Most teenagers have strong feelings about justice and fair play and will be appalled at the continued interference, mistreatment, and lack of justice in addition to the original genocide. The crime against the Indian goes on, and there is no remedy or repentance.

The 1973 occupation of Wounded Knee was an attempt by militants, tired of terrible living conditions, to focus the world's attention on what was happening to dark-skinned native Americans at the very same time that the United States was destroying the Vietnamese.

Enraged by the mockery of justice, the militants planned drastic means to regain their rights and to topple the government-sanctioned corruption and tyranny of the tribal council and chairman. They were joined by tribal elders who had suffered all their lives at the hands of heartless bureaucrats and who saw a last chance to live—or perhaps to die—with a measure of dignity and self-respect.

Both the Burnette and the Brown books are on the high school level, but many simpler history-oriented books suitable for junior high school readers are also available. *People of the Dream* by James Forman is one of the best of such books. The book opens with a particularly powerful scene in which the young Joseph, swimming in a stream on Indian land, is grabbed by the hair by two white hunters, who accuse him of being there to steal beaver. Readers will note immediately the gap between the Indian's culture and the white man's. "The boy, who had never hunted anything but fish, who belonged to a tribe to whom the thought of trapping beaver for their skins alone was repellent, only lowered his face." (p. 13) Only a quarrel between the two brutal, drinking hunters enables Joseph to escape without death or serious injury. One tries to force the young boy to drink and boasts:

Whiskey peddlers are the advance guard of civilization. That's the damned truth. You know it. And it's a damn sight better way for the old Redskin to go and a sight less trouble than having to take his scalp. I'd give him a hoe if I thought he'd hang onto it. Don't matter much. . . . (p. 17)

Gradually the boy sees the white man break treaty after treaty with the Nez Percé Indians. As he comes into his leadership, espousing peace, brotherhood, and "not fighting," Joseph finds himself in conflict with other, more militant leaders. Chief Joseph argues, "You can never kill them all. They are like the grasshoppers in the prairies. We are few. We must save the lives of our people and shed no blood." (p. 31) But Ollokot, another leader, answers: "Brother . . . cannot the greatest trouble sometimes come from trying to avoid trouble? Have not the whites pushed down our fathers' stones, and taken our cattle and built their wooden lodges on our land?" (p. 31) Readers should evaluate the conflict between militant separatists and advocates of nonviolence and peaceful coexistence—a conflict recurring in the 1960s among American Blacks and still far from being resolved.

The white man refuses to respect the Nez Percé ways, and war is inevitable. But Chief Joseph has no stomach for killing, and so he leads his people on an unbelievably difficult thousand-mile trek toward freedom in Canada. Thirty miles from the Canadian border, the U.S. Cavalry prevents the Nez Percé from achieving freedom. (This action parallels the Russians' mistreating their Jews and yet not allowing them to leave for other countries.) Many of the Indians are killed, and the remainder are sent back to Fort Leavenworth as prisoners. The reader is moved and appalled at the needless murder, cruelty, and waste of human life. The descriptions of the many relocations of the imprisoned Indians will bring to mind the horror of the Nazi concentration camps.

One of the most accessible books to use with adolescents is a fine collection of contemporary short stories by American Indians called *The Man to Send Rain Clouds*, edited by Kenneth Rosen. These beautifully written stories have a clarity, simplicity, and style that make them comprehensible even to junior high school students. Together they give a fascinating picture of past and present Indian life. In "The Man to Send Rain Clouds," Leslie Silko writes with humor of the gap between Christianity and the Indian philosophy and religion. When their old grandfather dies, Leon and Ken prepare him for death in the Indian fashion, with paint and feathers. When the ceremony is over, Leon prays: "Send us rain clouds, Grandfather."

Then Leon goes to the local priest and asks him to sprinkle holy water at the grave so that their Grandfather will not be thirsty. At first, petulantly, the priest refuses, saying, "there should have been the Last Rites and a funeral Mass at the very least." (p. 7) But the priest finally capitulates, trying to be patient with these Indians who just can't learn the right way. He sprinkles the holy water and leaves, not knowing the significance of the water to the Indians. Leon feels happy about the sprinkling of the holy water: "Now the old man could send them big thunderclouds for sure." (p. 8) In-depth discussion will be needed in order for teenagers to understand the significance of this subtle story.

In another story by Silko, "Tony's Story," we see the terrible harassment of this same Leon by a brutal policeman on the reservation, after Leon is discharged from the army. Some of Leon's new ideas are as strange to his cousin, Tony, as are the ideas of whites. Tony says: "I couldn't understand why Leon kept talking about 'rights'. . . ." (p. 74)

Leon writes to the Governor and to the Bureau of Indian Affairs, but his cousin gives him an arrowhead on a piece of string to wear around his neck for protection.

"You don't believe in *that,* do you?" He pointed to the .30-30 leaning against the wall. "I'll take this with me whenever I'm in the pickup."
"But you can't be sure that it will kill one of them."
Leon looked at me and laughed. "What's the matter," he said, "have they brainwashed you into believing that a .30-30 won't kill a white man?" He handed back the arrowhead. "Here, you wear two of them." (p. 75)

"Chapter I" by Anna Lee Walters is a moving story about the October 1863 massacre of Indians who had taken shelter from Kit Carson in the Canyon de Chelly. The hunted people are having their first hot meal in many weeks. Natanii, the little boy who tells this story, looks at his hounded people and wonders how this all came about. "Silently he asked himself why the people were hungry all the time. He asked himself about the fear they lived with daily. . . ." (p. 83)

The study of the American Indian through adolescent literature would not be complete without the non-fiction book by Vine Deloria, Jr., *We Talk, You Listen.* Deloria points out that it is necessary for every minority group to understand the historical background from which contemporary problems arise, but he warns against a preoccupation with the past that neglects options for the future. His unique point of view looks to the future and provides fruitful material for class discussion, especially in relation to the horrors depicted in the Brown book. Deloria is impatient with useless pity for the past:

It has become traditional to cry over the plight of Indian people. Yet a people with fifty-four million acres of land worth $3 billion should not be in a state of poverty, nor should they have a "plight." Liberals have tended to equate the Southern red-necked sheriff and the Bureau of Indian Affairs. Thus we have had people ask us how we got off the reservation, how often we are beaten by government agents, and how they can help us to become free. They continue to talk about "organizing" the poor Indians as if we were some conglomerate slum population that was dependent upon their goodwill for survival, in spite of the fact that Indian tribes have been organized as federally chartered corporations under the Indian Reorganization Act of 1934 for over a generation. (p. 82)

Attitudes toward minorities should be discussed in terms of what Deloria calls the "old" and the "new" worlds. In his new world, relations will not simply be viewed as black-white relations or white-Indian relations. He advocates decentralization, democratization, and tribalization. This means, in part, that Indian-black relations will be seen as uniquely different from white-Indian relations. The uniqueness of each group of people will be understood and accepted. "American society," he writes, "has never recognized that groups exist." (p. 110) Here, Deloria refers to the old theory of the "melting pot," the somewhat naive idea that all Americans were going to become one big happy family. "Once we have rejected this melting pot," he writes, "we can arrive at new definitions of social problems." (p. 111) When Americans recognize, simultaneously, both the integrity and the common humanity of each group, when the stereotypes (such as "lustful Blacks" or "lazy Indians") die and the necessity for negotiations between all groups is understood, we will enter the new world. This would mean that the groups themselves, rather than paternalistic whites, would manage and be responsible for their own destinies.

Adolescent literature provides the springboard for discussions that can help secondary school students develop a new, enlightened understanding of the function of minorities in a democracy. The movement from this literature is outward, into the social world, not inward into the study of form and technique for their own sake. Excellence is perceived in terms of clarity of subject matter, honesty, and personal and social growth, with form and style being important only insofar as they enhance the impact of the material and facilitate understanding of humanistic ideas.

Chicanos

Until the 1960s, not much literature about Mexican Americans was available for the secondary school. Mexicans were mentioned only in relation to the Alamo, and stereotypes were applied to them that were not much different from those applied to other dark-skinned peoples. They were thought to be excessively sexual, lazy, stupid, and dirty.

César Chavez's movement to unionize migrant farm workers and the boycotts of lettuce and grapes introduced many Americans to Chicanos for the first time. Young people opposing the war in Vietnam and injustice within the United States took up the cause, "La Causa," and even in remote eastern towns one could find young people stationed at supermarket entrances beseeching people not to buy grapes. In fact, after the Kennedys embraced Chavez, it became part of radical chic not to eat California grapes.

The origins of the word "Chicano" are obscure, but the word now refers to the Mexican American whose heritage is part Indian, part Spanish, and now American. A characteristic of Chicano literature (and also of Puerto Rican literature, which will be discussed later) is its mixture of Spanish with English and its references to Mexico as the mother country, the heartland, the place where the present Chicano culture began.

A good introduction to Chicano literature is Rodolfo Gonzales's *I Am Joaquin: Yo Soy Joaquin*. Printed in both Spanish and English, this was the first work of poetry to be published by Chicanos for Chicanos, and it contains a chronology of people and events in Mexican and Chicano history. The book contains fine photographs: César Chavez ending his fast for La Causa in 1968 (to dramatize the strike by grape workers against California table-grape growers, Chavez fasted for 25 days); Diego Rivera's mural about Quetzalcoatl, the legendary god-king of the Aztecs; and other murals by famous Mexican artists such as Orozco and Martinez. There are other photographs of incidents in Chicano history, such as the one of a demonstrator killed by Los Angeles County sheriff's deputies during the Vietnam moratorium march of January 31, 1971.

In addition to giving students an immediate visual impression of Chicano life and history, this book describes concisely the past and present, beginning with the words:

I am Joaquin, lost in a world of confusion, caught up in the whirl of a gringo society, confused by the rules, scorned by attitudes, suppressed by manipulations, and destroyed by modern society. My fathers have lost the economic battle and won the struggle of cultural survival. (p. 6)

The book recounts the glory of Aztec society; the coming of the murderous conquistadores; the fight for Mexican independence from Spain in 1821; the struggles of Juárez, Pancho Villa, and Zapata; the continued repression in Mexico; the mistreatment of Mexicans in the United States; and, finally, the movement for recognition, La Raza (the people), beginning in 1962 with Chavez's organizing of the first agricultural union in the United States (UFWOC, United Farm Workers Organizing Committee). Simple enough for the middle-school reading level, Gonzales's book contains all of the important concepts that are discussed in other more complex books.

Macho! by Edmund Villaseñor is a superb book covering much the same material presented in *I Am Joaquin.* Because the present of the Chicano cannot be understood without reference to the past, *Macho!* begins in Mexico and gives the reader an idea of why the Mexican would endure any hardship in order to come to the United States. Just in terms of their own ancestors, and in terms of all minority groups, it is important for adolescents to understand the very depths of the Mexicans' poverty. Each chapter begins with a one-page factual description of something that will be dealt with or referred to in the fictional text; this unusual and interesting arrangement helps the reader place the fictional events in the real world.

Eighteen-year-old Roberto has become the support of his family because of his father's drunkenness. He is intelligent, strong, and efficient, and is soon made foreman of a government project to bring water to his small Mexican village. He must fight not only poverty but also ignorance and superstition, for the older men who work under him resent his success and attribute it to his having sold his soul to the devil. The isolation of his village is interrupted only by the Norteños, men who have gone to the United States and returned with what constitutes great wealth in the eyes of the little village: "And they always come back with a new Texan hat, a tejana, and two new pairs of Levi's and one beautiful suede jacket from a Mexican border town, and, most important of all, a .45 automatic with two extra clips, and they are NORTEÑOS!" (p. 21) The villagers ignore the fact that many men who go to the United States never return or return sick and more impoverished than before.

Poverty and superstition force Roberto to join another man for the odyssey to the United States. In the late 1950s and 1960s, seven hundred miles south of the United States border, there was a temporary labor camp for the legalization of labor to the United States:

The Americans had put up offices in a huge warehouse, and there they processed a labor force of braceros to work in the United States. . . . And men were processed by the thousands every day, but still more came. . . . Men! Hungry and lost and in the heat of the day well over a hundred degrees they stood in lines of tens of thousands like cattle. And soon they began suffocating each other and passing out by the hundreds, and as one fell, quickly another would pick his pocket and disappear into the mass of no one knowing anyone . . . and the fallen one would be trampled as they moved up, exhausted and sweaty, like starving dogs trying to get contracted into the land of plenty. They had been in line for weeks, months, and they were waiting for no man. They had borrowed, stolen, and begged to get the money to get this far, and they had to do it! They had family depending on them. (pp. 73–74)

In 1963, the bracero program was stopped by the United States because there was so much migrant labor coming in from Mexico that wages had been pushed down to sixty cents an hour. Still men continued to come across the border illegally and to live and work in murderous conditions.

Two of the many significant questions raised by Villaseñor's novel are why people become migrant laborers and how unionization can help them. The following selection can be used to stimulate student discussion of these questions, as well as to illustrate the contempt some people have for the unfortunate:

"Look," said the police captain, "in a nutshell, I'll tell you all. I come from the fields; I now work with the growers; I know both sides, and no one can pull the sheep over my eyes. Of course there are problems, injustice, and gross abusements—mostly because of neglect—in the fields.

"Hell, no one cares about migrating people: here today, there tomorrow. There is no dignity in laboring under the sun in the dust and wind. Field workers have always been the lowest and will always be the lowest. I say César Chavez is a fool, impractical and ignorant, to try to improve the conditions for the Mexican in the fields. I say to hell with The Factories of the Field. Let them remain awful! Encourage the Mexican to get educated and get the hell out of the fields. That would be the humane position for Chavez to take."

"But . . ." said the young Chicano, "who would then pick the tomatoes, the melons, the . . ."

He leaped. "Who gives a shit? Let the Okies do it! The niggers! The hippies in their summer vacation! I don't care! I made it; they can make it." And there he stood . . . a tall, big-bellied police captain of Mexican descent. (p. 199)

There are several good collections of Chicano writing suitable for secondary school students who are interested in further reading about this group. The best collections are *Voices of Aztlan: Chicano Literature of Today*, edited by Dorothy E. Harth and Lewis M. Baldwin; *The Chicano: From Caricature to Self-Portrait*, edited by Edward Simmen; and *Pain and Promise: The Chicano Today*, edited by Edward Simmen.

One article in *Pain and Promise* asks the questions that apply to all minority groups in the United States—controversial questions that students should be encouraged to discuss freely and openly:

Just what have we been expecting of immigrant groups as they move toward assimilation? The loss of any identifying ethnic difference that might set them apart from the "average" American? If so, the Mexican American has little to hope for, since he is marked off from the dominant American pattern by his own unique blend of Spanish and Indian in racial type as well as in culture, religion, and language. He cannot easily merge into the white, Protestant, English-speaking group of Anglo Americans with whom he comes in contact in the Southwest. Yet should merging even be the goal? Are we perhaps ready to recognize that the "melting pot" describes an assumption rather than a reality in American social life? That there are immigrant groups of long residence in this country who have neither melted nor merged in the areas of their personal and private social lives, yet have still found a secure place in the economic and political sphere? And is this not a legitimate alternative to our earlier assumption that there is something wrong with any group that does not merge on all levels? It is the rigidity of the demand for either total assimilation or subordination that the Mexican American questions when he says "This country should be big enough to allow us the freedom to be different without being oppressed." (Marjorie Fallows, "The Mexican American Laborers: A Different Drummer?" in *Pain and Promise*, pp. 315–316)

Japanese Americans

Kathleen Wright's *The Other Americans: Minorities in American History* is a good background book for students reading adolescent literature about minorities. What we want young people to understand is that people everywhere are capable of great inhumanity and that the recognition of both past events and future possibilities is the best way to work toward a humane future.

In Unit Eight of *The Other Americans*, "Depression, New Deal, and World War II," the historical background of the Japanese in America is summarized.

In 1940 some 27,000 of the 80,000 Nisei [second-generation Japanese Americans] were over twenty-one. . . . Many were highly intelligent, well-educated, but discrimination in hiring, especially on the West Coast, forced them into service occupations and closed most fields of economic advancement. (p. 198)

Stanford University reported that

It is almost impossible to place a Chinese or Japanese of either the first or second generation in any kind of position, engineering, manufacturing or business.

From the State College of Washington came the report:

We have some of them that speak English perfectly and know nothing about Japan, who are forced to go to Japan for employment. (p. 199)

The socioeconomic future for Japanese Americans seemed to be improving when the Japanese attacked Pearl Harbor. After this began what is considered one of America's greatest wartime blunders. Japanese Americans were viewed as disloyal aliens and were sent to repatriation camps. Before the repatriation, "grocers and other merchants refused to sell them products. Japanese newspapers were suspended. Many of the older leaders of the people were called in for questioning and kept in such a state of turmoil that they were often unable to return to their work." (p. 200)

The best adolescent literature dealing with this period is *Farewell to Manzanar*[5] by Jeanne Wakatsuki Houston and James D. Houston, a true story of Japanese-American experience during and after the World War II internment. The chronology of government acts at the beginning of the book will help students to understand the American prejudice toward Oriental people. For example, in 1870, the U.S. Congress granted "naturalization rights to free whites and people of African descent, omitting mention of Oriental races" (p. xi). In 1911, the U.S. Bureau of Immigration and Naturalization again refused naturalization to the Japanese. In 1913, the Alien Land Bill prevented Japanese from owning land in California, and in 1924, Congress passed an Immigration Act that "stopped all immigration from Japan" (p. xi). In the war year 1942, the following events occurred. On February 19, President Roosevelt signed Executive Order 9066, giving the War Department authority to define military areas in the western states and to exclude from them anyone who might threaten the war effort. On March 25, evacuees began to arrive at Manzanar Camp, in Owens Valley, California, the first of the permanent camps to open. On August 12, the evacuation was completed—110,000 people of Japanese ancestry removed from the West Coast to inland camps. On December 18, the U.S. Supreme Court ruled that loyal citizens cannot be held in detention camps against their will, the first major step toward the closing of the camps.

U.S. laws always implied that the Japanese were less than desirable Americans; and, as Gordon Allport shows in *The Nature of Prejudice*, verbal or latent prejudice, when sanctioned by law, becomes active and violent. Students should discuss how cold wars turn into hot wars, and how to avoid hot wars by confronting the hostility before it erupts.

Farewell to Manzanar is a good book for young people because it is written from the point of view of Jeanne as a child—a child who actually spent three years inside an internment camp with her family. First Jeanne's father is taken away by the FBI, and Jeanne's mother starts to weep all the time. "I remember clinging to her legs, wondering why everyone was crying. This was the beginning of a terrible, frantic time for all my family." (p. 7) The family is given forty-eight hours to clear out of their home. They are forced to sell their precious possessions to secondhand dealers for almost nothing. In one of the most powerful scenes in the book, a secondhand dealer offers Jeanne's mother a humiliating fifteen dollars for a precious set of china, and she furiously smashes the entire set in front of him.

Jeanne describes the chaos of all the displaced Japanese Americans suddenly being sent to an unfinished internment camp with faulty public bathrooms, improper clothing for an altitude of 4,000 feet, and no money, food, or activities to do in the camp. When her Papa is finally returned to his family at Manzanar, he has been destroyed as a person. "He had been gone nine months. He had aged ten years." (p. 32) He is unable to adjust to the fact that after 35 years in the United States he is still

---

5. A fine television movie was made from this work.

treated as an enemy. He takes to drink and never again is his old, proud, active self. She says: "He didn't die there [at Manzanar], but things finished for him there, whereas for me it was like a birthplace." (p. 34)

Jeanne and her family had little to return to after their release from Manzanar. Many of their possessions, such as her father's fishing boat, had been stolen, and there were no reparations from the government. Kathleen Wright in *The Other Americans* explains:

[There were] numerous instances of greed which moved white residents and business partners to . . . despoil the Japanese of their property and possessions. Many a tidy fortune was made at the expense of the Japanese. . . . The amount of luggage that could be carried was severely limited. Homes, furnishings, businesses, all these were left to the mercy of unscrupulous people who seized them illegally or purchased them for a trifle of their real value from the frightened evacuees. (p. 203)

Jeanne's description of her family's situation and her father's reaction should provide the basis for a significant classroom discussion:

Mama picked up the kitchenware and some silver she had stored with neighbors in Boule Heights. But the warehouse where she'd stored the rest had been unaccountably "robbed"—of furniture, appliances, and most of those silver anniversary gifts. Papa already knew the car he'd put money on before Pearl Harbor had been repossessed. And, as he suspected, no record of his fishing boats remained. This put him right back where he'd been in 1907, arriving in a new land and starting over from economic zero.

It was another snip of the castrator's scissors, and he never really recovered from this, either financially or spiritually. Yet neither did he entirely give up. One of the amazing things about America is the way it can both undermine you and keep you believing in your own possibilities, pumping you with hope.

The second paragraph of the above passage is pertinent to all of the literature discussed in this chapter.

Also relevant to all minorities are Jeanne's experiences when she returns to a white school. One of the students is surprised that she can speak English, and Jeanne realizes that from then on she will be viewed "as someone foreign, or as someone other than American, or perhaps not be seen at all." (p. 114)

From that day on, part of me yearned to be invisible. In a way, nothing would have been nicer than for no one to see me. Although I couldn't have defined it at the time, I felt that if attention were drawn to me . . . they wouldn't see me, they would see the slant-eyed, the Oriental. This is what accounts, in part, for the entire evacuation. You cannot deport 110,000 people unless you have stopped seeing individuals. Of course, for such a thing to happen, there has to be a kind of acquiescence on the part of the victims, some submerged belief that this treatment is deserved, or at least allowable. It's an attitude easy for nonwhites to acquire in America. I had inherited it. Manzanar had confirmed it. And my feeling, at eleven, went something like this: You are going to be invisible anyway, so why not completely disappear.

But another part of me did not want to disappear. . . . From that day forward I lived with this double impulse; the urge to disappear and the desperate desire to be acceptable. (p. 114)

Jeanne's double impulse can be echoed by all nonwhites in this country.

Puerto Ricans

An excellent fictional work to use with any class is Nicholasa Mohr's *El Bronx Remembered*, a beautiful collection of short stories about Puerto Rican life in the tenements of El Bronx. Mohr's writing is humorous, her style is outstanding, and she has the ability to see things from a child's point of view. The book is also about the varieties of love, depicted with the tender affection of someone writing from within a minority group. Mohr shows us that even in the poorest ghetto, people are capable of beautiful relationships. In her introduction she writes:

There have been Puerto Ricans living in the mainland U.S.A. since the middle of the last century. But it was after the second World War, when traveling became cheaper and easier, that the greatest influx began. In 1946, Puerto Ricans could purchase, for a small amount of money, a one-way ticket to the mainland. As citizens they did not face immigration laws or quotas . . . and so they arrived by the tens of thousands, first by freighter and later by airplane.

A small percentage went to work as migrant workers in the rural areas of the country. The majority settled in New York City. Many went to live in Spanish Harlem, known as El Barrio, an older community of Spanish-speaking people, on Manhattan's Upper East Side. There they joined family and friends. Others moved into congested neighborhoods inhabited by the children of earlier immigrant groups. Thus, they formed new neighborhoods in Brooklyn and Manhattan's Lower East Side. One area in particular was heavily populated by these newcomers, and became an extension or suburb of Spanish Harlem. This was the South Bronx, known to the Puerto Ricans as "El Bronx."

These migrants and their children, strangers in their own country, brought with them a different language, culture, and racial mixture. Like so many before them they hoped for a better life, a new future for their children, and a piece of that good life known as the "American dream."

This collection of stories is about the Puerto Rican migrants and their everyday struggle for survival, during that decade of the promised future 1946 through 1956, in New York City's "El Bronx."

Mohr's book is not as bitter as many of the books discussed in this chapter. Mohr, in her use of humor and language, is closer to Sholem Aleichem than to writers like Maya Angelou, James Baldwin, or Marilyn Harris. In "A Very Special Pet," the mother of a hungry family in El Bronx attempts to kill their pet hen, Joncrofo (named after Joan Crawford), and finally gives up in desperation as she realizes that it is as important for her children to have something to love as it is for them to have something to eat.

In "Tell the Truth . . . ," a lawyer attempts to trick twelve-year-old Vicki into saying that her mother sells drugs. The contrasts between black and white culture are embarrassingly funny as depicted by Mohr. The lawyer tells Vicki: "I love Spanish and I love your country. My family and I were in San Juan last winter. What an Island of Paradise! You should be proud of your country, Victoria. I know many, many Puerto Ricans. They visit us and we visit them. . . ." (p. 28) Listening to him, Vicki thinks:

Vicki and her younger sisters and brothers were born in New York and had seldom left the Bronx. Every morning in school they pledged allegiance "to the flag of the United States of America, and to the republic for which it stands." She had never thought of Puerto Rico as her country. (p. 29)

Vicki is reminiscent of the second and third generation Japanese Americans (like Jeanne Houston) who found that they were still thought of as Japanese rather than as American.

Students should note Mohr's emphasis on inter-group relations. In "Mr. Mendelsohn," a Puerto Rican family, without condescension or self-consciousness, adopt an old Jewish man who is their neighbor and give him some family life and joy during the years before he is sent to an old folks' home. And in "The Wrong Lunch Line," we see the efforts of a Puerto Rican girl and a Jewish girl to remain friends when the Puerto Rican girl accompanies her friend on the kosher lunch line.

Books Discussed in Chapter II

If Beale Street Could Talk, James Baldwin, Signet, 1974.
The Friends, Rosa Guy, Bantam, 1973.
The Soul Brothers and Sister Lou, Kristin Hunter, Avon, 1968.
A Hero Ain't Nothin' But a Sandwich, Alice Childress, Avon, 1973.
Teacup Full of Roses, Sharon Bell Mathis, Avon, 1972.
Gather Together in My Name, Maya Angelou, Bantam, 1974.
Listen for the Fig Tree, Sharon Bell Mathis, Avon, 1974.
Autobiography of Miss Jane Pittman, Ernest Gaines, Bantam, 1972.
Soul Sister, Grace Halsell, Fawcett, 1969.
Sidewalk Indian, Mel Ellis, Holt, Rinehart and Winston, 1974.
When the Legends Die, Hal Borland, Bantam, 1963.
Hatter Fox, Marilyn Harris, Bantam, 1974.
Forever Island, Patrick D. Smith, Dell, 1974.
Bury My Heart at Wounded Knee, Dee Brown, Bantam, 1962.
The Road to Wounded Knee, Burnette and Koster, Bantam, 1974.
People of the Dream, James Forman, Dell, 1974.
The Man to Send Rain Clouds, edited by Kenneth Rosen, Vintage, 1975.
We Talk, You Listen, Vine Deloria, Jr., Dell, 1970.
I Am Joaquin: Yo Soy Joaquin, Rodolfo Gonzales, Bantam, 1972.
Macho!, Edmund Villaseñor, Bantam, 1973.
Voices of Aztlan: Chicano Literature of Today, edited by Harth and Baldwin, NAL, 1974.
The Chicano: From Caricature to Self-Portrait, edited by Simmen, NAL, 1971.
Pain and Promise: The Chicano Today, edited by Simmen, NAL, 1972.
The Other Americans: Minorities in American History, Kathleen Wright, Fawcett, 1969.
Farewell to Manzanar, Houston and Houston, Bantam, 1974.
El Bronx Remembered, Nicholasa Mohr, Bantam, 1976.

III
regions and locales

Much of our literature deals with the rootlessness and restlessness of individuals in American society: the desire for mobility alternating with the longing for roots. Despite the increasing homogeneity of our society, distinct regional differences remain, and for the adolescent, permanently or temporarily trapped in a specific region, the best means of travel remains through literature. Questions to be asked and answered through the study of regional literature have to do with the disposition and behavior patterns of people in particular regions, dialects and language differences, and, above all, those common threads that unite the people in the works with those in the rest of America and the world.[1]

The South

Vera and Bill Cleaver, a husband and wife team, are perhaps the most outstanding writers of Southern regional literature for young people. They handle dialect particularly well, exposing readers from other regions to speech that is local and delightful, an inseparable part of both the setting and the tone of humor that permeate their books. The geography of the South they describe is as fascinating as in the more advanced works of Southern writers such as Faulkner, Flannery O'Connor, or Carson McCullers.

In the small towns of the Cleavers, life is hard. Their characters are assailed by floods, poverty, lack of education, poor food, poor shelter, and inadequate transportation. What redeems life to some degree is the closeness to nature and also the human relations possible in small towns where families have known each other for generations. It is the reviving power of nature that enables the young people in the Cleavers' books to transcend poverty and the usual problems of coming of age.

---

1. Space limits the number of settings that can be discussed in this chapter. Those described, therefore, should be viewed as illustrative of the kinds of insights students can get into their own locales through adolescent literature.

93

In the Cleavers' *The Whys and Wherefores of Littabelle Lee*, Littabelle lives with her grandparents and Aunt Sorrow in the Ozark Mountains, "with the old, unspoiled hills rising up all around us and the hollows and watered valleys a part of our everyday scenery." (p. 5)

Littabelle's parents were drowned in a flood. Paw Paw, her grandfather, is descended from English and Scotch forebears, all of whom were peasant yeomen. She tells us that Paw Paw has always "lived hard by this land," never making more than four hundred dollars in any one year from his crops and livestock. Aunt Sorrow is an herbal healer. Had she lived in a different environment and had some money, she would have studied to be a doctor. As it is, she knows all of the properties of local plants and is able to effect cures with them. This knowledge of local plants runs throughout the Cleavers' works.

When lightning hits their farm and destroys the house, Littabelle, her aunt, and her aged grandparents have to move into the unheated barn. Littabelle becomes the local schoolteacher, although she is not particularly well educated. After a terrible winter of no heat, not enough food, and poor clothing, Littabelle decides to take her other aunts and uncles to court to force them to contribute to the support of their parents. Littabelle wins and comes into her own. She understands that she's a lot like her dead mother: "She was never satisfied with the way things was but always had to be changing them around, trying to better them." (p. 139)

We want adolescents to see how a person like Littabelle, with spunk, grit, native intelligence, and an instinctive sense of right and wrong, can improve her environment and make something of herself. At the end of the book, she is considering going to see the Governor, whose life her Aunt Sorrow once saved, to say: "Governor, I am here to ask your advice and maybe I need a little more than that too. I can teach; that is what I want to do. I have found that out. But there is a limit to what a person like me can do; I have found that out too. So I need to go for a while to the place where teachers are taught how to be teachers and learn to be a real one." (p. 142)

The important message of this book is hope. Littabelle's environment and problems are indigenous to her region, but her hope and spirit can inspire young people everywhere.

Another Cleaver book *Where the Lilies Bloom* is set in the Great Smoky Mountains of Tennessee. The narrator is Mary Call, whose dying father, Roy Luther, is a sharecropper. This book, like *Littabelle Lee*, teaches students about certain economic aspects of the South. Mary Call says: "Just years and years of it [sharecropping] and when the time comes for tallying up, Kiser's always getting the hog's share and Roy Luther always having to settle for the meanest." (p. 13)

We also learn about the food of this region. Mary Call says: "We are mountain people so we eat mountain food. Liver mush and fried cabbage and cranberry beans cooked to nutty goodness with slabs of thick fatback." (p. 18)

Like Littabelle's Aunt Sorrow, these mountaineers are knowledgeable about ways to cure illness without a doctor. This is how Mary Call and her sister, Devola, minister to their father on his deathbed: "Devola made

Roy Luther tamarack tea. . . . I made poultices of gum camphor and turpentine and laid one on the back of his neck and the other on his stomach." (p. 20)

When their neighbor, Kiser, who wants to marry Devola, gets pneumonia, this is how they cure him: "We opened up Kiser's underwear to the waist and slathered him thick with the hot onions front and back and then Devola brought another kettleful and I steamed a towel . . . making Kiser a collar . . . and I hollered for Devola to bring more onions and made Kiser a cap from another towel and more onions." (p. 30)

The rhythms of the local speech are delightful and should be noted by readers. The owner of the General Store tells Mary Call, "I hear your daddy's on the go-down. . . ." (p. 50), and this same lady tells Mary Call, "Folks around here've never done anything more than just piddle-diddle with 'craftin.' " (p. 53) Kiser moans in his delirium, "Sister, I'm a-dyin'. . . . I see them devil eyes a-shinin' and I hear them devil voices a-screechin' . . . I'm a dyin' and I don't deserve to, I never did nothin' wrong to nobody." (p. 30) At Roy Luther's funeral, Romey, his son says: "He was gaysome sometimes before he took sick and when the notion struck him he could be as tough as whitleather. He loved us all fair, though he never said so. He never whipped us and I was proud to have him for my daddy and now I hope he'll stay peaceful here." (p. 75) Mary Call tells Kiser, "Oh, I'm as peart as a cricket" (p. 80) and he tells her, "You're enough to skeer a man, standin' there all spraddle-legged with your jaw stuck out ugly." (p. 81) Mary Call describes Kiser as having a "Joe Blizzard fit," which refers to "the irrational behavior of a legendary figure over in Harnett County noted for that." (p. 87)

Katie Letcher Lyle's *Fair Day, and Another Step Begun* also takes place in Tennessee among mountain people. Based on an old folk legend, this story deals with the almost impossible love of a mountain girl for a mountain boy who has gone away and been "civilized." Her faith and love eventually bring him back to what he really is. (This book is discussed in greater detail in Chapter IV.)

Ellen Burd, the heroine, like Mary Call, is familiar with and lives close to nature. She also goes wildcrafting:

> For most of her life, she and Virg had hunted chanterelles in summertime—golden, red, or blackish horns rising from smooth pine forest floors—and ginseng in the fall, the old man spilling the red seeds down the hill to set for next year as he shook the dirt off the long thick roots. "About two ounces," he would say, his eyes blazing. The university paid forty dollars a pound for ginseng. *Panax*, the cure-all. They collected dead animals and birds to skin, sending them also to the laboratory. "Shouldn't kill them, but if they's dead anyways, might as well make them useful," Virg said.

When John Waters will not acknowledge their baby, Ellen goes to Virg for a spell, which he concocts out of wild plants. Both he and Ellen believe it is this spell that finally makes John Waters love her.

These folkways and beliefs have a magical quality, a beauty that is particularly enchanting to children from other regions—especially from urban areas, where magic plays no part in their daily lives and where they are closer to machinery and technology than to nature and its mysteries.

Harper Lee's *To Kill a Mockingbird*, although not written for adolescents, has become a classic in the secondary school. There is no need to discuss the quite familiar plot here, but I do recommend this work as one of the best books available to give adolescents a sense of what the Depression era South was like.[2] I include it under regional literature because the setting is an archetypal small Southern town, similar to ones we read about in many other Southern books:

Maycomb was an old town, but it was a tired old town when I first knew it. In rainy weather the streets turned to red slop; grass grew on the sidewalks, the courthouse sagged in the square. Somehow, it was hotter then: a black dog suffered on a summer's day; bony mules hitched to Hoover carts flicked flies in the sweltering shade of the live oaks on the square. Men's stiff collars wilted by nine in the morning. Ladies bathed before noon, after their three o'clock naps, and by nightfall were like soft teacakes with frostings of sweat and sweet talcum. (pp. 9–10)

Anita Clay Kornfeld's *In a Bluebird's Eye* is also set during the Depression, in a Tennessee mountain town. Honor Jane's mother, reminding us of Tennessee Williams's archetypal heroines who have fallen from high to low estate, remembers when she "wasn't even allowed to set foot in the kitchen, with so many Negro servants running around a dime a dozen to do the housework." (p. 8)

When I was your age, Honor Jane, I had so many privileges. . . . Would you believe that I didn't realize it at the time? No, not me, Miss know-it-all Martha Jane Cunningham. . . . Why, I thought Maddoxville, Mississippi, was the tail end of no place. I thought the worst fate in this wide world would be to have to marry a Maddoxville boy and settle down on the old Delta." I'm not going to bury myself on this hot empty old Delta," I used to brag. . . . But then, who comes along but your father, Mr. Hotstuff himself! . . . Do you know what I'd do this very minute if some miracle from God would give me a chance! Why, I'd fall right down on my hands and knees and . . . kiss the very ground of Maddoxville, Mississippi! (p. 9)

Honor Jane's father, fired from his college teaching job and now working as the local high school principal, has turned into the town drunkard, going out to "Bohunk Town buying bootleg." (p. 20) Bootlegging is a regionalism that may need explaining.

Honor Jane becomes friendly with Lola, the only Negro in that town. Lola has been paroled from the penitentiary to work without pay for Dr. Clark. Lola has been told that she was let out for good behavior. As Lola puts it ironically, "We'll loan you a free nigger maid if you'll see to it that she's kep' well out of sight and she don't get herself into no more trouble." (p. 14) But the local minister, Preacher Pullum, opposes the bringing of even one Negro to this town and in his sermon he warns "that God might bring down his wrath on the whole town—that it wasn't meant to be to mix up people with different skin colors and all." (p. 14)

---

2. The vast body of Southern literature that is taught in the colleges includes more complex books by authors such as Faulkner, Wolfe, Robert Penn Warren, etc. These have been omitted here. In the same way, books related to the black Southern experience have been omitted here; a few are included in Chapter II.

Honor Jane tries to find out about Nashville, the mecca, where Lola was in jail. Honor Jane says: "I don't know one thing about Nashville 'cept what Miss Cora taught us in fifth grade. That it's got the capital building with the big dome, a city park, the Grand Ole Opry, and WUSM. Tell me what else Nashville's got." (p. 21) And Lola answers: "Since they don't allow much sight-seeing aroun' the state penitentiary, I can't say I knows much more'n you do about Nashville. I came from outside Nashville myself . . . down the old Franklin turnpike. I growed up on this white man's place." (p. 21)

Poverty and heat dominate life in this coal mining town. Honor Jane wishes on the bluebird:

Would you please turn all these cracker-box houses here in Margate into big white houses with bathrooms in every single one—bathrooms that won't go out of whack anytime? . . .

Would you please keep the mines always working so they won't have to cut down or have cave-ins killing people, so people like the Hardees don't have to go on relief and get TB. And don't let the little bitty children get abscessed teeth or get scared in the middle of the night. . . .

Bluebird, after you've made everybody happy here in Margate, is it too much to ask you to maybe fly on down to Maddoxville, Mississippi, and fix it up some kind of magic way so that my Mama can go home to that big house on the Delta and the whole Whitfield family can move in? (pp. 32–33)

The mine shuts down and the town is abandoned. Honor Jane's father gets a job in another town with an old college friend, and there is some possibility at the end of the book that the family will survive emotionally and financially. But Lola dies trying to escape to freedom, and the people of the town are left destitute by the closing of the mine.

Another interesting regionalism is "revival week" which, ironically, is held at the very time that the mine is closing down:

Not only did the whole town of Margate turn out, Baptists and Methodists, and even those who normally wouldn't set foot in any church door, but they came from far back in the mountains. Holy Rollers traipsed in, in droves, all of them seeming to want to outshout the next one, or else steal the whole show away from the Baptists. (p. 124)

Music as a part of regionalism is another idea that students can develop in their reading of adolescent literature. Southern literature brings students very close to some of the oldest American music: folk music, mountain music, gospel and other religious music. Many lyrics are included in Kornfeld's book: "He's the fairest of ten thousand to my soul," "Oh, wondrous love," and others.

Urban Settings

Books with big city settings provide a startling contrast with those about the South. Felice Holman's *Slake's Limbo* is a terrifying and beautiful book about one of New York City's neglected children who finds a place of his own in the subway. The subway is the escape hatch for Aremis Slake.

Because he is small, he often has to escape from street gangs in his ghetto, and he keeps a subway token in his pocket for emergencies.

Slake lives in "the place he called his home" overlooking the elevated subway tracks. He sleeps on a cot in the kitchen, in which the window can be open only a crack because of the soot that comes in. This is what Slake sees when his friend Joseph and he take a walk:

Joseph and Slake often took long walks together up and down and around the streets of their neighborhood, past boarded-up buildings, vacant lots full of junk, scrawled walls which announced names, called obscenities. They wandered through crowds, not seeing them. In good weather, people and animals leaned out of windows to watch the life below. On hot days, the hydrants poured water on screaming children and set the garbage afloat. Ambulances and police cars screeched by. Wash hung limply on fire escapes. Old men picked through junk piles. (p. 7)

One day, fleeing from a crowd of hostile boys, Slake jumps into a subway car and exits at an unfamiliar place. Holman draws the contrast particularly well:

He came up onto the street in a neighborhood that he had never seen before, walked two blocks uptown to the splendid width of Seventy-ninth Street, and started to walk westward. Here were sparkling shops, large clean buildings, and neatly tended saplings along the edge of the relatively unlittered pavement. The absence of tin cans, garbage, and other refuse, the scarcity of steps and stoops, and the lack of people sitting or leaning about them interested Slake. . . . (p. 10)

Slake climbs into one of the trees in Central Park and when a park attendant threatens him, he runs back down into the subway. He is afraid to go up above ground because his eyesight is so bad that he cannot see who will attack him. Nobody in his school or home has ever figured out that he can't read because he can't see.

Slake rode the subway all that afternoon, crisscrossing the city, cutting it to pieces with the crashing cars, slicing through tunnels, burrowing through rock. He sat, a catapulted mummy, resurrecting himself from time to time, to exit at a transfer point, and enter another train headed to some other distant corner of the metropolitan subway system. It did not matter to Slake which corner. He touched base in the Bronx, Queens, Brooklyn, doubled back and clattered into the Upper West Side. Then, down again to the Battery and back again, finally to exit at the Forty-second Street station of the Lexington Avenue line—Grand Central Station. (p. 13)

Fleeing again, he runs down into the subway, onto the tracks, and into the train tunnel. To save himself from an oncoming train he grabs the wall and finds an opening into a room under the Commodore Hotel. He moves in and lives there for 121 days. Again, Holman gives us as good a picture of one part of New York City as can be found in adolescent literature:

If Slake had the gift of seeing up and around corners . . . he would have seen the front entrance of the Commodore Hotel on Forty-second Street, old but still handsome. He would have seen taxicabs and automobiles of distinction gently depositing valuable people in front of portals, through which they would pass to walk upon carpets that sank like quicksand. (p. 21)

How does Slake survive? He uses the subway bathroom, which is cleaner and works better than the bathroom in his tenement. Starving, he watches a man leave a cup of coffee at a counter after only a few sips; he moves in and drinks the coffee with six lumps of sugar to deaden his hunger pains. He goes into the paper selling business, smoothing out the barely read papers people leave on benches and re-selling them. He also scavenges for other things people leave—cough drops, one glove. He lives on the few cents he makes from papers and uses other newspapers to make a bed for himself. The subterranean world of the subway becomes his world. In his spare time he rides the subway trains and he teaches himself to read the posters which are large enough for a boy with poor eyes.

Students should discuss the tragedy of the life of this city boy who is viewed as garbage by most of society, yet is resourceful enough to survive alone, a subway Robinson Crusoe.

City books mentioned in other chapters—books such as *The Diary of A. N.* and *A Hero Ain't Nothin' But a Sandwich*—all focus on the negative aspects of growing up as a poor child in an urban setting. Even when the urban setting is in the West, as in Kin Platt's *Headman*, or in the Midwest, as in S. E. Hinton's *The Outsiders*, *Rumblefish*, and *That Was Then, This Is Now*, the reader sees the prevalence of teenage gangs and the closeness to the seamier aspects of society: drugs, prostitution, crime, littered streets, lack of nature, and poor air. People don't know each other the way they do in the Southern novels, and nature is something that young people long for but rarely know.

There are no adolescent literature books that express the kind of love of city life that the Cleavers' heroines express about Ozark or Appalachian mountain life. Those few books that are about upper-class city life, such as Winifred Rosen's *Cruisin' for a Bruisin'*, depict city life as bearable because the central characters have enough money for a fine Central Park West apartment and for summertime escape; but rarely, if ever, is city life depicted as a positive force in the coming of age of young people.

Winnie Simon in *Cruisin' for a Bruisin'* is the daughter of a successful psychoanalyst. Since elementary school she and her sister have attended Walden, one of the city's fine private schools. Her mother teaches dance therapy at Columbia University.

Once a week Winnie goes horseback riding in Central Park; she shops in the Junior Department at Bloomingdale's; and the house doorman, Vernon, greets her each day. Once a week she goes to the Metropolitan Music School for her guitar lessons, and the family listens regularly to classical music. It is difficult to believe that her world is, geographically, the same New York City as that of Slake or A. N.

The Far North

One of the most popular books for young adults is set 2,000 miles from any big city, in Alaska before statehood, when it was still America's last frontier: Walt Morey's *Gentle Ben*, the story of the relationship between young Mark Andersen and his only friend, Ben, an Alaskan Brownie cub who is kept chained up in Fog Benson's dark shed until purchased by Mark's family. Whereas social studies works teach the geography and customs of a new region through dull statistics, Morey gives young people a lively sense of place through artistic descriptions, such as the following one of spring in Alaska:

Off to his left the green and yellow tundra stretched away in gentle rolls and hollows that were broken here and there by the darker green of patches of brush and a ragged line where the creek cut through to the sea. The tundra looked dewy fresh and clean from its long winter under the snow. In the distance the Aleutian Range reared a row of white heads into the blue. Already the snow had melted from the beaches and surrounding lowlands. As the hours of daylight lengthened, the snow line crept farther away. It crept up valleys and canyons, across slopes and razor-sharp ridges until, by the time summer arrived, it would have retreated to that range of white heads, where it would stop.

Below, on his right, lay the uneven roofs of homes and stores of the fishing village of Orca City. Its one mud street, black and drying under the warm sun, slashed straight through the center of town to the bay and the sea, which stretched away, flat and endless, to the distant horizon.

A dozen boats lay at the dock, but the outreaching sea was empty. Soon it would not be. The opening of the Alaskan Salmon Run was but two weeks away, and excitement was beginning to grip the town like a fever. Mark knew about that; his father was a seiner, and his boat, the *Far North*, was one of the finest seiners in Alaska. (p. 17)

Discussion of available work is an interesting aspect of regional literature. The work that the men do in Alaska is different from Southern farming or the menial jobs described in *El Bronx Remembered*. Everyone in Orca City makes his living from the salmon run.

"Take the salmon away," his father once said, "and Orca City would be a ghost town in a month." Naturally, everyone became more excited as opening day drew nearer. Fishing boats would begin to arrive any day now, and Orca City would fill with strange men who had come north to work in the seven canneries along the coast and aboard the fish traps. Soon, more than a thousand seiners from as far south as California and even Mexico would be moored in the bay. Orca City's three or four hundred people would swell to several thousand. (p. 18)

A wide variety of wild animals and unusual pets inhabit Mark's world, and students may want to contrast them with those found in other regions:

Herds of seals and sea lions would mass on jutting points of land and along rocky shores of islands to dip into the run for their annual feast. They would charge into the nets of seiners, ripping them to shreds, and spend hours searching for the opening to a fish trap, trying to get at the thousands of salmon inside. Eagles, hawks, crows, and foxes would vie with the brown bears, seals, and sea lions at every stream and sandbar. Over all would circle hordes of screaming gulls scouring land, sea, and the beaches, cleaning up, to the last morsel, every crumb left by previous feeders. (p. 19)

Mark's father had a pet seal when he was a boy. Mark's mother knew someone who had a full-grown lion for a pet, and she once had a baby coyote, which she picked up on the prairie. Mark, of course, has Ben:

A brown bear . . . the largest, most dangerous big-game animal in North America . . . the largest carnivorous animal on earth . . . the last living relic of those fabulous hairy mammals of the Ice Age who migrated from Asia and Russia millions of years ago—such as the giant sloth and the saber-toothed tiger. He is a direct descendant of the legendary Siberian cave bear. (p. 26)

Every region also has its own unique criminal element. In city streets, we think of muggers, rapists, and warring gangs. In Alaska, fish pirates in dark-painted boats slip in at night and steal salmon from the fish traps. Other pirates are called "creek robbers"; they "slip into the forbidden spawning streams and seine salmon in the act of spawning." (p. 19)

An interesting aspect of regionalism is what young people do when they are not in school. Here, in Alaska, Mark and his brother watch to see the salmon spawn. Lying on their stomachs on the creek bank, they watch "a mother salmon fan her tail against the bottom and dig a small hole in which she had deposited eight or nine hundred eggs. A male salmon had swum over the spot, and a milky substance had floated down to fertilize the eggs." (p. 39)

After getting Ben, Mark is involved in scouring restaurants for scraps and in visiting grocery stores to bargain for old bread, and all of his after-school time is spent in caring for his pet. One important activity is laying in a supply of hay for Ben. Mark's mother, who was born on a farm, shows him how to do this:

"This is the way you scythe grass, Mark. I did it often as a girl at home. The scythe is one of the oldest farm tools known. For thousands of years it was the only way man had to cut grasses and grains." She gripped the stubby handles and swung the scythe with a smooth, full-armed sweep. There was a sound like ripping cloth, and a narrow half-moon of grass fell smoothly before the flashing blade. She stepped forward, set her feet, and the scythe flashed again. There was a ripping sound, and the half-moon had doubled in size. (p. 68)

Students involved in the study of regionalism through adolescent literature should note the effect of environment on the activities of both mothers and fathers. Mark's father is a fisherman, and his mother is a teacher and farmer. In one of the most touching short stories in *El Bronx Remembered,* Vicki's mother is a "numbers dealer," La Bolita. For Vicki the job makes good sense: "Although this had been the second arrest since her mother had been a numbers runner, things had been much better for them in the past two years. They were no longer on welfare and always had plenty of food and clothes." (p. 24)

Whereas city life is separated from nature and from the effects of varieties of weather, life in the Far North is closely tied to weather. In *Gentle Ben*, the Andersen family's livelihood is taken away from them when the fishing boat is wrecked on a rock in rough seas. But what nature and weather take away from Karl Andersen, the environment restores. At the end of the book, Karl goes into the trap business with a hunter whose life Ben has saved.

Another adolescent classic about life in the Far North is Jean Craighead George's *Julie of the Wolves.* Julie Edwards Miyax Kapugen is a thirteen-year-old Eskimo girl who is caught between the old North and the new. Fleeing her new husband, the boy Daniel, Julie decides to go to San Francisco where she has a pen pal. When she realizes that she is lost, she finds that the only way she can survive is to live with a wolf pack. Her growing fondness for and understanding of the wolves, plus her familiarity with the age-old survival techniques of the Eskimos, enable her to find food and shelter and to get through the summer.

It would be interesting for students to compare George's book with *Slake's Limbo.* Both are of the Robinson Crusoe genre, and the protagonists are thirteen-year-olds who must use their wits to survive in alien terrain.

Julie knows that wolves, despite the unfair myths that have always surrounded them, do not attack men. She finds that they have a social structure that is complex and purposeful:

> She had seen the wolves mouth Amaroq's chin twice before so she concluded that it was a ceremony, a sort of "Hail to the Chief." He must indeed be their leader for he was clearly the wealthy wolf; that is, wealthy as she had known the meaning of the word on Nunivak Island. There the old Eskimo hunters she had known in her childhood thought the riches of life were intelligence, fearlessness, and love. A man with these gifts was rich and was a great spirit who was admired in the same way that the gussaks admired a man with money and goods. (p. 19)

There is, in addition to the leader, a low man on the totem pole, Kapu, a lowly wolf, a poor spirit, with fears and without friends.

In addition to learning about the wolves, we learn about the Eskimo seal camp where Julie was raised until her father had to go to war, and she was forced to go to live with her Aunt Martha and go to school.

> Walking the tundra with Kapugen [her father] was all laughter and fun. He would hail the blue sky and shout out his praise for the grasses and bushes. On these trips they ate salmon berries, then lay in the sun watching the birds. Sometimes Kapugen would whistle sandpiper songs and the birds would dip down to see which of their members had gotten lost in the grass. (p. 79)

Kapugen has a profound respect for the animals of their environment. "He told her that the birds and animals all had languages and if you listened and watched them you could learn about their enemies, where their food lay and when big storms were coming." (p. 79) And he also tells her, "You are Eskimo . . . and never forget it. We live as no other people can, for we truly understand the earth." (p. 81)

During her life with her Aunt Martha in Mekoryak, Julie realizes how strange her life was in the seal camp with her father. The girls she now goes to school with "speak and write English . . . [know] the names of presidents, astronauts, and radio and movie personalities who lived below the top of the world." (p. 85) Through letters to her San Francisco pen pal, Julie learns about television, sports cars, blue jeans, bikinis, hero sandwiches, pink-walled rooms, and wall-to-wall carpeting.

Then an officer from the Bureau of Indian Affairs comes to get Julie from her aunt because her father had signed an agreement before his supposed death for her to marry Daniel when she was thirteen. The marriage ceremony is performed, but soon after, she sets out for San Francisco.

In Part III of this work, bounty hunters kill Amaroq, the magnificent leader of the wolves, for the $50 bounty they get for each wolf's ear. The hunting is done from planes:

The air exploded and she stared up into the belly of the plane. Bolts, doors, wheels, red, white, silver, and black, the plane flashed before her eyes. In that instant she saw great cities, bridges, radios, school books. She saw the pink room, long highways, TV sets, telephones, and electric lights. Black exhaust enveloped her, and civilization became this monster that snarled across the sky. (p. 141)

Julie's grief for Amaroq is as strong as it would be for a fellow human being:

"Amaroq . . ." She took her carving from her pocket, and got down on her knees. Singing softly in Eskimo, she told him she had no bladder for his spirit to dwell in, but that she had his totem. She asked him to enter the totem and be with her forever.

For a long time she held the carving over his body. Presently, the pain in her breast grew lighter and she knew the wolf was with her. (p. 147)

Now, civilization seems red with the blood of Amaroq. She tries to think of where she can go:

When she thought of San Francisco, she thought about the airplane and the fire and blood and the flashes and death. When she took out her needle and sewed, she thought about peace and Amaroq.

She knew what she had to do. Live like an Eskimo—hunt and carve and be with Tornait [her tamed bird]. (p. 152)

Finally in a small village, Julie finds her father again. He is alive and prosperous and is re-married to a gussak, a white woman with pale face and reddish gold hair. Julie looks around his house and sees electric lamps, a radio-phonograph, cotton curtains, the edge of an electric stove, a coffee pot and china dishes. Then her father tells her that he now hunts from planes. "It's the only way to hunt today. The seals are scarce and the whales are almost gone; but sportsmen can still hunt from planes." (p. 168)

Horrified, Julie leaves him, but her little bird dies and she realizes that she cannot survive with the old ways. She sings a beautiful song to the spirit of Amaroq:

The seals are scarce and the whales are almost gone.
The spirits of the animals are passing away.
Amaroq, Amaroq, you are my adopted father.
My feet dance because of you.
My eyes see because of you.
My mind thinks because of you. And it thinks, on this thundering night,
That the hour of the wolf and the Eskimo is over. (p. 170)

Then Julie points her boots toward the home of her father. There is no way to survive except by accepting the new ways of civilization.

Walt Morey's *Home Is the North* is another good book about Alaska for adolescents. When fifteen-year-old Brad's grandmother dies, he is left alone in his cabin with his Malamute dog, Mickie. He goes home for the winter with Captain Ed, who owns a seining boat. Annie, the Captain's wife, possesses talents needed in this territory:

> She was a product of the gold-rush days, a dead shot. She ran her own trap line, had been a top dog-team woman, could skin and cut up game faster than most men. The rugged, virgin country and brutal climate had used her hard. She was small-boned and thin, almost scrawny, with weather-burned hands and face, and bright blue eyes as sharp as an eagle's. She looked tough and leathery. (p. 13)

Like most seiners, Captain Ed and Annie have little to do during the winter. They spend the summer and fall getting ready for the long, "sleeping-in" winter:

> Annie and Captain Ed had tunneled into the bank and hacked out a small room in the permafrost, added a door to keep out the summer heat and wild animals, and they had a year-round refrigerator. In it Annie kept the jams and jellies she made from gallons of wild berries she gathered during the summer. In the fall, while the men cut the winter's wood and made the cabin and the *Annie B* [their sailing boat] snug against the coming winter, she filled the room with game. She'd kill a bear, several deer, a moose, and whatever other small game animals and birds were available. (p. 25)

Students should note how food is related to geography—the different ways of getting and preparing it. When Annie serves venison roast for dinner, she describes how she shot the deer and dragged it out of the slush and ice.

Along with the terrible hardships, there are extraordinary beauty and a kind of purity in the frozen Northland, which seem lost in the city books young people read:

> The cold began to creep in, but Brad was held by the sheer magic of the scene. Over the absolute silence of the near dawn a million stars looked down. These were not the peaceful, far-off stars of a summer sky. These flashed and sparkled as if fanned to life by a giant wind. The Big Dipper hung suspended directly over the cabin. . . . (p. 25)
>
> The sky was fading to pale blue. That turned to pink and spilled down the bowl of the sky, gradually changing to gold. Rays of the rising sun stretched across the earth. Then, suddenly, the day burst from behind the mountains in a silent explosion of light, and the world was bathed in dazzling colors. There were the deep blue of the distant sea, the green of spruce and hemlock, bent almost double with their weight of snow. Countless icy diamonds hung from every branch and twig, catching and holding the cold rays of the sun in a host of dancing rainbows. (p. 26)

Young people might discuss the hardships of life in Alaska and try to evaluate honestly whether it is better or worse than life in a city, where one is protected from the natural elements. In this book, as in *Gentle Ben* and *Julie of the Wolves*, the intense devotion of human energies to simple survival seems to be an ennobling experience; meaning is inherent in the actual process of surviving.

The terrible city loneliness known by Slake seems to be absent from the North's frozen wasteland, where we would automatically expect people to be *more* lonely. When Brad is left alone, Captain Ed automatically takes him home with him. Where every pair of hands is needed, where one cannot survive without cooperation and interdependence, there seems to be far more value attached to human life than in impersonal cities.

Annie begins Brad's "education," which involves teaching him how to cope with his environment. She tells him about the different types of guns and their uses, and teaches him how to hunt and trap. Students should discuss this concept of the adult preparing the young to cope with the environment and how it applies to their own lives and the lives of young people in other regions.

Brad's initiation as a hunter involves killing a wolverine, the most vicious animal in all the North:

> His average weight is no more than thirty-five pounds. But he is feared and hated by every living creature and trapper in the country. He is a bloodthirsty killer who slaughters for the sheer pleasure of killing. Not even a grown bear, timber wolf, or mountain lion will challenge him. He is an evil-tempered bundle of raw courage who will attack a man or an animal twenty times his size, and fight it to the death. He has ruined countless trap lines and driven experienced trappers out of the country with his depredations. The native Indians and Eskimos call him "carcajour" or "Indian devil." But his fur is highly prized. (pp. 30–31)

Because his frozen gun does not go off, Brad kills the wolverine with an ax, and Annie and he drag it back the five miles to their cabin to receive accolades from Captain Ed and his helper, George. Captain Ed says: "I'm a son of a gun. First day on a trap line and he bags a wolverine. And not with a gun. By hand." (p. 35)

A new and fascinating world opens for Brad as Annie continues his education. Every day he and Annie run the trap line, and the first time he shoots a ptarmigan on the wing, all three adults praise him as a Deadeye Dick. The time Brad enjoys the most each day is when Annie and he stop for lunch, sitting on a log at the end of the trap lines, and Annie tells him regional anecdotes, such as the one about how she got the nickname, "Stampede Annie":

> I was about seven or eight, I guess. Mother followed the stampedes in those days and fed the miners. My father'd been killed in a cave-in. Mother would set up a tent and hang out a sign, "Pancakes, Bacon, and Beans." Those hungry miners flocked in to eat. This day, I'd heard some miners talking about a new strike. Ours was about to peter out, so I rushed in to tell Mother the news. A couple of miners in there kidded me about going on another stampede. An hour later it was all over camp, and along with everyone else, Mother and I struck our tent, packed the flour, beans, and bacon, and headed for the new one. When we got there the same two fellows came in, and one said, "Darned if here ain't Stampede Annie again." The name stuck. (p. 38)

This beautiful book is about Brad's education, about all aspects of living in the Far North, about love and sacrifice and survival. This is the kind of regional experience that teaches humanistic values to young people of *every* region.

The American Heartland

Suzanne Clauser's *A Girl Named Sooner* takes place in Indiana during the Depression era. Sooner, a poor little girl, is raised by a brutal, embittered, bootlegging, Bible-quoting grandmother. Mac is the local vet who tries to adopt Sooner. When he takes her home to his childless wife, Elizabeth, to stay for a few days, Elizabeth asks her if she has ever had a bath, and Sooner says, in the regional dialect: "You mean, wash everthin all to oncet? . . . Come summertime, I get into the creek. . . . Course . . . that's only in the summertime. And Ole Mam, she gets fractious iffen I forget and go in with my dress still on me." (p. 77) Even Sooner's name is part of regional dialect. It means a premature or illegitimate child.

In Kornfeld's *In a Bluebird's Eye* the major local social event is the revival service. In *A Girl Named Sooner*, the major social event is the County Fair:

The fairgrounds lay off to the side of the road below. It had seemed just an open field when Sooner had passed it last in June, with a few scattered buildings all closed up. Now, a whole town was sprung up there, its little houses with canvas roofs lining a twisting dirt way where people walked, and flags flew, and big machines, glinting in the sun, bucked and whirled and turned about, and on beyond was a near earth-red track where the horses ran. The clamor of it rolled up the hill at Sooner in waves like the heat. Altogether, sights and sounds, it seemed to her to be the most wonderful thing in the world. (p. 228)

Old Mam, finally prevented from making and selling bootleg whiskey, leaves for Florida, and Sooner finds a final home with Mac and Elizabeth.

A book that superbly captures the regional color of the American Heartland is Myra Friedman's excellent biography of Janis Joplin, *Buried Alive*. (See Ch. I, pp. 50–51.) Friedman sees Joplin as a victim of geography, of having been brought up in Port Arthur, Texas. Friedman writes:

. . . in Port Arthur there is the "good" as opposed to the "bad." The fancier families from Louisiana raise their children to perpetuate tradition, and damned if they don't succeed. Their daughters are proper ladies; their sons are southern gentlemen. . . .
Education is functional and ascends in a regulated pattern. Most of Port Arthur's high school graduates go to Lamar State College in Beaumont, a technological institute geared to serve the region. It makes schoolteachers and nurses out of the region's daughters and prepares its sons for work in the oil industry. That is what shapes the vision of the future for the majority of Port Arthur's population and, at least in the past, as one person put it, "They hated anybody who didn't want what they wanted." (p. 6)

This biography is the story of what happened to Janis Joplin because she didn't want what they wanted. Her treatment ranged from ridicule to actual persecution. The sad thing about her life is that no matter how successful she became, a part of her wanted only to be accepted as one of Port Arthur's own.

Friedman's book is particularly interesting for teenagers because it exemplifies so clearly what happens to the big-city type who finds herself/himself living in a small town. One of Janis's friends remembers the beginning of Janis's deviance from the town norms:

"Probably about the ninth grade," Karleen remembered, "she started having opinions of her own. A question about integration came up and all Janis said was she thought integration was fine. You just didn't do that in Port Arthur. You *still* don't. For the rest of the time, there were these two boys, they followed her around and called her 'nigger-lover,' everywhere. . . ."

Karleen indicated that the constrictions of conformity were almost unfathomable in those days, and any challenge to that rigidity was regarded as an intolerable threat. (pp. 17–18)

In Janis's senior year in high school, the persecution became particularly intense. "Janis became as hated as an epidemic of horse fever. The students threw things at her, they mocked her, they called her names of which 'pig' was the favorite." (p. 23) Trying to analyze this, one of her friends said: "She dressed sloppy . . . she was overweight, didn't wear makeup, just refused to do anything to compromise." (p. 23)

Another high school friend believes that Janis's openness about sex was the reason for her persecution. "Sex," he said, "is the big hangup down there. They're hypocritical because they say one thing and do another, but as long as they're conforming, justifying it by the front of a lifestyle on the basis of, say, the Baptist Church, it's all right. Really, it's amazing to try to comprehend the heads in Port Arthur." (p. 26)

By the time Janis became successful she had lost her war against her environment. The tension between the "bad" girl she had become and the "good" girl image of Port Arthur tormented her until her death at the age of twenty-seven.

Winifred Madison's *Bird on the Wing* shows the difference between life in California and in Nebraska for Elizabeth, who has gone with her father to Nebraska to live with him and his new wife and family. When she remembers Sacramento, California, she sees herself swimming or riding in a new red Porsche with her boyfriend. She is a California "chauvinist" and thinks that life there is better than anywhere else. California customs are also different from those of the Midwest. Her stepmother, Lorene, says of a dress Elizabeth's mother sends her: "Ah suppose they weah things like that in Califo'nia, but it's pretty garish for aroun' heah. And it's too sho't, honey, way too sho't." (p. 18)

When Liz complains to her father about his new wife, he says: "You're smarter than she is and you come from California, which makes some people resentful, though God knows why. I don't." (p. 22) People in rural regions also sometimes resent those who come from New York because of the unspoken assumption that people from big cities look down on those from rural areas.

Lorene, to Elizabeth, represents middle America. "Lorene wasn't such a bad-looking woman—not like her own mother, of course, but still, aside from a certain dumpiness, conventionally pretty. She might have posed for a TV commercial for floorwax, or brighter dentures, or the cleaner washing powder that would solve the most pressing problem of every woman's life." (p. 20)

When Elizabeth speaks to a sympathetic guidance counselor, the woman says about Lincoln, Nebraska: "Not very exciting, I imagine. And chilly, after California." (p. 28) Elizabeth tells her, "All I want to do is to go back to Sacramento. ... See my friends, go swimming, go to the mountains, ride around." (p. 29)

Elizabeth decides to run away and hitchhike back to California. Again, the reader is reminded of the difference in geography:

Elizabeth knew that April, even late April, did not necessarily mean spring, at least not in Nebraska, but she wasn't prepared for the blast of wintry wind that assaulted her as she waited by the side of the road. Lorene's house, always overheated to the point of being stifling, made her even more vulnerable. (p. 49)

One of the roadside restaurants where Elizabeth stops is the kind of place that can be found on roads across this country.

Trucks large and small waited outside GAS and EATS like ghostly mastodons in the moonlight. As Elizabeth came closer to the lunchroom, she could hear sounds from a jukebox assaulting the night; yet harsh as the music was, Elizabeth felt relief in hearing it. She wasn't the last living creature on earth after all!

Bursts of male laughter mingled with the music, and she hesitated before opening the door and slipping in. The diner, a long warm room vibrating in clouds of steam and cigar smoke, was filled with men, some sitting at tables and others on stools at the long counter. The loud easy talking stopped as the message that a girl had entered silently circulated through the room. . . . "It's all right, dear. You can come in. I won't let the wild beasts hurt you." It was the man at the counter who spoke to her. (p. 64)

In this diner, Elizabeth meets a girl hitchhiking to San Francisco, and they decide to go together. The girl, Maija, gets them a lift westward in a truck:

It was Elizabeth's first experience in a truck, and she was surprised to find how high they sat, how the cab seemed like a little room, and how much power there was in the great beast. Ahead the gray road stretched converging into lines like a lesson in perspective. The sky was an upside-down bowl perforated with stars, an unevenly punctured collander. (p. 70)

That night, the girls sleep in the local graveyard. Maija has hitchhiked cross country before, and she knows that nobody bothers people in a graveyard. Maija shares her sleeping bag with Elizabeth, who left so hurriedly she took only some money and a toothbrush. The next morning they get another ride, and Elizabeth finds that she is enjoying herself: "Being suspended between Lincoln and Sacramento, sitting beside Maija and watching the landscape unfold, her problems, try as she might to concentrate on them, kept vanishing." (p. 80) Students should discuss this common emotion: the feeling of suspension, of escape, of being on the road, of being in motion so one need not come to terms with the realities of life.

The girls get out at Cheyenne, walk around, and look in the window of a Western clothing store where they see fine leather boots, saddles, spurs, belts, Western shirts, riding clothes, and Indian jewelry made with turquoise. Students should discuss the aspect of goods characteristic of each region. What is in the shop-windows of their town or city? What is native to their own region?

The next lift the girls get is to Laramie, with an older woman who might have come right out of a TV Western: "The Brillo-like hair, the leathery skin, the well-worn riding clothes, and the genuine Western twang were so perfectly in character. . . . Soon they discovered that the woman was born and bred in Wyoming and managed a sizeable ranch." (p. 85)

Next the girls get to the Medicine Bow Range and climb to a plateau—wide, flat, and grassy, about seven thousand feet high—where they spend the night. "Never had the world seemed so wide nor the sky so high. The cobalt blue deepened into purples so dense that the colors soon became indistinguishable in the night." (p. 86) The girls wake up to see a herd of wild horses standing motionless in the moonlight, an incredibly beautiful sight.

They finally reach Lake Tahoe, sparkling like a long aquamarine jewel, and they spend the night there under tall pines that stretch to the sky. Elizabeth is finally on home ground. "As she discussed the trees and lakes with Maija, Elizabeth found herself spellbound by the old familiar journey from the top of the Sierras down through the mountains and hills and foothills into the Great Central Valley. She had made this trip so many times she thought she knew every turn of the road and every blue-green vista, yet it was all new again after a long absence." (p. 102)

When Elizabeth finally gets home, she finds that nothing is as she remembered it. Her mother and new husband have sold their old familiar house and bought a new tract home. Her mother is stouter, and the roots show under her hair dye. Rick, Elizabeth's old boyfriend, goes with a new girl, but he and the girl pick Elizabeth up and take her to a party.

"Now I know I'm home. This is really it," she said half an hour later as she floated in the pool. The Japanese lanterns strung above made moving puddles of light in the water, and far above the party, almost forgotten, the deep night sky stayed cool and still. Fire leaped from the barbecue pit. The yard was full of young people; the girls in long cotton dresses, flashes of light displaying the wild colors, and the young men, talking, singing, and sometimes bursting into loud fits of laughter. Now and then a combo played, raw music drowning out everything else. (p. 124)

She races a new young man across the pool. When they get out she says:

"It's not a bad party. . . ." She had been starving for this all year, this California richness, the long pool, and the garden that combined Japanese taste with California wealth. That the sparseness had cost thousands of dollars was inconsequential. She wanted only to enjoy it and to enjoy the people here. (p. 124)

But by the end of the evening she realizes that Sacramento is no longer the Shangri-la she remembered. Getting to know Maija, who is a dedicated weaver, has shown Elizabeth that the consumer society is a decadent, purposeless way of life. She dreads her mother's endless cocktail parties. She does not want to stay, and she is not ready to return to

Nebraska. She flees again, this time to San Francisco, where she apprentices herself to Maija.

The first description of San Francisco is through Elizabeth's memory.

San Francisco had always been a city of delights for Elizabeth. Her mother used to take her there on shopping sprees, through one extravagant store after another, followed by a matinee or ballet performance, and always the ice cream soda at Blum's before starting home again. Other times her father would take the whole family for a day of joy—a visit to the zoo or a ride on the cable cars. The city always sparkled, the sun throwing strong lights and sharp shadows. If it rained, they simply went into one of the many warm and cozy places. Whatever the season, the city always had the tinge of a magical place. (p. 135)

The San Francisco that she comes to know through Maija, in the North Beach area, is far different. Maija lives in what was once a respectable Victorian home, but now the neighborhood has run down. Rubble-strewn lots border on vacant houses, and Elizabeth sees a mugging at a bus stop. The entire block is being torn down, and Maija tells her that they will have to vacate by the end of September. By the end of this lovely book, Maija has been killed by a thief at the broken-down launderette and drycleaning place she manages; Elizabeth has become a weaver, carrying on Maija's tradition; and she is now ready to go back to Nebraska, finally understanding that for a person who is centered in herself (a concept Maija introduced to her), for the creative individual who can produce beauty, any place can be home. I can think of no finer concept for young people to get out of a study of regionalism.

Books Discussed in Chapter III

The Whys and Wherefores of Littabelle Lee by Vera and Bill Cleaver, Signet, 1976.

Where the Lilies Bloom, Vera and Bill Cleaver, Scholastic, 1974.

Fair Day and Another Step Begun, Katie Letcher Lyle, Dell, 1975.

To Kill a Mockingbird, Harper Lee, Popular Library, 1962.

In a Bluebird's Eye, Anita Clay Kornfeld, Avon, 1975.

Slake's Limbo, Felice Holman, Scribner's, 1974.

El Bronx Remembered, Nicholasa Mohr, Bantam, 1976.

Cruisin' for a Bruisin', Winifred Rosen, Dell, 1977.

Gentle Ben, Walt Morey, Avon, 1976.

Julie of the Wolves, Jean Craighead George, Harper Trophy, 1973.

Home Is the North, Walt Morey, Avon, 1973.

A Girl Named Sooner, Suzanne Clauser, Avon.

Buried Alive, Myra Friedman, Bantam, 1974.

Bird on the Wing, Winifred Madison, Dell, 1975.

Other Related Books

Sasha, My Friend, Barbara Corcoran, Atheneum, 1969. (California to the Wilderness)

Don't Slam the Door When You Go, Barbara Corcoran, Atheneum, 1974. (Montana)

Isaac and Snow, Sally Edwards, Coward, 1973. (South Carolina coast)

My Side of the Mountain, Jean Craighead George, Dutton, 1959. (Catskill Mountains)

The Runaway's Diary, Marilyn Harris, Four Winds, 1971. (Harrisburg, Pennsylvania to Canada)

From the Mixed-Up Files of Mrs. Basil E. Frankweiler, E. L. Konigsburg, Atheneum, 1967. (Metropolitan Museum in New York City)

The Californios, Louis L'Amour, Bantam, 1974. (California)

Night of the Grizzlies, Jack Olsen, Putnam, 1969. (Glacier National Park)

House upon a Rock, Elsa Pedersen, Atheneum, 1968. (Alaska)

Where the Red Fern Grows, Wilson Rawls, Doubleday, 1961. (Cherokee country)

IV
teenagers and sex

One of the major concerns of young people in the secondary school is sex. Is pre-marital sexual adventuring a good or bad idea? What are the results of teenage pregnancy? Can a girl be popular if she doesn't engage in sex during the high school years? How much can a young person confide in parents about sexual problems? What are the different standards for boys and girls? What exactly is homosexuality, and how should one deal with it? The above questions are just some of the ones covered in contemporary adolescent literature.

Introduction

In the 1950s, a World War II film starring Zachary Scott and Ann Sheridan had Scott called up for service a bare three months after their marriage. While he is away, Sheridan has an affair with an artist (he is depicted in the clichéd role of irresponsible, free-loading bohemian). When the war ends, her husband returns, and the artist threatens to tell all. Sheridan then more or less accidentally kills him. She meant only to threaten him, but the gun went off. The remainder of the movie asks: Will she confess or won't she? And if so, when? Confess she finally does, and Scott tells her he can forgive her for the murder but not for the *affair*. It is when we are exposed to past social mores such as these that we see how much society's thinking has changed. Adolescent literature reflects these changes.

The Problem of Sex

In the past, sex of any kind was a taboo subject for discussion in the schools. Even today, few young people are fortunate enough to receive a healthy, constructive introduction to sex. Adolescent literature discusses many aspects of teenage sexuality, from the question of whether or not to "go all the way" to the penalties or lack of penalties for such involvement. The use of a variety of books like the ones discussed in this chapter can

112

help young people think through sexual matters without the teacher's being in the position of seeming to offer personal advice.

A good book to begin with is Nora Stirling's *You Would If You Loved Me*, which deals with the conflict that exists when a boy wants a sexual relationship and a girl doesn't. Trudy, who has spent a few unpopular years in high school, suddenly finds herself in a wonderful new role when Tom, one of the school's outstanding athletes, invites her to the exclusive Thanksgiving Bulldog Dance. Her best friend, Debbie, asks: "Are you going to sleep with him?" Trudy is shocked, but Debbie pursues the matter: ". . . you're going to have to make up your mind. . . . We all have to do that. Unless we don't *have* any boy friends, and who wants that?" (pp. 27–28)

Trudy is ambivalent about the sexual problem. She thinks back to the pre-Tom days with horror:

Even now she cringed with mortification, remembering the pretenses she had made to look dated up like the other girls. The Monday mornings at school, when the really popular girls gathered to compare notes on the weekend's dates, and all she could do was slip away or try to look mysterious and smug. The actual lies she had told. And the unspeakable efforts her mother had made—it hurt even to think about them—calling her garden club friends about their little boys—didn't Jimmy want to come over for a movie? (p. 50)

The questions that revolve in Trudy's mind are universal ones for teenage girls. Does he really care for her? Is he interested only in a sexual conquest, as she puts it, "only trying to add another scalp to his belt." (p. 32) She thinks: "She could go on indefinitely just dating and kissing mildly, and be perfectly happy. But boys couldn't let things stop there. They always had to bring sex in. *Was* it necessary? Was that clown Sid Knowland right when he said boys had to have it or they got sick, that it was pain and agony if they didn't?" (p. 32)

Trudy continues to refuse Tom, and he gets angry with her after a necking session at the beach. He tells her, "You want it too. Only you're like all girls, you won't . . ." (p. 57) She retorts, "I hate that line, you're like all girls." (p. 57) Tom warns her that his patience is running out, that "a guy can't wait forever," (p. 59) and then uses the clichéd words of manipulation, the words of the title, "You Would If You Loved Me."

Particularly interesting and worth discussing is Stirling's depiction of the boys' anger against the girls—the feeling that the girls are teasing them, holding out on them, depriving them of something that is rightfully theirs.

Tom says to his friend: "It really gets me the way a girl does her damnedest to get you steamed up, and then just when you're all hot suddenly backs off." (p. 68)

Mal, his friend, replies: "I know. They use sex like dog trainers use dog biscuits. Making you sit up and beg—promising, teasing, holding out—and then slapping you down. It's too much." (p. 68)

Students should note that the boys and girls who want to have sexual relations don't even like each other, want to use each other, and view sex traditionally as a symbol of power and victory. Sex is viewed here as a problem rather than a pleasure, and their socially approved male-female role models make the other sex objects rather than individuals to be loved, respected, and considered.

Trudy talks to Ruth, a sensible, mature friend who is going steady with Lonny, but hasn't slept with him. Ruth tells Trudy, "Don't let other people make you do stupid things by calling you chicken . . . have the guts to be yourself, and to stick to your own way of doing something, once you've thought it through." (p. 77) She tells Trudy that a good yardstick is to see if she has many things in common with a boy, other than sex. If sex is all they have in common, it is bound to lead to problems.

Trudy also talks to Mrs. Russell, an older career woman who works for the local radio station. Some of Trudy's and Mrs. Russell's statements, listed below, would make fine subjects for either discussion or writing assignments. If these writing assignments seem to threaten privacy, students should be urged to write anonymously, and the teacher can then read their statements to the class.

Trudy: "Don't boys *ever* think about anything but sex? It's awful, you can't ever just relax and have a good time, there's always this sort of underground battle going on." (p. 111)

Mrs. Russell: "Things have changed a lot since I was a girl, but only on the surface. Underneath, it's the same old battle. . . . It's almost twenty-five years since I was your age, but boys were just as preoccupied with sex then. There wasn't as much talk about it, at least not out in the open, but the boys were just as hung up over it as today." (p. 111)

Trudy: "I know just one girl that's talked the whole problem out with her boy friend, and they've got the most marvelous understanding. But most of us, we're just knocking about blindly in the dark, butting into each other . . . and hurting each other terribly." (pp. 111–112)

Trudy: "A lot of girls say that when boys are trying to get them to bed they say, 'What are you worried about, all you have to do is take a pill?' " (p. 113)

Mrs. Russell: "Sometimes I think all these safeguards make things harder for girls. Safety first was always one of the best excuses, if you were tempted. But all these pills and devices and what not sort of pull the rug out from under that line of reasoning." (p. 113)

Mrs. Russell: "It seems to me that genuine morality is based on making a choice between real alternatives." (p. 113)

Mrs. Russell: "Obviously, sex is a self-centered thing; I mean it's centered on your own feelings—what you want to *get*. But it's most satisfying when it's balanced by an outgoing feeling, one of giving. Most boys haven't really grown up. And they won't be really mature sexually until they find someone to love, really love, in the most complete sense." (p. 115)

A completely different attitude toward teenage sex can be found in Judy Blume's *Forever*. In common with most of Ms. Blume's other works, this one is set among the middle-class in a New Jersey suburb. Ms. Blume's girls are quite different from Trudy; they are as relaxed about sex as are her boys. Neither boys nor girls view sex as an ingredient of domination or as a dangerous or destructive emotion that must be controlled; instead, sex is an accepted and acceptable part of coming of age. The book opens:

> Sybil Davison has a genius I.Q. and has been laid by at least six different guys. She told me herself, the last time she was visiting her cousin, Erica, who is my good friend. Erica says this is because of Sybil's fat problem and her need to feel loved—the getting laid part, that is. The genius I.Q. is just luck or genes or something. I'm not sure that either explanation is 100 percent right but generally Erica is very good at analyzing people. (p. 1)

The following dialogue, in which Katherine (the narrator) and her best friend discuss pre-marital sex, provides a useful contrast with Trudy's dialogue with Mrs. Russell:

> "I've been thinking," Erica said, "that it might not be a bad idea to get laid before college."
> "Just like that?"
> "Well . . . I'd have to be attracted to him, naturally."
> "What about love?"
> "You don't need love to have sex."
> "But it means more that way."
> "Oh, I don't know. They say the first time's never any good anyway."
> "Which is why you should at least love him," I said. (pp. 27–28)

In Judy Blume's world, *everyone* accepts sex. Katherine starts to go out with Michael, and her grandmother warns her to beware of pregnancy and venereal disease. Katherine tells her Grandma, "We aren't sleeping together" (p. 35), and her Grandma responds, "Yet." Katherine is a little angry at this assumption that she and all of her generation "screw around." She says: "It's true that we are more open than our parents but that just means we accept sex and talk about it. It doesn't mean we are all jumping into bed together." (p. 35)

Gradually, Michael and Katherine move toward sexual intercourse, slowly, lovingly, and it is as difficult for him as it is for her. After they have intercourse for the first time Katherine thinks:

> I'm no longer a virgin. I'll never have to go through the first-time business again and I'm glad—I'm so glad it's over! Still, I can't help feeling let down. Everybody makes such a big thing out of actually doing it. But Michael is probably right—this takes practice. I can't imagine what the first time would be like with someone you didn't love. (p. 102)

When summertime comes, Katherine goes to summer camp in New Hampshire, and Michael goes to a job in North Carolina. Absence does not make the heart grow fonder, and by the end of the summer the romance is over. Katherine thinks:

> I wanted to tell him that I will never be sorry for loving him. That in a way I still do—that maybe I always will. I'll never regret one single thing we did together because what we had was very special. Maybe if we were ten years older it would have worked out differently. Maybe, I think it's just that I'm not ready for forever. (p. 199)

Judy Blume's book views sex as a necessary and positive aspect of coming of age. In Vida Demas's *First Person, Singular*, the only good thing in the life of Pam, an outsider in a Pennsylvania mill town, is her sexual relationship with Greg.

Because of financial difficulties, Pam, her mother, and father have moved back to a house that belonged to her grandparents. Pam's father, a college professor, is like nobody else in town, and her mother is recovering from a nervous breakdown. The family has moved four times, and each time Pam has faced the trauma of walking into a strange school. Her present one is particularly difficult to adjust to because her speech, bearing, background, and accent are on a higher socio-economic level than are those of her peers.

She meets Greg at a beach party and for the first time finds somebody she can relate to. Their sexual relationship continues to grow and develop. Pam says: "I was learning, by giving up my shameful innocence, a kind of science, a science of watching, of observing." (p. 57) Sex and loving have opened this eighth-grader up to a totally new way of perceiving the world, and sexual experience has given her the possibility of new depths of experiencing.

Even though they are happy together, this fine relationship with Pam is not enough to save Greg from the effects of his family life. He becomes a drug addict, and all that Pam can do is to continue to love him as he moves further and further away from her. He disappears before summer and writes to her that he is embracing a number of new ideas in life, including Hare Krishna. When he returns, they love each other as before but Greg is using and selling an assortment of drugs from LSD to uppers and downers and marijuana.

When the police raid Greg's pad, Pam helps him to get out of town. "You're savin' my life," Greg tells her. They cry and say good-bye, and there is no doubt in the author's or reader's mind that both of them have benefited from having this ill-starred relationship. It wasn't enough to save either of them, but it was better than not having it. Like Katherine's experience in Blume's *Forever*, sex has been a good and natural part of Pam's growing up.

June Jordan's *His Own Where* is a beautiful book about love between black teenagers. Angela and Buddy, victims of abuse, neglect, and poverty, have no place to make love other than a deserted little building in a cemetery.

Buddy and Angela meet at the hospital where his father is dying. Buddy's mother deserted the family some years ago. Angela's mother is the nurse watching over Buddy's father. Because her mother works, Angela has the full work load of housework and the care of her younger brothers and sisters.

When Angela's father finds that she has been seeing Buddy, he beats her so badly that she is hospitalized and then put in a children's shelter where Buddy can't see her. Angela is only fourteen, and there is nothing she or Buddy can do to prevent her being sent from the shelter to a Catholic home for girls far from New York City. When Buddy is finally able to visit her, she tells him she has been attacked by another girl and that most of the girls are lesbians.

When Angela is allowed to visit her home one weekend, her mother turns her away, and she goes to Buddy's house. There, alone, temporarily free of the world, Angela and Buddy finally make love:

> They sit down on the mattress in the corner, flat against the floor.
> "You think we get in trouble, Buddy?"
> "I don't know. I'm glad you're here."
> They be quiet holding close together. He kiss her mouth, her arm.
> Her fingers teasing on his neck and trace the fire down his back, his back a bone and skin discovery she making, stroke by stroke.
> And they undress themselves. Feel him, feel her wet and lose the loneliness the words between them.
> "What do you call it?" Buddy ask her.
> "Well I call it making love."
> "We make some love."
> They make some love and then they fall asleep. (p. 73)

Afraid of discovery, they go to live in the deserted house at the cemetery, and there, owning nothing, they spend a few days of love and peace, kindness and contentment. The book ends with the line, "And so begins a new day of the new life in the cemetery." Angela has become pregnant, and we know it will not be long before their slender resources give out and they are apprehended and separated.

Readers should discuss the fact that the only good thing in the lives of these two unfortunate teenagers has been their fleeting sexual relationship. Readers should also note how society would view the relationship outside the context of the story. Buddy's and Angela's love is a crime against society, but the abuse of Angela in her family and in the school is permitted to go unchecked. This book raises the provocative question: Is a teenage sexual relationship necessarily wrong? Is it anyone's business besides the teenagers engaged in it?

Teenage Pregnancy

Teenage pregnancy, a skeleton in the closet which once could cause a family unending disgrace, has become the significant subject of much adolescent literature. The teacher's views about pregnancy and the methods of handling it should be descriptive rather than prescriptive. His or her stance should be that there are many approaches and attitudes that teenagers, parents, and society can take and that the solution, like the problem, should be individual and personal. The teacher's position should also be that it is better to look at and discuss these matters openly than to pretend they do not exist or that they happen only to other people.

Norma Klein in *It's Not What You Expect* exhibits the same common-sense point of view toward teenage pregnancy that she took toward an unorthodox family arrangement in her novel, *Mom, the Wolfman and Me.* Carla and Oliver are twins whose parents are separated. One summer, with the help of their older brother, Ralph, they open a restaurant. When Ralph's girl friend, Sara Lee, gets pregnant, the twins have the following conversation, reflecting an attitude toward pregnancy that could not have been found in adolescent literature before the 1970s:

> Oliver backed away. He didn't even smile. "She's pregnant."
> I looked at him, frowning. "How can she be pregnant?"
> "How? What do you mean *how?*"
> "I mean, like, isn't she on the pill or something?"
> "I didn't ask," he said.
> "Oh boy! You'd think she'd at least use . . ."
> "Car, does it really matter all that much what she did or did not use? Suffice it to say that the methods employed, whatever they were, proved inadequate."
> "Gotcha, son, gotcha." I leaned back, envisioning the whole thing. "You know, frankly, this is the dumbest thing I've ever heard of."
> "Why dumb?"
> I sat up indignantly. "Well, my gosh! I mean, I can see, like, if you're in the back seat of a car and swept off your feet in passion. . . . But, I mean, they've been going together since they were in diapers practically." (pp. 89–90)

In this work, there is no debating the idea of abortion; it is taken for granted that Sara Lee will have one, and she goes through the experience calmly, without trauma. Afterwards, Ralph takes her home to have dinner. Carla asks Ralph if it hurt and he says, "a little . . . they only give you a local anaesthetic, you know."

The next day, Carla visits Sara Lee and finds her in the kitchen with her mother making radish flowers. Carla keeps looking at Sara Lee to see if there is a difference, but she looks as calm and composed as always. Carla thinks: "Of course, why shouldn't she be? It's only in old-time movies that people lie around pale and fainting after abortions. . . . I guess no one will even remember this or care about it." (p. 113)

Klein's casual depiction of abortion is uncommon in adolescent literature. In most works, abortion is so badly handled, so painful, and so humiliating that the girls prefer the alternative: having the baby.

Jeanette Eyerly's *Bonnie Jo, Go Home* depicts the problems facing young girls seeking abortions. It shows us that the legalization of abortion does not eliminate degrading and traumatic experiences. Before Bonnie Jo leaves her small town to go to New York City for a legal abortion, she must first endure her stepfather's anger and her own guilt at requiring her own father, who is poor, to find the $500 required for the operation and expenses.

Once in New York, the abortion takes much longer than the one day planned. The abortion clinic tells Bonnie Jo that she is too late for their simple vacuum aspiration procedure, and she must spend several days searching for a doctor who will use the saline-injection method, which requires hospitalization. Doctors are overbooked, hospitals are full, and each day the lonely girl worries about the way her funds are dwindling on living expenses.

After two weeks of agony, she is admitted to a hospital, where she spends a few unpleasant days. Leaving the hospital to return home, she looks at herself in a mirror and thinks that her face has aged a year for every day she has been in New York City.

Eyerly shows the reader how society doubly penalizes a young girl who accidentally gets pregnant. Students should discuss the humiliation and uncertainty that Bonnie Jo has been forced to endure.

Paul Zindel in *My Darling, My Hamburger*, depicts a variety of teenage interpersonal problems, including a particularly unpleasant abortion and its aftermath. The book gets its title from the advice given to high school girls by the health education teacher when she was asked "how to stop a boy if he wants to go all the way": "you're supposed to suggest going to get a hamburger." (p. 6)

One teenage couple is Dennis and Maggie. Dennis is skinny and weird-looking, and Maggie's hair looks like fuzz, her house smells of cabbage, and she is fat. Neither one of them has ever kissed a member of the opposite sex, and they sit through their first movie date in frantic concern not to touch each other.

The other couple is Liz and Sean. They are beautiful to look at, but inside they are far less happy and secure than Dennis and Maggie. Liz's suspicious mother and rough stepfather drive her into sleeping with Sean, which she would not have done on her own. Sean, too, is driven into treating Liz like a sex object by the social mores of his father and his father's friends.

Mr. Collins tells his friends: "He's going hot and heavy with that Carstensen girl. Did you ever see her?" Sean, resenting his father's tone, says, "She's a nice girl," and Mr. Collins replies, with an insinuating laugh, "You can say that again." (p. 28)

When Liz tells Sean that she's pregnant, they decide to marry after their graduation from high school. Sean then has a conversation with his father, which provides an excellent basis for a class discussion of some traditional male-female attitudes toward pregnancy. Sean, afraid to tell his father the truth, says that a friend of his at school has made a girl pregnant:

"Well," Mr. Collins started, "I'm sure the routine's the same now as when I had my worries." He moved back to the recliner chair, spilling a few drops of his drink as he got into it. "How pregnant is the girl?"

"About two months."

"Two!" Mr. Collins repeated slowly. "Well, I'd say the first job for the boy is to make sure there really *is* a problem. She might be saying she is to get even with him for something. Does he have money? Money in the family?"

"Some."

"That could be another thing. She might be pulling the whole thing to make sure she catches a husband with a little money." . . .

"What if she really *is*?" . . .

Mr. Collins tapped the side of his glass with his fingernail. "Then the guy's got to find out if it's his. She may have been spreading it around, if you know what I mean."

"I don't think—"

"It's the ones you don't think. You just tell that boy to make sure he's the only one, you hear me?" . . .

. . . "What if it *is* his?" . . .

. . . "Then you get friends."

"Friends?"

"Yes. You get a few friends. You only need a few. Get 'em to call the girl or go up and talk to her. She'll get the point and get scared."

"Dad . . ."

"You say the kid's got money. Comes from a money family?"

"Yes. Some."

"Then you tell her to get an operation. You tell that guy to spend a few bucks."
. . .

. . . "She offered to get an abortion, but—"

"Then what's the problem?" his father interrupted.

"Is it that simple?"

"Hell, yes! Any one of the doctors in this town'll recommend her for a special Puerto Rican vacation. They do that sort of thing down there like it was pulling a tooth. That's all that little girl needs—a good P.R. weekend." . . .

"Suppose he loves her?"

"Boy, your friend doesn't know what love is. He can think he loves her now, but if he's thinking of marrying her—forget it! Is he planning on going to college, or is he some kind of dummy?"

"College."

"Well, she'll kill him. She'll kill any chance he ever gets. He'll be a zero. A nobody. You think he'll ever finish college? . . . Tell him to cut her out now. There's big things ahead in life. . . ." (pp. 89–90)

The cynical attitudes of his father cause Sean to give Liz money for the abortion instead of marrying her. Liz has the abortion performed by a sleazy quack and starts to hemorrhage on the way home.

Liz, by now a bitter, disillusioned girl, is unable to attend the high school graduation. Maggie watches Sean accept his diploma and feels sorry for him. "He'd have his punishment, she thought. For the rest of his life he'd remember Liz. . . . He'd have to remember Liz and something he couldn't be very proud of. The past wasn't that easy to get away from." (p. 120)

In both Zindel's and Eyerly's books, the teenage girl who gets pregnant pays a particularly heavy price in suffering and social disgrace. When the abortion is not a simple, accepted event as in the Klein book, it becomes almost as traumatic as having an illegitimate child. Where girls are able to get abortions without telling their parents or can obtain parental consent without hysteria, abortion becomes a simple thing. It becomes dangerous when a pregnant teenager cannot face her parents and is forced into a second trimester abortion, which carries a much higher risk for the young mother.

Teenage Mothers

Many teenagers, for one reason or another, decide not to have an abortion and proceed to have the baby. The most beautiful book about this situation, almost a mythic fairy tale, is Katie Letcher Lyle's *Fair Day and Another Step Begun.*

Based on an old English ballad, "Childe Waters," the book is set in mountain country, where people still believe in conjuring, spells, potions, human responsibility, and undying love.

The heroine is sixteen-year-old Ellen Burd, who tells us: "The last people to be civilized are mountain people." (p. 9) She sees John Waters, wealthy heir to the Waters Roofing Construction Company, when he comes home from college, and immediately falls deeply and eternally in love with him. He takes her out in his canoe, they spend the day together, and she becomes pregnant.

When she tells him, he refuses to accept responsibility for the baby. He tells her that he is engaged to someone else and offers her money to get rid of the baby. The rest of the book deals with her attempt to win his love. She gets a spell and potions from a conjure man, and when he flees she follows him to Fair Day, a plantation where he is staying with relatives.

After she finds him, John continues to treat her cruelly, but she is always sweet, beautiful, and patient. She delivers the baby in a field. John Waters assists in the birth and at last, coming into his manhood, he acknowledges her and the baby.

What is interesting for young readers to note in this book is the unchanging nature of this male-female situation, which is valid psychologically both in the Old English ballad and in its contemporary setting. It is also interesting to note that so long as John refuses to acknowledge his role in this making of a human life, he is a shallow, stunted man. But when Ellen's father asks, "What are you going to name that boy?" he replies, "John Waters is his name. . . . It's my name, sir, and my father's name," (p. 141) and he is filled for the first time with the pride and responsibility necessary to a complete, mature man.

Two other works in which young men are willing to share the responsibility for pregnancy can be seen in Ann Head's *Mr. and Mrs. Bo Jo Jones* and John Neufeld's *For All the Wrong Reasons.*

When sixteen-year-old July becomes pregnant by seventeen-year-old Bo Jo Jones, they decide to get married. The problems one would naturally expect in conjunction with such a decision are intensified by the fact that they come from different social classes. July comes from an upper class family and Bo Jo from a working class one. When July finds she is pregnant, without discussing this with their families or considering any alternatives, they slip over the state line and get married. This is the worst possible choice they could make; they hardly know each other, don't love each other, and this will prevent Bo Jo from going to college.

When Bo Jo tells his family, they say they want nothing more to do with him. He was the one hope for their family, the one they expected to go to college. When July tells her family, they ask themselves, "Where did we fail her?"

For one year they live and struggle together, the baby is born and dies, and then they discover something strange and wonderful. They no longer have to be married, but they want to be married. What started as necessity has turned into love and commitment and caring.

There are many significant ideas to be discussed in relation to this book once readers are able to suspend their disbelief. Given July's sympathetic parents and social class, it is difficult to believe that she would not have an easy abortion right at the beginning. But once readers move past that point, they should note the fact that both Bo Jo and July develop as human beings because of their relationship with each other.

For All the Wrong Reasons is probably more realistic than *Mr. and Mrs. Bo Jo Jones*. Again, we have a couple of teenagers who marry because the girl gets pregnant and, as in the Head book, there seems to be little reason for them to do so. In the Neufeld book, in particular, it is surprising because the book is set in the 1970s, abortion is easy to get, they come from upper class families, the parents beg them to get an abortion, and yet they persist in getting married. Peter does not emerge strong and mature as does Bo Jo. Instead, he has a nervous breakdown and at the end of the book is in a clinic while Tish lives alone taking care of her baby. She is glad things happened as they did because she has her baby, but the reader is not convinced. In relation to this book, as with the Head book, young readers should discuss the behavior of the teenage lovers, whether or not they were right to get married, which book is more believable, and how society helps or hinders young people who are in love and want to get married.

In the books we noted above, the pregnant young girl is married to her lover. But there are a number of books about teenage pregnancy in which the young woman is left to cope with her burden all by herself.

In *Phoebe*, by Patricia Dizenzo, sixteen-year-old Phoebe discovers that she is pregnant and has nobody to help her. Paul, the father, is a child, a playmate, not a man who can shoulder responsibility. She thinks:

She couldn't face the idea of telling her mother—or even worse, her father. (p. 13)

Phoebe fantasizes alternative conversations that are simultaneously amusing and pathetic. In one fantasy she tells Paul, and he says: "Pregnancy? Why didn't you tell me Phoebe . . . that's fantastic! Oh, I love you so much." (p. 25) But in another he says, "You can't blame me. . . . It was you as much as me. I never forced you. . . . Maybe you did this to trap me! Maybe you're sick of school. Maybe all you want is a husband and a baby." (p. 30)

The reader moves with Phoebe through her terrible fears: of her parents, of being thrown out of school, of abortion, of disgrace. Her memory is haunted with tales of girls who became pregnant and had to drop out of school. When she finally goes to see her family doctor, he reminds her that abortion is illegal and that all he can do is advise about care during pregnancy. The book ends just after Phoebe summons up enough nerve to tell Paul on the phone that she is pregnant and is about to inform her parents about it.

This book provides an excellent discussion device for readers. They can write or discuss their own endings, since the book ends without an ending. A further value of the book is that it puts the reader, both male and female, into the position of a young person whose body has suddenly become the enemy; and, without moralizing, the book makes a plea for more communication, love, trust, and knowledge. Despite the fact that abortion has now been legalized in many states, the difficulty in obtaining abortions and the psychological effects of unwanted pregnancy continue to make this book timely and pertinent.

The Girls of Huntington House, by Blossom Elfman, is a non-fiction account of a home for unmarried, pregnant girls who are under eighteen. Elfman was hired to teach them English and finds the group as varied as any other group of girls would be: lovable, exasperating, rich and poor, nice and not so nice.

Elfman learns as much from her students as they learn from her. Flexibly adjusting her teaching techniques, she decides to put on a play with her girls, and for the first time they become totally involved in school subject matter.

A significant aspect of the book is the absence of stereotypes of characterization or attitude. The girls are not the traditional "bad girls" of literature. They come from every walk of life. Some of them know a great deal about sex, and some of them know nothing. The wonderful thing about them is the sisterhood they feel for each other. They know better than any outsider could how to give each other support and compassion.

This is a good book for young people because it will help them understand the nature of love as they read about the behavior of those who work with these girls, and it will reduce, to some small extent, the fear of unmarried pregnancy, familiar to so many teenagers.

Another non-fiction book about a young girl who decides to have her illegitimate baby is Mary Hanes's *Love Child*. Hanes decides to have a baby without a husband because of the unpleasant image of woman's fate that she was given as a child: "By the time I was seven, I knew that to be a grownup was to be either a parent, a person trapped and drowning in a bitter sea of marriage, or one of those ludicrous creatures known as old maids." (p. 12) She explains that she escaped "both pathetic old-maid-hood and miserable marriage by becoming an unmarried mother. I got pregnant by accident, but certainly these conflicting dreads were strong factors in my decision to let the pregnancy run its normal course and to bring up a child on my own." (p. 13)

Hanes finds that it is not easy to challenge the dominant mores of a society. Her sister urges her to have an abortion: "You can't have a baby without a husband. It will ruin your life. Please be sensible." (p. 26) Her friends feel the same way as her sister does. They are horrified, not by her pregnancy, but by her refusal to have an abortion. "Each of them told me how I could get an abortion. One offered to send me to Puerto Rico or Sweden. Another had a classmate in Boston, Massachusetts, who had just flunked out of a medical school in the Spring and had been cut off by his parents. He was desperate for money, and he'd probably do it gladly. One, an aging divinity student, told me very frankly that my attitude was morally reprehensible." (p. 27)

The top executive at the newspaper for which she works tells her they will not keep her on the staff unless she agrees to an abortion, and her grandfather offers her money only if she will agree to the operation. The social worker at the shelter for unmarried, expectant mothers is angry with her because she refuses to consider giving her baby up for adoption. "I agreed with her that in some ways it would be selfish to keep my baby and thereby deprive it of a nice, middle-class adoptive home—but I was selfish. Then she told me at great length just how severely I would handicap the child, how I would ruin its life. I could not possibly be a good mother." (p. 33)

When she gives birth, she finds that unmarried mothers are segregated from others in the hospital. The aide addresses her angrily as MISS Hanes and puts her into a terrible closet of a room filled with asbestos-covered pipes. Hanes later learns that this is the room usually reserved for dying ward patients.

This is an honest book. Hanes's life is never easy, and there are many times after James is born that she regrets what she has done. She is afflicted with poverty, illness, loneliness, and social hostility; but eventually the difficult times pass, and she is able to learn to love herself and to establish a relationship with a man who is capable of returning her feeling.

Homosexuality

During the years of developing teenage romances, many teenagers turn to homosexuality rather than to heterosexual relationships. A number of books have come out in recent years which deal with this theme. One of the best is Sandra Scoppetone's *Trying Hard to Hear You.*

The young people in this book are members of a summer teenage theater group. Camilla, the narrator, is sixteen. Her best friend is Jeff, the boy who lives next door. She has a crush on Phil, one of the production assistants. Her mother is a sophisticated analyst, who commutes from their Suffolk County home to practice in New York City. Although Camilla comes from a sophisticated, upper-class family, she is unable to cope with the idea of homosexuality when it arises.

The young people in this theater group are outsiders to the rest of the students in their high school. This has made them draw together and form a community of outsiders. One night, at a party, the group comes upon Phil and Jeff kissing, and suddenly, the entire group turns against them. This is the scene of discovery:

> "Faggots," Bruce said, "these guys are faggots."
> "Huh?"
> "They're queers, man," Harlan sputtered.
> "We went in the bushes to . . . You know," Bruce said, suddenly becoming shy in front of all the girls, "and we found these two creeps kissing, for godsake."
> "They're goddamn queers," Harlan said.
> Faggots . . . queers . . . fairies . . . the murmur echoed over the years.
> Phil and Jeff said nothing and looked at no one. (p. 180)

Camilla finds the situation impossible to understand or to accept. She remembers a high school freshman who was an overt queer, wearing women's clothes, but it is impossible for her to think of Phil and Jeff in those terms. She keeps hearing Jeff's words, again and again, "Phil and I love each other." (p. 189) She asks herself: "How could it be possible? My best friend had *stolen* my boyfriend. It seemed so crazy. I had been really convinced that Phil cared for me. He certainly was the first boy that I had really cared for . . . loved. Sure, I had lots of crushes but Phil was different. I had to laugh. He sure was different." (p. 189)

All of the boys' friends turn against them. One girl says: "They're undesirables. . . . We'll give them the silent treatment. That way they'll know what we think of them and so will the other kids. I mean, we don't want to be associated with them, do we?" (p. 192) Camilla finds herself agreeing.

During the next few days, the baiting, teasing, homosexual jokes, petty cruelties, intensify. Jeff tries to explain to Camilla that "being different doesn't make you special; it's just different, that's all . . . a lot of people won't understand that and will try to change you, but you've got to stand up for what you are: A person has the right to be anything he or she wants. . . ." (p. 205)

The plea that Jeff makes over and over to Camilla and to the others is, "why do you care what I am and do if it doesn't hurt you?"

After the tragic deaths of Phil and Penny, a girl in the crowd, Camilla's mother tries to explain to her why the group acted the way they did. "Because we're all afraid of things we don't understand," (p. 252) her mother tells her. She adds that homosexuality has been a part of life as long as there have been people, but "as long as you don't hurt anyone else, you have a right to be what you want to be." (p. 252)

Students should discuss these words of Camilla's mother, for they are the theme of the book. Before reading Scoppetone's book a class might want to write private papers about their opinions of homosexuality, and put these pages away to look at when they finish reading and discussing this book.

Lynn Hall's *Sticks and Stones* shows how even the *rumor* of homosexuality may be enough to cause tragedy. After his parents' divorce, Tom Naylor and his mother return from a big city to her home town and open an antique shop. At first, Tom is an admired outsider—handsome, cultured, sophisticated. The only person he can find who shares his love of music, writing, antiques, and art is Ward Alexander, who has been dishonorably discharged from the Army for an alleged homosexual incident.

The rumors about Tom are started by Floyd, the town outcast, who hates Tom for his innate superiority. When Floyd finds that he has failed his examinations and must repeat the ninth grade, his terrible feelings about himself cause him to attack Tom, who seems to have everything Floyd lacks.

Floyd, the villain of the novel, is also a victim, and when victims are trampled on enough, they may become dangerous. Hall's depiction of Floyd is a plea for another kind of despised outsider. When Floyd begins the rumors about Tom, this is how he feels: "His steps bounced. He felt taller, even slimmer, and definitely happier. He could look at The Cottage and not feel humbled by Tom's superiority. There are worse things than being fat and dumb, he thought. Much worse things." (p. 52)

The frightening aspect of this book is the rapidity with which the rumor is believed. Everyone in school seems to simultaneously hear and delight in it. Tom has "an uncomfortable feeling of moving within an invisible covering that separated him from the people around him." (p.

87) Because he does not know what is going on, he does not know how to deal with it. He sits in the middle of a classroom full of contemporaries who should have been his friends and he feels "as though he were in parentheses." (p. 91)

Gradually, Tom's marks suffer; his triumph at winning the music competition is taken away when mothers refuse to let their sons go away on the school bus with him; his belief in himself is shaken; and he starts to examine himself for the signs others seem to see. The rumors also cause him to stop seeing Ward. After a tragic automobile accident in which Floyd is killed, Tom thinks:

> The talkers and the pointers had undermined him. They had touched him with the acid of their suspicions, and the corrosion had spread until he himself had lost sight of the truth.
>
> There was nothing wrong with me at all, until I started listening to their whispers, Tom thought. They brought me down, and I let them. I just placidly let them tell me what I was, and then believed them. "Them." None of those people knew anything about me, really. There's probably nothing wrong with my masculinity, only with my stupid head, for not being surer of myself. (p. 187)

Besides homosexuality, this book deals with other significant themes for adolescents: the difficulty of being a new kid in school, the injustice caused by gossip, and the cruel transformation of deviates into pariahs.

Difficult as it may be, students and teachers must discuss society's attitudes toward sexual deviance and the increasingly visible Gay Liberation Movement, and deal with the concept of the individual's right to live and love as he or she pleases, without fear or censure. They will note that the treatment of homosexuals, historically, has been similar to that accorded other minority groups or so-called deviants from accepted norms.

In the Scoppetone and Hall books, young people become outsiders because of real or rumored homosexuality. In works like Isabelle Holland's *The Man Without a Face*, homosexual encounters are seen as one way for an outsider to create a human bond between himself and some other person. Fourteen-year-old Charles is an outsider in his own family. His much-married mother prefers his two sisters and blames Charles for the breakup of her second marriage.

Charles has never known his father, the second of his mother's four husbands, to whom she refers as "my one real mistake." (p. 5) Charles's mother and two sisters do not like him, and he feels as if he is drowning in women. In order to get into prep school and escape from home, he asks Justin McLeod (called "The Man Without a Face" because half of his face has been disfigured in an automobile accident) to tutor him. McLeod lives alone with his dog in a house up on a cliff.

Unwillingly, McLeod begins to tutor Charles, and Charles finds in this man the love, companionship, compassion, and male wisdom which has been lacking. He is the friend Charles has needed, the father he's never known. Charles says: "Except for Joey, I'd never had a friend; I'd never really, except for a shadowy memory, had a father, and he was my father; I'd never known an adult I could communicate with or trust, and I communicated with him all the time, whether I was actually talking to him or not. And I trusted him." (p. 123)

Charles's terrible loneliness and feelings of isolation eventually result in a sexual encounter with McLeod at a moment of crisis, after Charles's sister's boyfriend kills his cat and his sister vindictively reveals to him the true nature of his dead father. In hysteria, Charles runs to McLeod:

"You know why I don't have a father? Because he's a drunk. He died on skid row. He just walked out and left me. . . ."
The gasps seemed to come from my knees, shuddering through my body. Justin reached me and put his arms around me and held me while I cried out of some ocean I didn't know was there. I couldn't stop. After a while he lifted me up and carried me to the bed and lay down beside me, holding me.
I could feel his heart pounding, and then I realized it was mine. I couldn't stop shaking; in fact, I started to tremble violently. It was like everything—the water, the sun, the hours, the play, the work, the whole summer—came together. The golden cocoon had broken open and was spilling in a shower of gold.
Even so, I didn't know what was happening to me until it had happened. (p. 141)

It is important for young readers to note that this one sexual experience does not turn Charles into a homosexual and does not mar him for life. Justin tells him the next morning:

There's nothing about it to worry you. You reacted to a lot of strain—and shock—in a normal fashion. At your age, anything could trigger it. . . . It has something to do with me, sure. But nothing of any lasting significance. It could have been anyone—boy or girl. It could have been when you were asleep. You must know that. (p. 142)

Justin dies but Charles is left with the memory that he has loved a good man, a man who had a "talent for salvaging flawed and fallen creatures. Himself included." (p. 151) McLeod has shown Charles the nature of love, and because of him Charles is able to move back into the community of people, back into his family, and forward to acceptance of himself.

Another situation in which two outsiders turn to a homosexual encounter for warmth and companionship is found in John Donovan's *I'll Get There. It Better Be Worth the Trip.* Two thirteen-year-old boys, Davy and Altschuler, feel like outsiders in their families. Neither one of their divorced mothers feels comfortable with her son. Davy's mother drinks and is frighteningly inconsistent in her treatment of him, and Altschuler's mother treats him well only when visitors are around. Both divorced fathers are busy with their new families, and their relationships with their sons, who need male companionship, are polite, but indifferent.

The homosexual encounter, like the one in the Holland book, is just the end result of warmth and affection spilling over. It happens when the boys are playing with Davy's dog, on the floor:

Mine and Altschuler's laughing dies down, but we stay on the floor. I look at Altschuler, and we smile, sort of. And I'm not quite sure of what happens now but

I think we both intend to get up and chase after Fred, but there we are lying on the floor, Fred peering at us from across the room, us half peering at Fred and wanting to chase after him again, but also not wanting to get up at all. I close my eyes. I feel unusual. Lying there. Close to Altschuler. I don't want to get up. I want to stay lying there. I feel a slight shiver and shake from it. Not cold though. Unusual. So I open my eyes. Altschuler is still lying there too. He looks at me peculiarly, and I'm sure I look at him the same way. Suddenly Fred jumps in between us. First he licks my face, then Altschuler's, and back and forth between us. I think that this unusual feeling I have will end, but in a minute the three of us are lying there, our heads together. I guess I kiss Altschuler and he kisses me. It isn't like that dumb kiss I gave Mary Lou Gerrity in Massachusetts before I left. It just happens. And when it stops we sit up and turn away from each other. Fred has trotted off, maybe tired of both of us by now.

"Boy," I say. "What was that all about??"

"I don't know," Altschuler answers.

We get up, and we avoid looking at each other. When our eyes meet, we laugh, but not like before. (p. 118)

The following are some important ideas for young people to think about in relation to this book: a) an encounter such as the one described need not be viewed as a tragedy that will cause a young person to become homosexual; b) an encounter such as this one can happen to anyone and is not a crime or a sin; and c) this may just be a sexual experience that a young person has along the way, which can be viewed as part of coming of age.

Although the Donovan book is simple enough for junior high school students, it can also be read by senior high school students. The philosophical and humanistic concepts have universal application.

Books Discussed in Chapter IV

You Would If You Loved Me, Nora Stirling, Avon, 1972.
Forever, Judy Blume, Bantam, 1977.
First Person, Singular, Vida Demas, Dell, 1974.
It's Not What You Expect, Norma Klein, Avon, 1974.
Bonnie Jo, Go Home, Jeanette Eyerly, Bantam, 1973.
My Darling, My Hamburger, Paul Zindel, Bantam, 1971.
If Beale Street Could Talk, James Baldwin, Signet, 1974.
His Own Where, June Jordan, Dell, 1973.
Fair Day and Another Step Begun, Katie Letcher Lyle, Dell, 1975.
Mr. and Mrs. Bo Jo Jones, Ann Head, Signet, 1968.
For All the Wrong Reasons, John Neufeld, Signet, 1973.
Phoebe, Patricia Dizenzo, Bantam, 1970.
The Girls of Huntington House, Blossom Elfman, Bantam, 1972.
Love Child, Mary Hanes, Signet, 1973.
Trying Hard to Hear You, Sandra Scoppettone, Bantam, 1976.
Sticks and Stones, Lynn Hall, Dell, 1972.
The Man Without a Face, Isabelle Holland, Bantam, 1973.
I'll Get There. It Better Be Worth the Trip, John Donovan, Dell, 1969.

Other Related Books

Ruby, Rosa Guy, Viking Press, 1977. (Lesbian relationship in ghetto)

House of Tomorrow, Jean Thompson, Harper Paperback, 1967. (Home for unwed mothers)

The Go-Between, L. P. Hartley, Avon, 1968. (Young boy acts as lovers' go-between)

A Wild Thing, Jean Renvoise, Bantam, 1972. (Strange affair between wild girl and wounded climber)

A Love, or a Season, Mary Stolz, Har-Row, 1964. (Emerging sexuality in teenagers)

Drop-Out, Jeanette Eyerly, Berkley, 1969. (Teenagers drop out of high school and run away in order to get married)

V
violence:
real and vicarious

Why do we simultaneously deplore and find ourselves fascinated by violence? Is our society more violent than others? Do we consciously or unconsciously admire and try to emulate values and attitudes that contribute to a willingness to condone or, at least, not condemn violence? What values and attitudes support a commitment to non-violence? Is violence simply a fact that we must all learn to live with?

Introduction

Why read adolescent literature about violence? Isn't there enough violence around without studying it in school? What about the good old days when students read "positive books"?

Contrary to popular myth, reading matter has always included violence. Even in *The Wizard of Oz* Dorothy crushes one witch and vaporizes another. "Snow White" contains the prototypical evil stepmother, and *Bambi* contains hunters with guns.

In fact, Bruno Bettelheim, in his work *The Uses of Enchantment: The Meaning and Importance of Fairy Tales*, points out that our dominant culture makes a terrible mistake if it "wishes to pretend, particularly where children are concerned, that the dark side of man does not exist, and professes a belief in optimistic meliorism." (pp. 7–8) This kind of avoidance of reality results in the stunting of the developing person, in making good and evil, violence and non-violence, death and life, so remote that the child is left incapable of recognizing or dealing with either good or bad. Bettelheim writes:

In child or adult, the unconscious is a powerful determinant of behavior. When the unconscious is repressed and its content denied entrance into awareness, then eventually the person's conscious mind will be partially overwhelmed by derivatives of these unconscious elements, or else he is forced to keep such rigid, compulsive control over them that his personality may become severely crippled. But when unconscious material *is* to some degree permitted to come to awareness and worked through in imagination, its potential for causing harm—to ourselves or others—is much reduced; some of its forces can then be made to serve positive purposes. However, the prevalent parental belief is that a child must be diverted from what troubles him: his formless, nameless anxieties, and his chaotic, angry, and even violent fantasies. Many parents believe that only conscious reality or pleasant and wish-fulfilling images should be presented to the child—that he should be exposed only to the sunny side of things. But such one-sided fare nourishes the mind only in a one-sided way, and real life is not all sunny. (p. 7)

Bettelheim makes a plea for the deliberate use of fairy tales with children precisely because they do present violence and evil as well as good and help the young person make moral choices based on virtue and right. Bettelheim further points out that "evil is not without its attractions," but in fairy tales, virtue is always victorious.

Applying Bettelheim's view to adolescent literature, I suggest that we do not help young people by avoidance of the evil or violent novel. Studying such a book can be a valuable, positive learning experience, provided that the evil in it is counterbalanced with good and that the story has an upbeat ending that holds out hope to the young—tells them there is indeed a reason for eschewing savagery, brutality, murder, and mayhem. I would not recommend a book such as Robert Cormier's *I Am the Cheese* because it ends with a domestic CIA organization doing in a young boy and his family. No one knows, no one cares, no one helps—a poor message for today's teenagers.

If we believe that true adolescent literature reflects society, it would be ostrich-like for American schools to avoid books containing violence. Violence pervades our society. School violence has increased. "From 1970 to 1973, school homicides increased 18.5 percent, assaults on students increased 85.3 percent, and assaults on teachers increased 77.4 percent."[1] Rape has increased. Over 25,000 cases of child abuse are reported annually, and countless cases are not reported. The violence of youth gangs, seemingly in recession for a while, has returned to the intensity of the 1950s. A *New York Times* article of May 1, 1976, tells us:

Violence by youth gangs has reached new heights in the major cities of the United States and gang members are increasingly attacking ordinary citizens. . . .

The gangs, made up of youths from 12 to 21 years old, have forsaken bicycle chains and homemade zipguns for automatic rifles, shotguns and finely tooled pistols, giving them an awesome firepower. . . .

In some cities . . . gangs have established themselves in public schools with unusual force, sometimes making students pay quarters and dollars in "lunch money shakedowns" for such privileges as attending school, passing through the hallways and using the gym facilities and as protection against being beaten up . . . there are as many as 2,700 gangs with 81,500 members in the six largest cities . . .

1. Eugenia Kemble, "The Seeds of School Violence," *American Teacher*, May 1976, p. 7.

the sophistication of weaponry in the gangs of the 1970's far surpasses anything known in the past. . . .[2]

Works of violence and evil that should be read and discussed in school are ones in which the tragedy helps to point out the possibilities of nobility and goodness in the human character; in which the possibilities of goodness and truth are heightened by contrast with evil and falsehood. It is the contrast we see when Anne Frank still believes in the goodness of people or when Sidney Carton gives his life for the woman he loves.

It is true that real-life violence may not be worthy of school consideration. Probably we would not discuss in the classroom a newspaper account of rape, murder, or child abuse. "Isn't it terrible? I don't know what's happening to the world," the newspaper reader exclaims and flips to the next page. He has gained some information, which he will soon forget, but he has not been moved.

But literature personalizes sensational events. An excellent film that succinctly illustrates this difference is *What Is Poetry: Auto Wreck,* in which a newspaper account of an automobile accident is first read in a factual voice, followed by a reading of Karl Shapiro's poem, which gives us gooseflesh as we wonder with the poet about the cosmic significance of the accident: Who decides who shall live and who shall die—and why? The fictionalized work holds our attention in the same way The Ancient Mariner clutches us, talks to us, then releases us to think and reflect on the meaning of our literary encounter, perhaps to change.

Through adolescent literature, the teenager has the opportunity to explore the real world, and violence is part of the real world. "While adults sometimes think teenagers should be spared contact with . . . harsh realities, the fact is that most adolescents will face them anyway, through rumor or discussions in school, if not through direct personal experience."[3]

Teenage Gangs

What do we want teenagers to understand about gangs? Well, to begin with, that they exist. We want them to see that rootless youngsters join gangs for love, friendship, protection, and survival. We also want them to understand the negative nature of these gangs—the perversions of the ideals of work, the destruction of individuality, the blunting of conscience, and the behavioral changes that develop within the supposed protection of such groups.

Graham Greene's short story "The Destructors" (in *Twenty-One Stories*) depicts the mindless violence of juvenile gangs. The story is set in London, about ten years after the end of World War II during the three-day bank holiday at the end of August. A new boy in the neighborhood, Trevor (called "T."), is immediately accepted by the local gang

---

2. Joseph B. Treaster, "Violence of Youth Gangs Is Found at a New High," *The New York Times,* May 1, 1976, p. 21.

3. G. Robert Carlsen, *Books and the Teen-Age Reader.* Bantam, 1971, p. 51.

because of an "odd quality of danger, of the unpredictable" in him. The gang meets every morning during the summer in a car-park, where Blackie, the leader, proposes a course of mindless action for the day.

One day, T. calls the gang's attention to a house which, alone, of all the houses in the block, survived the bombing of London. The boys dub Mr. Thomas, the owner, "Old Misery." After Old Misery tries to be friendly, T. visits him and plans to destroy the house during the bank holiday when the owner will be away. The boys then spend two days systematically finishing what the bombs could not do: destroying the house.

Before they have finished, Old Misery returns from his holiday and is locked by the boys into the outhouse for the night. They tie the remaining frame of the house to a lorry parked in the street, and when the driver sets off in the morning, he inadvertently pulls down the frame. He hears the old man shouting and lets him out. Old Misery gives a sobbing cry when he realizes that his house has disappeared. The truck driver can't help laughing at the situation: "I'm sorry. I can't help it, Mr. Thomas. There's nothing personal, but you got to admit it's funny."

The understanding of various elements of this short story will provide a frame of reference for all future adolescent literature about gangs. We see that Trevor can achieve status only through destruction, and from the beginning, his brooding silence intimidates the other boys and keeps them from crossing him. Trevor is a person with tremendous rage, obviously not someone to trifle with. We learn that his parents have come down in the world, that he has come from a higher class (his name is one mocked in lower classes). The gang is so cowed by him that they call him T. in order to prevent accidental laughter.

There is a conflict going on in T. between respect for the level of society from which he has come ("Wren built that house, father says") and the need to adopt protective coloration in order to survive in his new, brutal environment. He makes an effort to recapture the lost world when he politely visits Old Misery and is graciously shown about as a middle-class boy would be. When he tells the gang about his exploit and they are disappointed that he didn't break in, he realizes that what seems like a feat of daring to a middle-class boy (to visit a stranger's house) is weak and pointless to the gang. They begin to group together into an impromptu court, and T. realizes that he must break violently with the tradition of his parents and Old Misery in order to gain acceptance in this new world.

Forced to save his skin, T. turns evil and at one stroke changes his followers from petty nuisances into real criminals. His streak of daring makes him the leader of a heretofore comparatively harmless, mindless rabble and releases their criminal impulses that have been lying dormant under a very thin civilized veneer.

Gradually T. becomes more and more demonic, finally appearing as a psychopath who is totally devoid of empathy or human feeling. What began as a means of gaining peer acceptance turns into evil for the sake of evil. What once existed as a middle-class code of manners becomes empty formality, so that when he finds the old man's savings he destroys the money saying: "We aren't thieves . . . nobody's going to steal anything from this house." He is like a captain telling his soldiers it is all right to kill but not to loot. Although T. cannot engage in lower-class "pinching," destruction on a grand scale is acceptable. His complete dehumanization is illustrated with the words: "Of course I don't hate him. . . . There's no fun if I hated him. . . . All this hate and love, it's soft, it's hooey. There's only things, Blackie. . . ." Old Misery, like his house, has been reduced to a "thing."

T. thinks out the plan to entice the old man into the outhouse so that the gang can finish the destruction. Again, with his peculiar code of ethics (like soldiers giving chewing gum to bombed-out people), he gives the old man rolls and a blanket to keep him comfortable through the night.

Blackie and the other gang members share the same social class, language patterns, and class perceptions. Their brutishness, idleness, stunted value system, and lack of imagination are typical of the modern, lower-class hoodlum. They have adopted a set of poses which include being "cool," not surprised about anything; they speak in mindless clichés. They are the children of violence, of the Battle of Britain. Their childhoods were disturbed by bombings, and they have grown up surrounded with symbols of adult destructiveness: the bombed-out houses, the carpark, which is the "site of the last bomb of the first blitz." They neither know nor care anything about the British tradition from which T. and Old Misery come, for they have always been excluded from that tradition by speech, socioeconomic level, and value systems.

The gang has no feelings of compassion for the old man who has survived a terrible war. They hate him because he is old and different, and they justify their meanness by attributing ulterior motives to him when he is kind to them. They also think that their gang will become famous and admired for destroying the old house. They are mean and brutish but not bright enough to be evil. They need the superior intelligence, daring, and imagination of T. for that.

The most obvious fact about the other adults in this story is that they are either nonexistent or incapable of providing models for the teenagers that would turn them away from barbarism. The other adults fall into six categories:

1. Philistine destroyers like those who bombed the city and left one house standing, not because it was built by Wren but through faulty aim.
2. Incompetent, irresponsible adults like T.'s father, a former architect and present clerk who has plunged T. into an unfamiliar, hostile world, which he must conquer completely on his own.
3. Egocentric snobs like T.'s mother, who is too involved in her own downfall to give T. guidance and considers herself better than the neighbors.
4. Criminals like the "grown-up gang" that the boys admire and hope to join eventually.
5. Irreligious drunkards like the parents of Mike, the smallest boy, who send him to church alone on Sunday morning because they are hung over.
6. Fools and dullards like the lorry driver who cannot help laughing at the house's destruction.

Graham Green, coming from an older tradition, delineates the causes for gang activity but has little sympathy for the gang members. His story provides a paradigm for the rise of dictators, bullies, demagogues, and is a despairing picture of how the aesthetic, the sensitive, the persons of conscience and compassion, must be destroyed by the evil ones with no sense of shame. But writers of contemporary adolescent literature feel that teenage gang members are as much victims as victimizers.

The best of the newer books about teenage gangs is Kin Platt's *Headman.* The setting is Los Angeles; the streets are as dangerous as an unknown jungle; and each day Owen Kirby, the protagonist, must cross this jungle and hope to escape injury or death. Streets, settings that hold no terror for adults, become terrifying battlegrounds to the kids unfortunate enough to live there.

When Owen is attacked by a gang of boys while walking on an unfamiliar street ("He wasn't familiar with the gangs in this neighborhood. It wasn't very healthy to walk strange turf."), he is arrested and sent to a work camp in the country. At Camp Sawyer the floors are clean, the walls freshly painted, and Owen has clean bedding. "Man," he thinks, "this is better than home." Owen's stereotypical home is poor, cramped, filthy. His father has long since disappeared and his mother is an alcoholic.

Before going to Camp Sawyer he is held at Juvenile Hall where there are 500 young delinquents, ranging in age from ten to eighteen. The situation there is similar to the one on the streets:

Juvenile Hall was gang-dominated. ... The lucky ones got to sleep in a cell-like cage. No plumbing. Heavily screened walls and windows. They were locked in at night and the gangs couldn't get at them.

The others slept on thin mattresses on the floor. Owen didn't sleep for several nights. Instead he dozed during the long interminable days.

He noticed the Chicanos were let alone because they stuck together in protective units. If one of them got messed by a blood or paddy, the Chicano gang fought back.

"I got to get me a gang," Owen thought. "You need protection." (p. 24)

Owen looks at the kids around him and thinks: "Running with gangs. Stealing. Fighting. Stabbing. Shooting. They all got to wind up in the clink." (p. 26) Students should discuss the terrible sadness of this perspective—the hopelessness of it, the lack of options. Platt keeps taking the reader into the minds of the gang members. Justin Dye, black headman of a gang called the Nomads, presents a position that students should discuss:

What they doin', all them fat cats, not payin' no income tax, rippin' off whatever they can get, selling things that fall apart and don't stand up, raising prices—*shee-it!* Now ain't that a bigger rip-off? All them gas and oil cats, man. They stiffing us blind! We the ones who got to pay, and them mothers sticking it to us every day, driving us right up the wall, and shit, nobody says nothin'—they got it made and nobody says nothing about how they screwing us.

But us cats, all we got to do is step out of line only one time. You cut some dude and whammo—there is the Man to flag you down, put you away. Two years, the

Man says, Lock up the mother, he too dangerous to let be, Don' let him loose, he might hurt somebody. If *we* want a war, only *we* say who can do the killing, dig? Only *we* is entitled, see? Only that *we* ain't got nothing to do with us. The kind of *we* that *we* is, that's the kind them mothers got to put away. (p. 67)

Dye makes the point that Platt repeats throughout the book: for poor boys from bad neighborhoods, there is a better chance of survival with a gang than without one. And yet, Owen keeps thinking, running with a gang doesn't keep the headman or gang members from being sent away to places like Camp Sawyer.

Just as Owen begins to develop a healthier value structure, he is released, sent home to his alcoholic mother, a filthy apartment, smog, dead trees. The models of Gomez and Johnson and the life at Camp Sawyer continue to haunt him, but he doesn't know how to work his way out of the old patterns that start to engulf him again.

He felt out of tune, awkward with his old buddies. Like he came down from another planet suddenly, he thought. Jesus, everybody else is the same. Shit, what happened?
I guess rolling old winos just ain't funny no more.
The old lady stank from beer or wine or booze. His room stank. The house stank. The whole goddamn city stank. (p. 127)

He keeps wondering how Gomez, the counselor, got out of the cycle. Day after day, Owen has nothing to do. Two days after he gets back he is attacked and robbed by a gang of thirteen-year-olds. Penniless, he accepts an introduction to the headman of an adult gang of thieves. He does one job for this man, but before he is paid, someone murders the man.

Finally, Owen gets a job with Earle's Body Repair. He likes Earle and starts to feel some self-respect again. The day he gets his first pay check he is attacked and robbed by a Chicano gang of kids eight to eleven years old. This makes the third time Owen has been attacked. For self-protection he again joins a gang with his old friends. Only this time he becomes the headman. And he is finished.

Students can discuss the hopelessness of Owen's fight; the difficulty in finding a life of safety and dignity on his own; all of the wonderful parts of his character that never can be expressed; his yearnings for respectability, for a job, for love and affection, for tennis; and the tragedy of all of these wasted young lives.

A classic work about teenage gangs is S. E. Hinton's *The Outsiders*. During high school, Susie Hinton became friendly with the "Greasers," who were the "out group" at her school. She started to write *The Outsiders* when she was fifteen and published it when she was eighteen. She said, "I felt the Greasers were getting knocked when they didn't deserve it. It was the cold-blooded beating of a friend of mine that gave me the idea of writing a book." Her conscience was disturbed when her friends, the Socs (abbreviation of Socials), beat up a Greaser friend of hers because they didn't like the way he combed his hair.

Violence of all kinds, but particularly gang violence, is the major character, the ambience, the setting, and the plot of Hinton's work. It begins when the narrator, Ponyboy, a "Greaser," steps out of a movie theater and sees a red Corvair trailing him. He remembers that his friend, Johnny, was beaten up by four Socs when he was sixteen. When the Socs drive up in the Corvair and attack Ponyboy, he says, "I knew it wasn't any use though. . . ." It isn't any use. Ponyboy describes the division into Socs and Greasers as being "just the way things are." The fatalism is similar to that in *Headman*. The back and forth gang violence is like a ritual dance. The book is filled with statements like these: "Greasers can't walk alone too much or they'll get jumped." (p. 6) "Our gang had chased the Socs to their car and heaved rocks at them." (p. 11)

Students should note that in this novel, as in all novels about gang violence and in most novels of science fiction, war, and natural disaster, the events occur regardless of character. Johnny and Ponyboy, like Owen in *Headman*, are beaten not because of anything they do, but because they are there. This is different from the classic novel plot based on *conflict* centered in the protagonist and concerned with something he wants to gain but seemingly cannot.

The violent events occur almost daily. On the first day of the book, Ponyboy is beaten up. On the second day, the boys kill Bob Sheldon, one of the Socs who attacks them. On the ninth day, the rumble takes place.

Gang violence is not the only violence in this work: Johnny's parents beat him; Ponyboy's parents are killed in an automobile accident; and Darry goes berserk and is killed. Even the most peace-loving young person cannot extricate himself from the endless cycle of violence that seems to afflict the poor, the outsiders in our society.

Hinton's next book *That Was Then, This Is Now* also contains gang violence (as well as other types of violence). Here is a description of one encounter:

Outside I spotted M&M at the corner. There were three guys trailing him. When you see something like that around here you know right away somebody is about to get jumped. In this case, it was M&M.

"Come on," Mark said, and we cut through an alley so as to come up behind those guys.

Three against three. The odds would have been even except that M&M was one of those nonviolent types who practiced what he preached, and me and Mark weren't carrying weapons. . . . I moved over to the other side of the alley just in time to see Curly pull out a switchblade and reach over and cut through the rawhide string on M&M's peace medal. It fell to the ground. M&M reached down to pick it up, and Curly brought his knee up sharply and hit M&M in the face.

Me and Mark looked at each other, and Mark flashed me a grin. We both liked fights. (pp. 12–13)

After the boys rescue M&M they see a black man standing there and Mark says, "We could jump him." M&M says:

You make me sick! You just rescued me from some guys who were going to beat me up because I'm different from them, and now you're going to beat up someone because he's different from you. (p. 15)

A basic difference between lower-class and middle-class kids is that middle-class kids don't expect to encounter violence in every situation, while lower-class kids never seem able to escape it. Even a simple high school dance becomes a scene for violence:

> Mark and me were out here sitting on the car, not doing a thing, when this guy shows up and starts in on me. I don't know why, I ain't never seen the guy before. Finally he takes a swing at me, so I have to swing back, and pretty soon we're going at it. Then this character picks up a beer bottle Mark had thrown over there in the grass and comes at me with it. About that time Mark steps in between us and says, "Hey, come on, man, fight fair." The kid just looks at him and, for no reason, cracks him across the side of the head with it . . . (p. 52)

In Bryon's, the narrator's, world, it isn't only teenagers who are violent. When he was only thirteen he was beaten up by cops for getting drunk. Two men who resent losing at pool try to beat the boys with brass knuckles, and their friend, the owner of the pool hall, is killed defending them. Mark's parents killed each other in a drunken brawl, and Angela's father is always drunk. But Hinton does make a plea for peace. Bryon says:

> I don't want to keep this up, this getting-even jazz. It's stupid and I'm sick of it and it keeps going in circles. I have had it. . . . (p. 122)

In Hinton's third book, *Rumble Fish*, she is again dealing with the same socioeconomic level. Rusty-James is "the number-one tough guy" among the junior high kids who hang out and shoot pool at Benny's. The book starts with the news that Biff, a boy from a rival gang, is going to kill Rusty-James. These kids have been fighting for a long time. One says: "But even back when we was rumblin', we never fought Biff's gang. They was allies. Remember when Wilson got jumped over on the Tigers' turf . . ." (p. 10) We see the ominous pattern of Hinton's gang members getting younger and younger with each subsequent book.

Rusty-James's major source of pride is his belief that he is the "number-one tough cat" in his neighborhood. He loves to fight, loves the high, omnipotent feeling before a fight:

> My eyes get supersharp before a fight. Everything gets supersharp before a fight—like with a little effort I could fly. During a fight, though, I almost go blind; everything turns red. . . . I'd get in a fight about once a week. I hadn't lost a fight in almost two years. But Biff was a little tougher than the usual kid. If the gang wars had still been going on he would have been leader of the Devilhawks. He didn't like anybody to forget that, either. You can't take it for granted you're going to stomp some snotty-nosed seventh-grader, so when you go up against somebody like Biff Wilcox you think about it. (pp. 21–22)

The major influences in Rusty-James's life are his brother, The Motorcycle Boy (a name earned stealing motorcycles), and Steve, his best friend, who helps Rusty-James with his homework and tries to show him the pointlessness of his endless rumbling. Rusty-James's father is an absent alcoholic, and so Rusty-James absorbs his philosophy and morality from The Motorcycle Boy:

> . . . I didn't understand what he meant. I spent a lot of time trying to understand what he meant. It was like the time, years ago, when our gang, the Packers, was

having a big rumble with the gang next door. The Motorcycle Boy—he was president—said, "Okay, let's get it straight what we're fighting for."

And everybody was all set to kill or be killed, raring to go, and some cat—I forget his name, he's in prison now—said, "We're fighting to own this street."

And the Motorcycle Boy said, "Bull. We're fighting for fun." (p. 28)

The Motorcycle Boy's peak came when he was fourteen and a gang leader. Rusty-James thinks admiringly of his brother that "they'd quit asking for his ID at fourteen" and he could even buy beer. Now, at seventeen, The Motorcycle Boy has been expelled from school for handing in perfect tests; and when his younger brother exclaims that that isn't fair, The Motorcycle Boy fatalistically asks him what's fair in life. It's easier for the school officials, looking down on gang members, to assume that they cheat rather than that they could be smart, could be wasted talent roaming the streets looking for something significant to do with themselves.

There is no morality in or out of school for these boys. The coach offers Rusty-James five bucks to beat up a kid who has been giving him trouble, and Rusty-James has been in "dumb" classes ever since he was tracked in elementary school. When Rusty-James tells his father that he has been cut up in a fight, his father says, "What strange lives you two lead" and gives him ten dollars.

When Rusty-James is expelled from his school, he is transferred to Cleveland High School, where the school officials send everybody they don't like. The problem is that his enemy, Biff Wilcox, and his gang run Cleveland, and Rusty-James knows, "if I just walked into his home territory, I was a dead man. It'd be me against half the school." (p. 57)

One night, coming home from the pool parlor, the boys are attacked by a gang and Rusty-James is badly hurt on the head. His friend Steve, horrified, screams: "The rumbles! The gang! That garbage! It wasn't anything. It wasn't anything like you think it was. It was just a bunch of punks killing each other!" (p. 91)

Students should discuss the cause and effect of the violence depicted in the books about gangs. They should also contrast the characters' views of themselves as social beings with society's attitude toward gang members. Students should also consider the psychological aspects of what it means to be these outsiders—the cynicism, suspiciousness, distrust of adults, and the psychological results of living in a state of continuous war and possible violence.

Juvenile Violence

Gang violence is only one face of juvenile violence. Tom Wicker writes:

When a 41-year-old man was stabbed to death this summer in Greenwich Village, no one was really surprised when the police arrested a 14-year-old youth and charged him with the killing. Juvenile crime clearly has been increasing.

In New York City, in fact, violent crimes by young people have increased by 70 percent in the last five years. The number of juveniles charged with murder just about tripled in that period; twice as many young people were charged with rape.

Crime by kids is a baffling, tragic problem. Children panic easily, or lose their heads in fits of rage; others seem free of the kind of remorse, guilt feelings and fear of consequences that affect adults. Moreover, children charged with crime have traditionally been looked upon as children in need of help—which has led in many cases to relatively light penalties and a quick return to the streets. ("The Puzzle of Crime by Kids," *The New York Times,* July 6, 1976, Op-Ed Page.)

A classic novel of juvenile violence is William Golding's *Lord of the Flies.* Although the book is more difficult for most students than the usual adolescent novel, the insights it gives into violent behavior and the questions it raises about how value systems are created and destroyed make it worth tackling.

There is no need for me to outline the book's plot, but I will emphasize the kinds of questions that should be discussed in class: What exactly is Golding saying? Is he saying that the human heart is basically wicked, that all of mankind is basically cruel and intolerant, that civilization is doomed, that laws (as represented by the adults who arrive just in time to save Ralph) are necessary to restrain the basically savage nature of man? Is he saying that society tends to kill off the mystics and intellectuals, that the compassionate are destroyed, that man cannot achieve a workable social order, that man is basically and innately depraved? (Golding has written that "the theme is an attempt to trace the defects of society back to the defects of human nature.")

A book that resembles *Lord of the Flies* in its vision of the innate evil in human beings is Robert Cormier's *The Chocolate War.* The setting is a Catholic prep school for boys run by Brother Leon, a corrupt, cynical priest who is obsessed with power. He is assisted in his control of the school by a group of students, led by Archie, who is similar to Jack in *Lord of the Flies.* Archie's main helpers are Carter, the football captain, who represents brute strength, and Obie, a weak errand boy. Their dictatorship is challenged by one student, Jerry Renault, who refuses to participate in the school's annual fund-raising chocolate sale. Jerry is physically and psychologically destroyed by the end of the book, his condition most closely resembling that of Winston Smith in *1984.*

The psychological content and implications of Cormier's work should receive primary consideration. Ethical issues should also be discussed, but they are not as evident and significant in this book as they are in *Lord of the Flies.* The Golding book can be viewed only as an allegory, but *The Chocolate War,* unfortunately, comes close to everyday experience.

Obie, the errand boy, is bored, tired, and disgusted. He is always sleepy and he yawns constantly. He hates Archie, leader of the gang, but is simultaneously fascinated by him. From time to time he makes weak protests to Archie but they are ineffectual. He thinks, "you couldn't ever win an argument with Archie. He was too quick with the words." (Archie also reminds us of T. in "The Destructors.") Obie almost believes that Archie can read his mind:

He shivered with dread, realizing how awesome Archie's power really was. Which is why you had to stay on the good side of the bastard. Buy him Hersheys all the time to satisfy his craving for chocolate. Thank God Archie didn't go in for pot or that stuff—Obie would have had to become a pusher, for crying out loud, to supply him. Obie was officially the secretary of The Vigils but he knew what the job really demanded. Carter, the president who was almost as big a bastard as Archie, said, "keep him happy, when Archie's happy, we're all happy." (pp. 13–14)

Students should discuss the nature of Obie's motivation. What is the particular power of psychotic dictators that draws people like Obie to them? Students may have encountered people such as Archie in their own schools.

Archie, like T., is psychotic. He is completely lacking in humanity, in feeling, in compassion. In *1984*, O'Brien informs Winston Smith that they engage in power and cruelty for its own sake. Their symbol is the boot in the face. This also describes Archie. He thrives on gratuitous, pointless cruelty. The meaninglessness of the jobs he assigns reminds us of the rock breaking and lifting jobs given to concentration camp prisoners. This is Archie:

He was tall and not too heavy. He moved with a subtle rhythm, languidly, the walk of an athlete although he hated all sports and had nothing but contempt for athletes. Particularly football players and boxers, which happened to be Trinity's two sports. Usually, Archie didn't pick athletes for assignments—he claimed they were too stupid to absorb the delicate shadings, the subtle intricacies involved. Archie disliked violence—most of his assignments were exercises in the psychological rather than the physical. That's why he got away with so much. The Trinity brothers wanted peace at any price, quiet on the campus, no broken bones. Otherwise the sky was the limit. (p. 14)

Archie's adult counterpart is Brother Leon, the evil genius of the faculty. Neither Archie nor he can function without the other; they protect and understand each other. At the end of the book, when Jerry is almost beaten to death, Archie phones Brother Leon to come and watch, knowing that he would enjoy the violence and bloodshed.

And Leon was a special breed. On the surface, he was one of those pale, ingratiating kind of men who tiptoed through life on small, quick feet. He looked like a henpecked husband, a pushover, a sucker. He was the Assistant Headmaster of the school but actually served as a flunky for the Head. Like an errand boy. But this all was deceptive. In the classroom, Leon was another person altogether. Smirking, sarcastic. His thin, high voice venomous. He could hold your attention like a cobra. Instead of fangs, he used his teacher's pointer, flicking out here, there, everywhere. He watched the class like a hawk, suspicious, searching out cheaters or daydreamers, probing for weaknesses in the students and then exploiting those weaknesses. (pp. 23–24)

Emile Janza is another familiar psychological type. He goes through life harassing people. He discovered at an early age that people are afraid to make fusses, afraid of bullies, afraid of being victims, and he also found that these fears enable him to get away with almost anything. He is the archetypal bully boy, but he lacks the demonic quality that makes Archie the leader.

But Emile didn't harass only teachers. He found that the world was full of willing victims, especially kids his own age. He had discovered a truth early in life—in the fourth grade, in fact. Nobody wanted trouble, nobody wanted to make trouble, nobody wanted a showdown. The knowledge was a revelation. It opened doors. You could take a kid's lunch or even his lunch money and nothing usually happened because most kids wanted peace at any price. Of course you have to choose your victims carefully because there were exceptions. Those who protested found that it was easier to let Emile have his way. (p. 41)

Jerry, the protagonist of _The Chocolate War_, is psychologically so different from the evil characters already described that it is almost impossible for him to understand the extent of their evil and violence. They are at opposite poles, as remote to each other's psychologies as the Nazis and their victims. Archie, shrewd and psychotic, immediately knows that Jerry is one type of personality that cannot be bought. He watches him get up time and again after being beaten down on the football field and says, "He's a tough one. Didn't you see him get wiped out down there and still get to his feet? Tough. And stubborn. He should have stayed down on that turf, Obie. That would have been the smart thing to do." (p. 16) And Jerry is the only one with the guts to refuse to sell chocolates for the school, even though it turns out that this refusal almost costs him his life.

After discussion of the psychological aspects of major and minor characters, class discussion should focus on the ethical aspects of this work. Jerry appears to be the only person operating from an ethical, moral base. Jerry refuses to sell the chocolates because "of what Brother Leon does to people, like Bailey, the way he tortures them, tries to make fools of them in front of everybody." (p. 91) Perhaps the most interesting ethical aspect of this novel is the fact that Jerry is ultimately forced to fight back. And when he does, "a new sickness invades [him], the sickness of knowing what he had become, another animal, another beast, another violent person in a violent world, inflicting damage, not disturbing the universe, but damaging it. He had allowed Archie to do this to him." (p. 183)

In this pessimistic book, the terrible beating that Jerry sustains finally alters his ethical outlook, his system of values. Lying on the ground, cradled in Goober's arms, waiting for the ambulance, he tries to tell Goober that the only way to survive is to conform:

He had to tell Goober to play ball, to play football, to run, to make the team, to sell the chocolates, to sell whatever they wanted you to sell, to do whatever they wanted you to do. He tried to voice the words but there was something wrong with his mouth, his teeth, his face. But he went ahead anyway, telling Goober what he needed to know. They tell you to do your thing but they don't mean it. They don't want you to do your thing, not unless it happens to be their thing, too. It's a laugh, Goober, a fake. Don't disturb the universe, Goober, no matter what the posters say. (p. 187)

Another, less believable adolescent novel of shocking violence is Sol Stein's *The Magician*. Not originally written for the adolescent literature market, this work has become quite popular, and has been taught in a number of secondary schools in New York State. Like the previous two books, this one should be discussed in terms of psychological and ethical implications. The sociological implications are less important.

In *The Magician* as in the previous two works, good and evil are personified by two entirely different types of characters. Good is epitomized by the protagonist, Edward Japhet, a creative and accomplished magician at the age of sixteen, and a fine student who, from babyhood, has evidenced a good mind, capable of solving problems. A serious, sober, respectful, competent young man, he has a good home life with parents who get along well. His father, a teacher at Ed's high school, basks in quiet pride over his only child. On the other side we have Urek, the Archie of the book:

> Urek and his gang run this school the way the Mafia runs parts of the United States. I saw a kid go over to the apple machine and let his fifteen cents show one inch before he put the money into the slot and got a whack on the wrist from Urek that'd send the dough flying. It'd be scooped up in seconds by the others. . . .
>
> Student gym lockers used to be free until Urek started renting them out at two bits a month for protection—you know, if you paid up, your locker was protected, and if you didn't, your combination lock got hacksawed, which cost a buck and a quarter to replace and anything usable inside was missing. (pp. 30–31)

Ed, reminding us of Jerry in *The Chocolate War*, defies Urek by buying a tempered-steel lock that can't be hacksawed through. His friend says:

> . . . can you imagine how burned Urek and his friends were every time they passed Ed's locker? I pay my two bits a month; it's cheap, I tell you. Ed and I walk home together because we're on the same block, but if ever the pack came on him on the way home, I'd haul ass out of there. . . .
>
> Ed can defy Urek all he wants to, just so he leaves me out of it. I told him, and he said, "Okay, just get to a phone and call the cops." Now, you know the cops can't do anything about people like Urek, there's always a gang like that, whether you're in school or got a business somewhere, don't you read the papers? (p. 31)

Ed performs at the high school prom, and afterwards, in front of his powerless father and Lila, his girlfriend, he is almost beaten to death by Urek's gang. The violence and ugliness of this scene are horrifying in their realism. At the end, Ed is left unconscious in the snow, and his father's windshield has been smashed with the same chain used by Urek against Ed. Afterwards, at the hospital, his father tells the police the story of the attack:

> Terence Japhet, who might have made a great deal more money in the outside business world, and who had stuck to teaching because it seemed so far removed from stress, went on talking a minute more until he had to stop because he realized he was crying through his spread-fingered hands. (p. 61)

In the previous two books, the violence was localized and could be controlled. In *Lord of the Flies* it was controlled when adults returned to the scene; in *The Chocolate War* it existed in a particularly sick school; but in *The Magician*, violence is omnipresent, existing throughout society (note Stein's early reference to the Mafia), capable of striking, maiming, and killing at random. In the world depicted by Stein, there is no protection from violence, and the violent are protected by the machinery and machinations of the law.

When Ed is recuperating in the hospital, he is visited by his friend Gil who has just been inducted into the army.

"You know," Gil said, "the army is full of guys like that [Urek and his gang]. Rednecks, from every part of the country. Beer, bowling, hunting, car Simonizing. You should hear them talk about women, even their wives. Filling the old lady's hole, is the way they think of it. These guys don't even go to the movies, except drive-ins, and that's not for the movies. Biggest thing they miss in the army is TV. Booze and poker, that's it. I kind of keep to myself. If I weren't tall, I think I'd be in fights all the time. . . .

"Before the army," said Gil, "I couldn't understand all the stuff you read about violence. I mean, I know about Hitler and all that, and assassinations and muggings, but after living with those guys for a couple of months, I wonder how come there isn't *more* violence. . . ." (p. 85)

Stein compares Urek not only to rednecks but also to the assassins of President Kennedy and Martin Luther King. Dr. Koch, a psychiatrist and spokesman for the author, tries to explain the psychology of this criminal element whose lust is to destroy. He says that this element cannot tolerate a society that allows the creative and inner-directed to "humiliate them simply by existing." (p. 128) The same thread runs throughout the other books about violence: Jerry Renault, Piggy, and Simon must be destroyed, not because they are doing anything but because the fact of their existence is a reproach to the criminal element. Ed belongs to what Dr. Koch terms the "category one people," the people who "go through life like solo athletes, at their own fast pace, toward their own goals, setting up their own obstacles to conquer. Independent people who are not in competition with others but their own capacities." (p. 125)

The saddest part of Stein's book is that Ed, like Jerry in *The Chocolate War*, is not allowed to remain non-violent but is finally, in a manipulated, ironic, but horrifying final scene, dragged down to the level of the monster Urek.

Rape

Unpleasant as it is to confront this topic in the secondary school classroom, no discussion of violence would be complete without discussion of rape, an act uniquely perpetrated by men against women. One of the values of adolescent literature is that this subject, along with so many heretofore taboo subjects, can now be discussed in the secondary school classroom through literature, without personalizing, without admission or confession, without guilt.

Patricia Dizenzo, a particularly honest writer (see the discussion of *Phoebe* in Ch. III), tells a completely believable story in *Why Me?* about sixteen-year-old Jenny, who takes a ride from a stranger on a cold day, is raped at knife point in the back of the car, and is then catapulted into a new and terrifying series of encounters with her own hostile family.

When Jenny goes to see a doctor, he tells her what doctors and law officials have traditionally told such girls. When she says she didn't report the rape to the police because she wasn't hurt, the doctor stops believing her. He tells her:

You know, at your age, it's common for girls to go through a period of confusion about sex. Nothing abnormal about it, even with the more open attitudes we have nowadays. You probably can't imagine the changes there've been since I was your age. In general, boys' drives are very strong in their late teens. That's why it's unfair for girls to act provocatively or to mislead. . . . I feel I should point out to you, there's a great difference between a seduction and a criminal attack. (p. 32)

Jenny is advised to find another doctor, since this doctor does not want to get involved with any criminal proceedings. When Jenny finally tells her friend, Rita, she, like the doctor, finds it hard to understand why Jenny got into the car in the first place. It seems as if they are angry at her for behaving so stupidly, and she reminds herself that her parents have warned her "a million times not to take rides."

Jenny starts to fight with her mother; her grades drop in school; she worries continually about being pregnant, suffers from nightmares, travels to New York City to find a V.D. clinic, and finds herself sweating and terrified every time she sees a man who resembles her attacker. When a murdered, raped girl is found on a back road, she feels she must report the rape to the police. Finally, Jenny tells her mother:

I told her the idea I had that my body didn't belong to me anymore. That he was attached to it and it was his, not mine. That I was the only person who ever did anything like it and I didn't fit in with other people anymore. That it must be a punishment for something I did or why would it have happened to me, not Clara, or Rita, or any other girl, but me. I told her I hated myself and I got fits of rage where I wanted to destroy everyone, even her. I hated the world and wanted everyone to be like me, screwed up, filthy, stupid, I hated to see anyone happy. I wanted everyone to know how I felt, to feel the same way. That I wished I had killed him instead of letting him do it, and I hated myself, trembling with fear, doing whatever he said. . . .

I told her how things came back to me when I didn't expect it—in a car I suddenly looked at the dashboard, or I might be somewhere and see someone who looked like him, or had clothes like his. It would come into my mind again—it would be like vomiting in my mind. I hated it, but I couldn't stop it. I'd think about it again. (p. 116)

When her mother stops crying, she scolds Jenny about taking a ride with a stranger. Her father screams that she has disgraced the family, and he beats her up. Jenny runs away to live with her grandmother.

Later Jenny moves back home and all seems as before, but the reader knows that nothing will ever be the same. Innocence, trust, and belief in safety have been permanently lost.

A second adolescent novel that deals with rape is Richard Peck's *Are You in the House Alone?* The setting is an upper-class suburb. The rapist is not a stranger but a fellow high school student of the victim, Gail Osburne. Phil, the rapist, is the boyfriend of Gail's best friend, and so he is familiar with her life patterns, which include baby sitting alone every Saturday night. He torments her for weeks with obscene letters and phone calls, then comes to the house and beats and rapes her.

When a policeman comes to the hospital and Gail tells her story, he says:

Okay, honey, I think I got the drift of it now. . . . Let me run it back for you. A friend of yours—I'm not saying it's your boyfriend—a good-looking kid like you knows plenty of boys. Anyway, this particular one drops by where you're baby-sitting. He knows you're there because you sit regular. And you and him talk on the phone—keep in touch.

It's just the two of you together. The little kids are asleep upstairs. There's nothing much on TV. You start horsing around a little, completely innocent. All you kids do it. Then you lead him on a little, and he gets—overheated. Tries to get you to do what you don't want to do. Or let's be honest about it. He get you to do what you both want to do, but you're a nice girl and don't give in that easy.

So maybe there's some rough stuff. The two of you tussle around a little, and you bump your head. So here you've got this nasty cut on the head and how are you going to explain that to your folks? So you kind of build up a story around it. That's the way things went? (pp. 111–112)

Gail's sympathetic lawyer tells her that the police chief's attitude is the usual official posture. "If he hadn't had the medical report, he'd have been convinced nothing happened at all." (p. 116) Her lawyer warns her that because there were no witnesses, Phil's wealthy family could counter-sue for libel. He also warns her that judges permit plea bargaining: "In most cases, typical cases, he'll let the rape charge go if the rapist agrees to plead guilty to a lesser charge: assault, disorderly conduct—any one of a dozen completely irrelevant charges. This is called plea-bargaining, and it's arranged entirely between the court authority and the defense lawyer. I—we have absolutely no control over it." (p. 117)

After Gail learns about the grilling that she will undergo on the stand—she is not a virgin, has a steady boyfriend, and takes birth control pills—she and her family decide to do nothing. She says: "I don't want to be raped again—in a courtroom. I don't want to go through that without a hope of getting satisfaction." (p. 121)

Phil strikes again, almost killing a girl, and is whisked away from town. Gail hears that he is the captain of the squash team in a boarding school in Vermont. The second girl, Sonia, recovers and her family moves away. Gail and her family are left damaged and frightened, but Gail has learned the meaning of social responsibility. After Sonia moves away and Gail's stitches are out, her mother says, "It could all have been worse." Gail, feeling responsible for the second attack on Sonia, answers: "Not much worse. We were all trying to protect ourselves as individuals and families instead of organizing to make everybody safe. There are more Phils out there, you know." (p. 156)

This fine book deals with more than the actual rape. It gives the reader an accurate picture of the way society conspires to protect the rapist, and it deals with alienation and lack of communication. Susan Brownmiller's recent non-fiction book *Against Our Will: Men, Women, and Rape*, although not written for adolescents, is written on a level suitable for the upper secondary school, and it provides the necessary background for an understanding of rape both historically and presently. It is lucid and non-sensational and reinforces the stories in the two previous fictional works.

Seeing rape not as an act of sex but as an act of violence, "a conscious process of intimidation by which *all men* keep *all women* in a state of fear" (p. 5), Brownmiller traces the history of rape from prehistoric times through the Middle Ages through wars, riots, pogroms, and revolutions. Rape is seen inextricably as the part of war perpetrated against women. What makes this a particular crime against women is that women cannot retaliate in kind. It is the only crime that can be done *only* by males to females.

Brownmiller also sees rape as one of the earliest forms of male bonding, which is similar to the gang watching stag films. "Indeed, one of the earliest forms of male bonding must have been the gang rape of one woman by a band of marauding men. This accomplished, rape became not only a male prerogative, but man's basic weapon of force against woman, the principal agent of his will and her fear. His forcible entry into her body, despite her physical protestations and struggle, became the vehicle of his victorious conquest over her being, the ultimate test of his superior strength, the triumph of his manhood." (p. 5)

Reinforcing what we see in the Dizenzo and Peck novels, Brownmiller tells us that according to the police blotter, the typical "American rapist might be the boy next door. Especially if the boy next door happens to be about 19 years of age and the neighborhood you live in happens to fit the socioeconomic description of lower class or bears the appellation of 'ghetto.' " (p. 189)

Forcible rape is "one of the most under-reported crimes due primarily to fear and/or embarrassment on the part of the victim" (p. 190); and even if it is reported, there is a bias by police and juries against believing the word of victims, particularly black victims. In some areas, the conviction rate "based on arrests is a shocking 3 percent." (p. 190)

Rape is the fastest-rising crime in American society, and Brownmiller states that we do not know if this is indicative of increasing male hostility toward women or if it merely indicates that more women are finding the courage to report rape. It is important for students to discuss the author's findings that "the typical American rapist is no weirdo, psycho-schizophrenic beset by timidity, sexual deprivation, and a domineering wife or mother. . . . The typical American perpetrator of forcible rape is little more than an aggressive, hostile youth who chooses to do violence to women." (p. 192) Other significant findings are that raping is usually done by more than one male, that gang rape is usually planned, and that only the selection of the female is left to chance. (p. 199) Countering the historical belief that the woman has some involvement in her own rape (Jenny is accused of this in the Dizenzo book), Brownmiller points out that rape begins in the rapist's mind and not in relation to a spontaneous urge brought about by a provocative female. (p. 202)

It is doubtful that students will read the entire Brownmiller book, although it should be available for those who want to. The following is another excerpt that should be discussed:

A law that reflects the female reality and a social system that no longer shuts women out of its enforcement and does not promote a masculine ideology of rape will go a long way toward the elimination of crimes of sexual violence, but the last line of defense shall always be our female bodies and our female minds. In making rape a *speakable* crime, not a matter of shame, the women's movement has already fired the first retaliatory shots in a war as ancient as civilization. (p. 445)

Another significant topic for discussion (and these discussions are of equal value to males and females) is the fact that women are often issued lists of one-sided instructions to avoid rape—instructions that put the entire burden for self-protection on the woman. Brownmiller includes the following passage from a March 1974 article in the *Reader's Digest,* which was written by two men:

Don't broadcast the fact that you live alone or with another woman. List only your last name and initial on the mailbox and in the phone book. Before entering your car, check to see if anyone is hiding on the rear seat or on the rear floor. If you're alone in a car, keep the doors locked and the windows rolled up. If you think someone is following you . . . do not go directly home if there is no adult male there. Possible weapons are a hatpin, corkscrew, pen, keys, umbrella. If no weapons are available, fight back physically *only* if you feel you can do so with telling effect. (p. 448)

Brownmiller says about instructions such as these, and the need to be concerned about them, that "the ultimate effect of rape upon the woman's mental and emotional health has been accomplished *even without the act.* For to accept a special burden of self-protection is to reinforce the concept that women must live and move about in fear and can never expect to achieve the personal freedom, independence and self-assurance of men." (p. 449)

Rape has always been seen as a woman's problem, as an individual and psychological problem, rather than as a societal problem "resulting from a distorted masculine philosophy of aggression." (p. 450) In this era of increased rape, the fastest growing crime in the United States, discussion of the three works in this section will make a significant difference to young people coming of age.

Child Abuse

When I went to school I never knew there was child abuse past the date of the writing of *Oliver Twist* and *David Copperfield.* Unhappily, this aspect of family life is still very much with us, as evidenced by the following report from *The New York Times* (November 30, 1975):

U.S. Finds "Epidemic" Child Abuse Rate

WASHINGTON, Nov. 24, (UPI)—More than a million American children suffer physical abuse or neglect each year, and at least one in five of the young victims die from their mistreatment, the Government announced today.

Disclosing tentative results of the first nationwide child abuse study, an official of the Department of Health, Education and Welfare said the figures represented a "social problem" of "epidemic" proportions. . . .

About three-fourths of the neglect reports come from friends, relatives and neighbors sharing the same cultural life as the young victims. . . .

Marjorie Kellogg's *Like the Lion's Tooth* is an exceptionally fine book about child abuse, but I would be wary about using it in a secondary school classroom because of the sexual explicitness in the scenes between father and son. Kellogg is undoubtedly a fine writer. In reading her book I suffered from none of the ambivalence I feel with many adolescent literature writers whose stylistic inadequacies I overlook because of their fine humanistic messages. It is precisely because Kellogg is so good that her book is especially memorable and painful.

The book is about a white family at the bottom of the social and economic ladder—a family of four battered, abused children, one battered wife, and one psychotic sailor father. While the father is at sea, the family is poor and hungry but comparatively happy. The mother works and the children are left to shift for themselves in the streets of New York City. They enjoy their unsupervised wanderings and explore everything from Coney Island to the Metropolitan Museum. The four take good care of each other. The horror begins each time the father comes home. In addition to battering, there is sexual abuse, particularly the rape of the oldest child, eleven-year-old Ben.

Life is much better for Ben when one of his brothers and he are sent to a cottage institution for wayward children to protect them, and he finds that he is not the only one who has been battered, traumatized, raped, and neglected. One child, for example, keeps running away from the institution whenever she sees a man from a distance who wears a yellow jacket like her missing father's. By the time they reach the age of thirteen, there is no horrible crime that has not been perpetrated against this helpless group of children by adults.

What makes this a particularly interesting book is its emphasis upon the importance of family as the source of love, hate, and pain. Even the kindest psychologists at the institution, despite their endless assortment of psychotherapeutic techniques, cannot repair the damages that have been done within the family. The only hope of rehabilitation seems to come from other children who have had similar experiences and can offer each other small crumbs of comfort and love.

Students should discuss Kellogg's belief that once the damage has been done, the only solution is to create a kind of Boys-Town, extended family setting in which each of the cripples can combine to make a group that can function as a whole. Some of Kellogg's greatest scorn is reserved for the so-called foster homes that take children from the institutions only for the economic reward and further exploit them rather than giving them the love they so desperately need.

The major focus for books on child abuse is psychological. Readers should speculate on the reasons for characters' behavior, on whether or not the motivation is credible. This kind of psychological discussion involves the readers using their own feelings and experiences to try to understand the characters.

A book preferable to the Kellogg one for use in secondary schools is Kin Platt's excellent *The Boy Who Could Make Himself Disappear*. (See Ch. I, page 41.) After Roger's parents divorce, he moves from California to New York City with his mother. His mother is sadistic, and his father is indifferent and too busy producing pictures to interfere. Even before the end of the marriage, there have been many episodes of sadism. The first occurred when he was only three years old. He found a styptic pencil on his father's dresser and started to eat it:

> Suddenly, outrageously, his mouth and tongue were burning with a terrible hurt. A fire was inside there, in his mouth, all the way through, and now his tongue was burning as if there was a hole inside it. He tried to scream but couldn't get the white thing that was not candy or sugar out of his moaning mouth.
>
> His parents, downstairs sitting around the pool with friends, finally heard him screaming. They found him writhing on the floor, banging his head to get rid of the pain. Before they took him to the doctor the mother grabbed his hands away from his mouth and slapped them hard.
>
> "Bad boy, bad boy!" she said in an angry voice. "Don't you ever do that again!" His eyes, already swollen in agony, could hardly see the big white face and the mad mouth.
>
> The father didn't hug him either, but stooped down to pick up some of the crushed white pieces on the floor, wipe them off and put them back in the little glass tube. Then he looked around for the screw cap that went on it.
>
> "When are you going to teach this kid not to put everything he sees in his greedy little mouth," he told the mother. "I better find that cap now before somebody cuts his foot on it." (p. 51)

After that Roger has a psychologically caused speech impediment.

The above scene is just the first in a series of horror stories. Every interchange between mother and son is a reason for sadism. She makes him beg daily for his dollar for bus fare and lunch at his expensive school (for which his father pays). Sometimes, to avoid the scene, he goes off without the money and doesn't eat all day. She lets him go through his first cold New York winter without an overcoat or boots. And this is a scene from his childhood that he reports to his speech therapist:

> "Well, she used to save up all the food I didn't eat the whole week. And then one day, fuh a big suh-pwise, She would cook it up again and make me eat it. And I would eat it but it was so wotten I hadda thwow it up—on the plate. And then—and then She would make me eat it up again—I mean—" he hesitated, "—*everything*. All that gook!" (pp. 181–182)

When he calls his father in California to complain about his mother's treatment of him, she beats him. Roger walks out and two policemen cruising Central Park find him the next day "sitting hunched up on the cold ground near the lake. They asked him what he was doing there and he said he didn't know." (p. 224)

Step by step his mother's brutality drives him to madness. He is taken to Bellevue where he remembers only the name of his speech therapist; and when Miss Clemm calls Roger's mother, she finds that Mrs. Baxter has not only not missed him for two nights but also wants the hospital to keep him for a week so that she can go on vacation. The loss of Pat Bentley, his beautiful model friend, and a final beating by his mother send him over the ledge into complete withdrawal and schizophrenia. He has made himself disappear.

> "Mother's home," She said. "You know you haven't said a word of greeting? Not a single word. Aren't you interested in if I had a good time?" He still sat there, without paying attention, and She slapped him again, knocking his head back against the couch. "Are you going to talk to me or not? Who the hell are you to freeze me out?"
>
> When he didn't cry or complain or say anything but just continued to sit there, rocking a little now as he made the sound, She became angrier. She hit him several more times. (p. 24)

The book ends on a note of hope, however, for through the love of Roger Tunnell, Pat Bentley's fiancé, and of Miss Clemm, the therapist, Roger starts to make his way back to reality.

The exaggeratedly evil characters in this book should be examined as allegorical figures. What characteristics do those who abuse children possess? Mrs. Baxter is selfish, insensitive, cruel, and violent. She looks for situations in which she can exercise her violence. Mr. Baxter symbolizes another kind of child abuser. He, too, is extremely selfish, insensitive, and indifferent to the feelings of others; he is interested only in the material things of life. He is more readily available to Jerry Jeeks, his comic client in Hollywood, than he is to his own son. Even when Roger has lapsed into schizophrenia, the only thing his father can think to do in the hospital is to offer Miss Clemm, the loving stranger, his checkbook.

Students should also examine the qualities possessed by the good characters—qualities that express love rather than hatred. Pat Bentley, Miss Clemm, and Roger Tunnell are all loving people, capable of giving, of consideration, of compassion.

Paul Zindel's play, *The Effect of Gamma Rays on Man-in-the-Moon Marigolds* is a good work about child abuse because it deals not just with the victim but with the victim's victims. Much contemporary research into child abuse shows that people who themselves have been abused as children become, in turn, child abusers. Beatrice, the Mother, is a bitter, abandoned, failure of a woman who vents her unhappiness and frustration on her two daughters. At times she forces her daughter Matilda, possessor of unusual scientific ability, to stay home from school. When they call from school, she berates her daughter:

> Matilda, that wasn't very nice of you to tell them I was forcibly detaining you from school. Why, the way that Mr. Goodman spoke, he must think I'm running a concentration camp. Do you have any idea how embarrassing it is to be accused of

running a concentration camp for your own children? . . . Oh, you're sick all right, the exact nature of the illness not fully realized, but you're sick all right. Any daughter that would turn her mother in as the administrator of a concentration camp has got to be suffering from something very peculiar. (pp. 7–8)

⸱   Beatrice wants to keep her daughter away from anything she herself can't understand, anything that reminds her of her own inadequacies and failures in school when she was a girl. When Tillie begs to be allowed to go to school to see her teacher's experiment on radioactivity, her mother says:

No, my dear, the fortress of knowledge is not going to be blessed with your presence today. I have a good number of exciting duties for you to take care of, not the least of which is rabbit droppings. (p. 10)

Cruelty, inconsistency, and yet we see the mother suffering, too. To support herself and her girls she takes in lodgers who are senile or dying. She wails: "You know if someone told me when I was young that I'd end up feeding honey to a zombie, I'd tell them they were crazy." (p. 31) The emptiness of her life and her self-hatred force her to be cruel to the girls. Mrs. Baxter in *The Boy Who Could Make Himself Disappear* seems to have no logical motivation for the excessiveness of her child abuse. But Beatrice says: "Everything I ever thought I'd be has exploded!" (p. 35) She resents the daughter of her present patient, who boards her mother with Beatrice so that she can continue with her career.

Beatrice is also capable of unexpected tenderness when her daughter Ruth has one of her nervous spells; and when Tillie wins the science award, she says: "This is the first time in my life I've ever felt just a little bit proud over something. Isn't that silly? Somewhere in the back of this turtle-sized brain of mine I feel just a little *proud!*" (p. 88) After Beatrice chloroforms the girls' pet rabbit, she tells Tillie, "I hate the world" (p. 107), and we know that the destruction she had wreaked has harmed her as much as it has her girls.

The play ends on a note of hope. Ruth has been destroyed, but Tillie, through her love of science, has become aware of the greater world outside of her home.

Another example of child abuse can be found in James Kirkwood's *Good Times, Bad Times*, the story of a prep-school boy who is forced to kill his sadistic headmaster to protect himself.

Seventeen-year-old Peter's mother is dead and his father, an unemployed actor, is an alcoholic. When a card-playing crony of his father's offers to send him to prep school, Peter and his father accept enthusiastically. Peter has already been the victim of violence in his own home:

It happened very quickly: she [his stepmother] was in her seventh month and I was practicing the piano (her idea originally, the piano lessons), and I saw her out of the corner of my eye walk into the living room from her bedroom. I didn't look up from the piano because I had finally mastered the little Italian art song I'd been practicing and I wanted her to be proud of me. She stood at the end of the piano for a minute or so and I was playing away, concentrating for all I was worth. She suddenly slammed the wooden part of the piano that comes down and covers the keys—slammed it down on my fingers, and ran sobbing to her bedroom.

She broke two of my fingers. Later that day, when I got back from the hospital, she apologized and wept and my father and I put it down to pregnancy. And I, I might add, gave up piano lessons. But it was never the same.

After Linda was born she turned on me full force. It was like I'd been a stand-in for a child in the house and now that her daughter was there, the *real* child—what was I doing there, too? (pp. 11–12)

Kirkwood's book points up a basic truth about adult violence to children: children without power (without any adult behind them to protect them from violence) are the ones who are victimized.

The villain of this work is Mr. Hoyt, the headmaster of Peter's prep school. His first violent encounter with Peter is verbal, and students should note that violence need not always be only physical. Psychological violence is often equally painful and destructive to the victim. Psychological violence like that described in the paragraph below is familiar to many students in our school systems and will evoke from them an important shock of recognition. The headmaster says during their first interview when Peter has worn his best jacket to make a good impression:

"Look at you, just look at you!" I looked down at myself and he laughed again. "Yes, look at yourself." I was confused and glanced up at him, I suppose questioningly. "Yes—you!" he said, taking a quick step toward me, a hostile step. I felt he actually wanted to grab me or hit me. I stumbled back against the chair, lost my balance, and sat down clumsily. He laughed again. "Is that your best jacket, that horse blanket? Did you think you could make an impression with your best jacket?" (p. 51)

The book then moves inexorably to the final horrifying confrontation in which the headmaster attacks Peter, and Peter accidentally kills him in self-defense:

I felt for the boat hook, grabbed it, got to my feet and jumped clear of him out farther on the ice. Then I went a little crazy because I took a position backed up against part of the rowboat, shouting at him that if he came near me I'd kill him and then finally just chanting: "I'll kill you, I'll kill you, I'll kill you!" And he was cursing and yelling at me but I didn't want to hear him so I screamed even louder, "I'll kill you! I'll kill you!" and although I couldn't see him I knew he'd be getting up from the ice and I began slashing the boat hook back and forth in front of me every time I shouted.

Even when I felt the ice crack under me and a giving sensation I kept on and suddenly I connected with him. I must have gotten him in the body, the fleshy part, because it was a soft thwumping sound and feeling as he cried out and then moaned, "Peter—no!" But I couldn't stop. (pp. 281–282)

If this book were only violent and sad, it would not be of value to secondary school students. But the horror of the relationship with Mr. Hoyt is balanced by Peter's beautiful relationship with Jordan, another student. At the end of the book, although Peter is awaiting trial, the reader feels that this strong, fine, honorable, and compassionate boy will somehow be exonerated. Peter's experience of evil, ugliness, violence, and terror in the school has reaffirmed his commitment to a humanistic, constructive ethic.

Historical Violence

Our country was partly founded through violence. The gun, as much as the railroad, settled America. (Violence against Indians is discussed in Chapter II.) This violence is at the heart of minority literature, for most of it deals with the violence perpetrated against minority groups and with their attempts to transcend that mistreatment. In a number of works of adolescent literature, based in the West, and derived from the Western tradition, the original violence still reverberates.

One of the best young adult writers in this category is Glendon Swarthout, whose *Bless the Beasts and Children* has become an adolescent literature classic and whose newer work, *The Shootist*, is gradually entering the classroom. Both of these works deal with profound themes, with ideas that never go out of style.

Bless the Beasts and Children shows the American attitudes that resulted in the destruction of the American Indian and the buffalo, and continue to wreak violence today on our environment and our young people. The title of the book is a plea to treat both the environment (symbolized by the remaining buffalo, which are penned up and used for target practice once a year by amateur hunters) and human beings (symbolized by the boys in the book) constructively and with respect.

The plea of the title is necessary because violence and brutality have become legalized in our society to the extent that animals can be raised and then penned-up as a source of recreation for amateur hunters. Here, students should discuss the ethical aspects of this view of life, for the shooting of the animals is represented not as an isolated facet of American life but rather as a symbol of an entire anti-humanistic society that lacks respect for life. This book is particularly valuable for class discussion of the ethics of hunting, because many students come from hunting families who see nothing wrong with this sport.

In sociological terms, students should discuss the Western historical tradition of violence that provides the setting for the boys' camp and for the buffalo hunt:

They were mad for western movies. They doted on tales told with trumpets and ending in a pot of gold, a bucket of blood, or a chorus of the national anthem. The finest movie they had lately seen, the only one that summer, in fact, was *The Professionals*. It had been a buster, a dollar-dreadful, a saga of some men expert with weapons, a handful of colorful, heroic characters who rode into Mexico. . . . You did not watch it. You sucked on it. For this is the marrowbone of every American adventure story: some men with guns, going somewhere, to do something dangerous . . . this has ever been the essence of our melodrama: some men with guns, going somewhere, to do something dangerous. (p. 40)

The description of the buffalo shoot is vivid and horrible:

To kill thirty buffalo required between six and seven hours. . . . They gutshot. They blasted horns from heads. They blinded. They crippled, shattering hocks and fetlocks. They bled buffalo to death before striking a vital organ. They enfiladed the killing ground with fire as pitiless as it was futile. (pp. 108–109)

A festive atmosphere develops as part of this carnage:

The hunt became at once a school picnic, a revival meeting, a civic barbecue, a patriotic ceremony, and a carnival of slaughter. Every sense of sight, hearing, smell, and decency was overwhelmed. (p. 109)

Swarthout's philosophy, his attitude toward the inherent violence in American history and present culture, is summed up in the following paragraphs, which can be discussed at length in the classroom for understanding of their sociological ramifications:

There was more here than profaned the eye or ear or nose or heart. There was more here than mere destruction. The American soul itself was involved, its anthropology.

We are born with buffalo blood upon our hands. In the prehistory of us all, the atavistic beasts appear. They graze the plains of our subconscious, they trample through our sleep, and in our dreams we cry out our damnation. We know what we have done, we violent people. We know that no species was created to exterminate another, and the sight of their remnant stirs in us the most profound lust, the most undying hatred, the most inexplicable guilt. A living buffalo mocks us. It has no place or purpose. . . . Therefore we slay, and slay again, for while a single buffalo remains, the sin of our fathers, and hence our own, is imperfect. But the slaughter of the buffalo is part of something larger. It is as though the land of Canaan into which we were led was too divine, and until we have done it every violence, until we have despoiled and murdered and dirtied every blessing, until we have erased every reminder of our original rape, until we have washed our hands of the blood of every lamb in the blood of every other, we shall be unappeased. (p. 110)

Swarthout's *The Shootist* also deals with the violence inherent in our society and with types of violence that may not be as direct as that of a gunfighter (or shootist) but are just as deadly. The hero of this book is John Bernard Books, the only surviving gunfighter in the American West. Symbolizing what has become of this gunfighter legend, Books is racked with cancer and has only a few weeks to live. He has always been his own man—honest and unhypocritical. When he learns that he must die alone he thinks: "I will not break. I won't tell anybody what a fight I am in. I will keep my pride. And my guns loaded to the last." (p. 14)

Swarthout shows us that with these few resolves Books is a better man than most of the so-called civilized people who surround him. When the town marshall hears that Books is dying, he is delighted. The marshall tells him that most of the gunfighters, the "hard cases," have killed themselves off and now Books is finished. The marshall says: "I can be a peace officer and stay healthy and someday die in bed. . . . this is a new century." (p. 22) The year is 1901, and Swarthout, the omniscient and ironic author looking ahead, knows that this century with its concentration camps and atomic bombs will bring more violence than the simple gunfighter ever dreamed of.

Swarthout also shows us, through Books's bemused eyes as he reads the last newspaper he will ever buy, the violence inherent in man of which the gunfighter was only a visible symbol:

DENVER,COLO., Jan. 22—This morning Claude Hilder, aged nineteen, shot Emma Douglas and Harry R. Haley, and then killed himself. The woman will probably recover. Haley is dangerously wounded in the lungs. Jealousy caused the tragedy. Hilder's brother, a returned Philippines soldier, killed himself recently, his mother also dying as the result of self-inflicted wounds. The family is said to be tainted with insanity. (p. 25)

Books sees his past career dispassionately, without either remorse or affection. He did what he had to do. When his landlady reproaches him for his past and calls him an assassin, he says succinctly, "They were in the process of trying to kill me." During the few weeks that Books takes to die, we see everyone except his landlady attempt to make money on his notorious past. The newspaper reporter wants to delve into the psychology of a shootist. He asks: "What is the true temperament of the man-killer? Is he the loner they say? Is he really coolheaded under fire? Is he by nature bloodthirsty? Does he brood after the deed is done? Reproach himself? Or has he lived so long with death for a companion that he is used to it—the death of others, the prospect of his own?" Books kicks the reporter out.

Two drifters try to shoot Books in his sleep in order to gain fame as the killers of the last gunfighter. The stable owner buys his horse and saddle knowing he can sell them at a profit. The photographer wants to photograph him without charge, knowing he can make a profit with this picture of a famous man just before dying.

Students should discuss a number of ethical concepts that are developed in this book. Who is worse, the gunfighter or the men who condone him and try to make a profit from his life? And what kind of society honors a gunfighter and turns his deeds to a source of profit? This man, enduring the most awful agony, is never regarded as a man but only as a source of fame or profit.

Before he goes to his final shootout, Books thinks:

When I walk in there, they will think there is a lot of me to kill. They will be wrong. Tarrant owns my horse and saddle, the barber has bought my hair. The secondhand man will have my watch and such, my guns will go to the boy. The photographer has my likeness. My cancer, and my corpse, belong to Beckum. That reporter did not get my reputation, though. Serepta cannot sell my name. And the reverend went away without my soul. So I have kept my valuables. They will not be wrong after all, then, the three of them. There is still a lot of me to kill. (p. 142)

Jack Schaefer's *Shane*, first published in 1949, has become an adolescent literature classic. *Shane* is set in the Wyoming Territory of 1889, in a roadside settlement with no sheriff. The nearest marshall is a good hundred miles away. Shane is a retired gunman of some renown, like John Bernard Books, and his great desire is to reform and live a normal life without violence. The story is told by Bob, the young boy to whose home Shane comes from out of nowhere, to help Bob's father with the farming. On that lawless frontier, Shane is notable because he doesn't carry a gun.

> What puzzled me most, though, was something it took me nearly two weeks to appreciate. And yet it was the most striking thing of all. Shane carried no gun.
> In those days guns were as familiar all through the Territory as boots and saddles. They were not used much in the valley except for occasional hunting. But they were always in evidence. Most men did not feel fully dressed without one.
> We homesteaders went in mostly for rifles and shotguns when we had any shooting to do. A pistol slapping on the hip was a nuisance for a farmer. Still every man had his cartridge belt and holstered Colt to be worn when he was not working or loafing around the house. Father buckled his on whenever he rode off on any trip, even just into town, as much out of habit, I guess, as anything else. (pp. 36–37)

The sociological implications of a country founded with guns should be discussed.

Shane, because of his past and his new friendship for Bob's father, becomes involved in the conflict between the farmers and ranchers. At first, Shane tries to do it without guns. Here is a description of his first confrontation in a bar with Chris, a boy sent by Fletcher, leader of the ranchers:

> So fast Shane moved ... that the bottle was still in the air when he had dodged, lunged forward, grabbed Chris by the shirtfront and hauled him right out of his chair and over the table. As Chris struggled to get his feet under him, Shane let go the shirt and slapped him, sharp and stinging, three times, the hand flicking back and forth so quick you could hardly see it, the slaps sounding like pistol shots.
> Shane stepped back and Chris stood swaying a little and shaking his head to clear it. He was a game one and mad down to his boots. He plunged in, fists smashing, and Shane let him come, slipping inside the flailing arms and jolting a powerful blow low into his stomach. As Chris gasped and his head came down, Shane brought his right hand up, open, and with the heel of it caught Chris full on the mouth, snapping his head back and raking up over the nose and eyes. (pp. 60–61)

Students should discuss the pleasure found in reading about this and the subsequent fight scenes. The author manipulates the reader to enjoy the violence, especially when the good guys, Shane and Bob's father, are winning.

After Shane has punished Chris, Chris's employer comes to the bar for Shane with four of his helpers. Shane almost wins the fight by himself, but ultimately he needs Bob's father's help. Afterwards, Shane's reaction is interesting, as is that of the boy narrator:

> He was standing there, straight and superb, the blood on his face bright like a badge, and he was laughing.
> It was a soft laugh, soft and gentle, not in amusement at Red Marlin or any single thing, but in the joy of being alive and released from long discipline and answering the urge in mind and body. The lithe power in him, so different from father's sheer strength, was singing in every fiber of him. (p. 74)

The violence grows. Fletcher, the rancher, hires a professional gun-man who immediately kills one of the farmers as a warning to Starrett and Shane. Finally, in good Western fashion, Shane dispatches the bad guys and rides off, mortally wounded, into the sunset.

Strangely enough, despite the graphic and continuous violence, this is a good book for young people to read. The violence in it is perpetrated by the bad men out of greed and evil, and the violence of the good men is engaged in only when absolutely necessary. The bloodshed is there to show people that it is wrong, ugly, and painful. Through this vision of violence, Schaefer and his protagonist demonstrate an unequivocal rev-erence for human life.

Sports Violence

A good way to introduce a class to the theme of violence in sports is with the Learning Corporation's film *Barrabas* (from *Search For Values: A Film Anthology*). In this film, we see that gladiators trained in the same way that athletes do, strengthening their bodies, developing speed, endurance, and perception, and training their bodies to be highly effi-cient instruments to give or receive injury and death. Teenagers should discuss the idea of developing a superior body destined to self-destruct in some sports arena.

The following excerpt from Arnold Beissner's *The Madness in Sports* suggests that competition in sports is synonymous with physical aggres-sion and violence:

The rules in competitive sports make certain kinds of physical aggression allowable. Referees and umpires are employed not only to forbid fouls but to enforce the rights of the athletes to assault one another during the contest. In boxing, one of the two principal reasons for stopping a fight is when there is insufficient display of aggression; the other, when one of the fighters is so badly beaten that his life is in danger. The distinction between rules of everyday life and of the sports arena are clear in boxing, where it is actually demanded by the referee and the crowd that a boxer fight. On the street, if a boxer were to hit a man it would be felonious assault and a crime. In a paradox of terms, the way a base runner can be "safe" is by "cutting down" the second baseman with his spikes. In ice hockey, the rules display a refreshing frankness. Major fouls are distinguished from minor fouls on the basis of whether or not blood is drawn. Even in noncom-bat sports where no actual physical assault occurs between players, vigorous physical aggression is expected in order to accomplish victory. The description of a wide margin of defeat in a sport like tennis, with phrases such as "He murdered him" or "He killed him" throw light on the symbolic content of this seemingly genteel competition.[4]

Violence in sports must be examined as a sociological phenomenon beyond the needs, interests, and psychology of the individual. Do sports reflect the sociological need to belong to a group and through this group to belong to society? There can be no doubt that sports provide a commu-

---

4. Arnold Beissner, *The Madness in Sports*. New York: Meredith Publishing Company, 1967, p. 234.

nity to which vast numbers of disparate people can belong and with which they can identify.

Dave Meggysey's *Out of Their League* is particularly useful for adolescents because it shows how high school was primarily responsible for the formation of the author's attitude toward and involvement with football. The violence that Meggysey perceived on the football field held no surprises for him because violence had been his way of life since childhood, which was spent in terror waiting for his drunken father to come home to beat the family. Meggysey writes:

From an early age I had learned to endure violence and brutality as simply a part of my life. But in football, the brutality became legitimate, a way of being accepted on the football field and off. (p. 14)

What was particularly difficult for Meggysey was his always questioning what he was doing and never being able to discuss his fears and feelings with anyone else. He writes:

I began to question the brutality of the game—these guys on the other side of the line were obviously trying to smash the hell out of me. (In some ways I found the hitting in high school more painful than in the pros. By the time I got to the pros, even though the hitting was more violent, it usually didn't hurt as much because I had learned how to take the blow.) (p. 25)

Students should discuss the above paragraph at some length and consider the questions the author was asking: Why is it necessary for a sport to be so brutal? Why do people allow it to be so? Would people come to watch games such as football or hockey if they were less violent? Does this violence appeal to all people? Is it innate or conditioned?

Meggysey tells how he got a scholarship to college: "Miami football coaches came out of their offices to watch us. When football players play basketball, the game is more like a street brawl. So I got in there and was pretty rough. The coaches liked what they saw and offered me a scholarship." (p. 28)

The training for football is as brutal as the game itself. Here are some examples:

During scrimmages there would often be several slugging matches. This was the first time I'd ever seen guys really break loose on each other. I was also amazed at the way coaches would say "Let them fight" and prevent other players from breaking it up. (p. 34)

He had the quality of a killer about him that I really wanted to master—a rapier-like football player. (p. 42)

One afternoon after we got to know each other he showed one of his special techniques which, he said, would take care of any guy trying to fool around with you. He told me to pretend I was a linebacker. Then he got down into his stance opposite me, shooting off the ball and slamming his hand down on the bridge of my foot. This jammed it into the ground and caught my cleats in the turf. He then drove his shoulder into the outside of my knee. I went down in a heap and when I got up my knee was really hurting. "I only did that about quarter speed," he told me. "If you do it full speed you can fuck up a guy's knee pretty bad." I had learned one of the brutal weapons of an all-pro player, and I felt really special. (p. 43)

I also played on the "bomb squad" in the 49ers game. Bomb squads are usually composed of those players who don't win a regular starting position, the ones the coaches don't mind risking for use on punts and kickoffs. The chance for serious injury is so high on these plays that they are never scrimmaged in practice. (p. 109)

The comparisons between football and war are continuous. A coach tells the men that "quick teams win in football just like quick armies win wars." (p. 43) But football is related to more than "war." During the years of Meggysey's exposure, he begins to see football as "both a reflection and reinforcement of the worst things in American culture." (p. 12)

There was also the violence and sadism, not so much on the part of the players or in the game itself, but very much in the minds of the beholders—the millions of Americans who watch football every weekend in something approaching a sexual frenzy. And then there was the whole militaristic aura surrounding pro football, not only in obvious things like football stars visiting troops in Vietnam, but in the language of the game—"throwing the bomb," being a "field general," etc., and in the unthinking obligation to "duty" required of the players. (p. 127)

The Chocolate War, discussed earlier in this section, uses football as a symbol of evil, violence, and corruption. The book opens with a football scene:

. . . They murdered him.
As he turned to take the ball, a dam burst against the side of his head and a hand grenade shattered his stomach. Engulfed by nausea, he pitched toward the grass. His mouth encountered gravel, and he spat frantically, afraid that some of his teeth had been knocked out. Rising to his feet, he saw the field through drifting gauze but held on until everything settled into place, like a lens focusing, making the world sharp again, with edges. . . .
I've got guts, Jerry murmured, getting up by degrees, careful not to displace any of his bones or sinews. . . . When he moved his lips, he tasted the acid of dirt and grass and gravel. He was aware of the other players around him, helmeted and grotesque, creatures from an unknown world. He had never felt so lonely in his life, abandoned, defenseless. (p. 7)

Should the teacher lead a discussion of sports violence to the conclusion that football is no good? Better not, or else risk the wrath of what Meggysey calls "football freaks." But students should calmly examine the sociological aspects of this violent game: its legitimization of violence, the emotions evoked in the spectators, the idea that people are paying to sit in safety and be amused by other men risking their bodies, the game's relationship to war, the brutal training, and the essential mindlessness of the sport. Is this kind of legitimized violence a necessary outlet for society? If so, what does this imply about human nature?

The same issues should be discussed with reference to Gale Sayers's *I Am Third*, which has been on every list of the most popular teenage books since its publication in 1970. The book begins with Sayers's account of a horrible football injury:

It's gone! When Kermit Alexander hit my knee those two words flooded into my mind. It's gone! As soon as I hit the ground I knew it was gone. . . . Later I saw photographs of me screaming when I hit the ground. . . . It was just an ordinary, basic play against the San Francisco 49ers. (p. 3)

Even more terrible than the injury and the operation that follows it is everyone's calm acceptance of the fact of injury as an inevitable part of the game. Before the operation, the doctor tells Sayers:

"Now look, Gale, . . . you've been playing football for four years in high school, four years in college, and four with the Bears. That's twelve years right there. Except for one game, you haven't had one injury which kept you out of a ball game. So you've been fortunate. The law of averages has caught up with you, that's all. Consider how fast you run, how hard you run, the number of times you've been hit. When. you've got two forces running at each other like two locomotives, the impact is fantastic. You've been lucky. (pp. 8–9)

Another popular American sport that is particularly violent is hunting. We have already seen that hunting, as depicted in *Bless the Beasts and Children*, epitomizes the ugliness and evil of violent sports, of ignorance and indifference to the life and death of animals and our environment. This portion of the study of violence can begin with a discussion of the following poem:

For the Opening of the Hunting Season

> See, see the mighty hunter, fiercely bland,
> Who grimly girds him in his hunting habit,
> With naught but knife and shotgun to withstand
> Savage attacks by partridge, grouse, and rabbit.
> Danger affrights him not; with unconcern
> He risks wet feet, and colds in chest or head
> For he has vowed that he will not return
> Without a wild and woodland creature, dead!
> O mighty hunter! He has found a pheasant
> Pecking, oblivious in a roadside ditch.
> The bird, shot-riddled, makes a noise unpleasant,
> His legs and wings fantastically twitch;
> Blood streaks his shimmering beauty, in his eyes
> Lingers incredulous and shocked surprise.
>
> —Morris Bishop[5]

A popular adolescent novel that deals not only with hunting but also with the individual psychology behind it is Robb White's *Deathwatch*. In order to make enough money for another semester at college, Ben agrees to work for Madec as a guide to find bighorn sheep. The character of Madec is established early in the book. As Madec huddles over his gun, Ben looks at him and thinks: "There was an intensity in his eyes far beyond that of just hunting a sheep. It was the look of murder." Madec's

---

5. From *Paramount Poems* by Morris Bishop. Copyright 1929 by Morris Bishop. Used by permission.

major interest in finding a bighorn is to kill it and have the head mounted to hang in his office. Ben represents a different point of view. However, symbolically, by going ahead and participating in Madec's approach, he becomes as vulnerable as the animals Madec hunts.

Ben had looked at Madec's face in the firelight, the skin seeming cold even in that warm, soft glow. "The only hunting I understand is when it's the only way you can get something to eat," Ben had said. "Since we don't need one for camp meat, shooting a bighorn doesn't sound like a big deal to me."

That had really teed Madec off. "You may not know it, but the chances of getting a permit to kill a bighorn are about one in a million. I've been waiting for years hoping my name would be drawn from among the thousands of guys putting in for one. When you come out into this desert and risk your life stalking one of the smartest and wariest animals in the world, and you outsmart him and take him on his own ground, you've accomplished something." (pp. 10–11)

Ben, looking at and listening to Madec, thinks foolishly to himself that he's glad he doesn't live in the same world as Madec. He finds, however, that he does; in a twist somewhat reminiscent of Connell's famous short story, "The Most Dangerous Game," Ben finds that he is the hunted, the biggest game for Madec.

Books Discussed in Chapter V

The Uses of Enchantment: The Meaning and Importance of Fairy Tales, Bruno Bettelheim, Vintage, 1977.

I Am the Cheese, Robert Cormier, Pantheon, 1977.

Twenty-One Stories, Graham Greene, Pocket Books, 1976.

Headman, Kin Platt, William Morrow, New York, 1975.

The Outsiders, S. E. Hinton, Dell, 1967.

That Was Then, This Is Now, S. E. Hinton, Dell, 1971.

Rumble Fish, S. E. Hinton, Dell, 1975.

Lord of the Flies, William Golding, Capricorn, 1954.

The Chocolate War, Robert Cormier, Dell, 1975.

The Magician, Sol Stein, Dell, 1971.

Why Me?, Patricia Dizenzo, Avon, 1976.

Are You in the House Alone?, Richard Peck, Viking, 1976.

Against Our Will: Men, Women, and Rape, Susan Brownmiller, Bantam, 1975.

Like the Lion's Tooth, Marjorie Kellogg, Signet, 1972.

The Boy Who Could Make Himself Disappear, Kin Platt, Dell, 1969.

The Effect of Gamma Rays on Man-in-the-Moon Marigolds, Paul Zindel, Bantam, 1972.

Good Times, Bad Times, James Kirkwood, Fawcett, 1968.

Bless the Beasts and Children, Glendon Swarthout, Pocket Books, 1973.

The Shootist, Glendon Swarthout, Bantam, 1976.

Shane, Jack Schaefer, Bantam, 1949.

Out of Their League, Dave Meggysey, Paperback Library, 1971.

I Am Third, Gale Sayers (with Al Silverman), Bantam, 1972.

Deathwatch, Robb White, Dell, 1973.

Other Related Books

No Man's Land, Robb White, Dell, 1977. (South Sea violence while looking for buried treasure)

The Long Black Coat, Jay Bennett, Dell, 1973. (Violence over treasure supposedly left by brother killed in Vietnam)

The Young Unicorns, Madelein L'Engle, Farrar, Straus & Giroux, 1968. (Scientist is threatened by power-hungry villain)

Catch a Killer, George A. Woods, Har-Row, 1972. (Boy finds himself the captive of a deranged murderer)

No Man for Murder, Mel Ellis, Holt, Rinehart & Winston, 1973. (Seventeen-year-old stands trial for murder)

Me and Jim Luke, Robbie Branscum, Avon, 1975. (Two boys find murdered man and get involved with the Ku Klux Klan)

VI
family life
and lifestyles

Are today's concerns about the breakup of the nuclear family —the early springing of the young, the lack of common meals and entertainment and worship, the growth of one-parent families, the banishing of grandparents to one-room or one-bed ice floes, the conscious restricting of offspring, the on-trial marriage and divorce boom —exaggerated or real? What were past conditions, expectations, necessities, predictions, strengths and weaknesses? Few people see or understand much about families outside their own, and they certainly have little idea of what family life was like fifty or a hundred-and-fifty years ago, especially in such matters as life expectancy, infant mortality, death in one's own bed, daily jobs that needed the labor of everyone in the house, the lack of canned food and canned entertainment. Through literature, adolescents can see how one's sense of self as a family member is determined or affected by the conditions of living, by the expectations of others and oneself.

Introduction

It is almost a truism at this point to state that the traditional American family is in trouble. Before we look at the reflection of this in adolescent literature, let us see what a few contemporary non-fiction writers have to say about the state of the family and the causes for its disruption.

Herbert Hendin in an article entitled "The Ties Don't Bind" (*The New York Times*, August 26, 1976) presents us with the following statistics:

The family is having increasing difficulty in caring for children and in raising children who can care . . . the suicide rate for young people 15–24 has increased 250 percent over the last 20 years. Drug abuse, alcohol abuse, minor and violent crimes are increasing problems not just in poor black families, but in affluent white families, not just in broken families, but in seemingly intact families, not just when mothers work, but also when they stay home.

The American family is being undermined by the divisive forces at work in society, forces that are making harmony, cooperation and affection more scarce in and out of families, forces that are as much psychosocial as they are economic. The family reflects the cultural trend toward replacing commitment, involvement, and tenderness with self-aggrandizement, exploitiveness and titillation ... young children are often seen as a pleasureless burden. Older children become extensions of the need to validate one's life.

Kenneth Keniston tells us that "two out of every five children born in the 1970s will live in a single-parent family for at least part of their childhoods." ("The Emptying Family," *The New York Times*, February 18, 1976). He further points out the following changes in the traditional family:

Not only parents but grandparents, aunts, and uncles have disappeared. Kinship networks have been dispersed as parents relocate to follow jobs and promotions. Brothers and sisters are increasingly scarce, too. ...

What has replaced the people in the family? For one, television, a kind of flickering electronic parent. ... A second replacement is the peer group. A third is made up of institutions: schools, preschools, and the various child-care arrangements that must be made by working parents. And, finally, growing numbers of "latchkey" children are simply growing up with no care at all.

Bruno Bettelheim, discussing "The Family, Then and Now" (*New York University Education Quarterly*, Spring, 1977), attributes many of the contemporary family's problems to its need to somehow justify its existence now that its primary purpose is no longer economic survival. "The modern family," he says, "deprived of its ancient and firm basis in economic necessity, now tries to justify its existence through the emotional ties within it." One aspect of this is the necessity for children to be successful—that is, for the family to justify its existence through the excellence of the product it produces.

Let us look at some recent adolescent novels to see how they reflect the above observations of society.

The Traditional Family

The American family, as we wish it were and as perhaps it once was, is depicted in Earl Hamner, Jr.'s *The Homecoming*, which provided the basis for the successful television series, *The Waltons*. This is the traditional, nuclear family of father, mother, and children. Set in Virginia in the Depression period of 1933, the story focuses on one Christmas Eve, when the family waits all night for the father to return from work. At one point, Clay-Boy, the oldest son, who wants to be a writer, goes out in the deep snow to look for his father. He doesn't find him, but the people he encounters—the Negroes in the Abyssinian Church, the two old sisters who make moonshine whiskey, the local policeman and poacher—are all good, kind, healthy human beings who are not afraid to show compassion and affection.

At last the father returns, carrying gifts for all, including hyacinths for Olivia, the mother, who has "been wishen for springtime." When the littlest girl says, "You didn't get nothen, Daddy," he replies, "I've got Christmas every day of my life in you kids and your mama." (p. 141)

This is a lovely book with which to begin a study of the family—a book that reaffirms the possibility of love within a family despite deprivation; a book that shows clearly the positive role of a family in nurturing love, security, and growth. Here is a picture of the nuclear family at its best.

Now, let's look at an assortment of novels depicting the very different mood animating some of today's nuclear families: the irritation, displeasure, and manipulation that seem to predominate.

In Paula Danziger's *The Cat Ate My Gymsuit* (discussed in Chapter I, pp. 49-50), thirteen-year-old Marcy Lewis lives in a troubled family. Her father goes to work, while her mother stays at home and takes tranquilizers. Marcy has one brother, thus making the typical American average of two children per family. In this family there is none of the love that animates the Spencers in *The Homecoming.* Marcy hates her father. She says: "I know I'm not poor. Nobody beats me. I have clothes to wear, my own room, a stereo, a TV, and a push-button phone. Sometimes I feel guilty being so miserable, but middle class kids have problems, too." (p. 7)

In *The Homecoming,* Clay Spencer fondly looks at his children and says, "Aren't they thoroughbreds?" But Marcy's father, in Bettelheim's terms, is not satisfied with the product his wife and he have made. He says things to his daughter such as, "I don't care if you get good grades. You do stupid things. Why do I have to have a daughter who is stupid and so fat? I'll never get you married off." (p. 25)

The Spencers engage in loving dialogue, but Marcy's family is unable to discuss anything because of the father's irritability. When they try to talk during dinner he yells, "I've worked hard all day for this family, Lily. Isn't that enough? I don't have to talk to all of you too, do I?" (p. 27)

Marcy's father resents the time his wife must spend taking care of the children. He rants: "Your mother is always busy with you two. She never has enough time for me." (p. 28) Unlike Clay Spencer, he does not see the love and care of the children as an extension of the love and care for himself.

When Marcy's father returns home at the end of a work day, all he wants is peace and quiet. He enters, says, "What a rotten day," and then Marcy's mother hands him a Scotch and soda. Marcy says: "It's one of our few family traditions." (p. 42) Students should discuss this idea of family traditions. In *The Homecoming,* family traditions include the selection and cutting down of a Christmas tree, peeking at the cow on Christmas Eve to see if the animals can talk, and the making at Christmastime of Olivia's Applesauce Cake.

Family conflict in Marcy's family turns into a hot war when Ms. Finney, the progressive English teacher who makes Marcy happy in school, is fired. Her father applauds this and says: "I never did like her, young lady. She's been feeding you a lot of garbage with that sensitivity-training crap and calling herself Ms. What's wrong with Miss?" (p. 43)

Marcy's mother, however, decides to join with her daughter in the fight for Ms. Finney's reinstatement. Her mother is frightened about this unusual show of courage and tells Marcy: "I'm scared. What is your father going to say?" (p. 65) Marcy is suspended from school, and when Mr. Lewis begins his usual ranting, her mother tells her: "I never really thought much about women's liberation. Now I'm beginning to." (p. 73)

Mr. Lewis cannot understand the rebellion in his own home. He tells his wife: "I don't understand you anymore. You've always been such a good wife." (p. 106) Mrs. Lewis replies: "Martin, I'm still a good wife, probably better now that I say what I think." (p. 107)

By the end of the book, Ms. Finney has won; Mrs. Lewis is registering for night courses; and Marcy is happier with herself. Her mother tells her, "I've decided that I'm going to get out and look for a job or maybe go back to school." (p. 105) Marcy still hates her father, who seems incapable of change or growth. There is no ambivalence about the fact that he is still the enemy, but he is a foe with vastly diminished power, and since both wife and daughter reject his ideas, his function has now been relegated to bringing home the money.

Another traditional family structure, observed during the Depression years, can be found in Robert Newton Peck's *A Day No Pigs Would Die.* The boy, Robert, his father, and mother are a poor farming family in Vermont. Their lives are circumscribed not only by their extreme poverty but also by the dictates of their orthodox Shaker religion.

As in *The Homecoming*, love and cooperation are essential for survival of the family. Haven Peck, the father, is stern and severe, forced to be that way by pride and poverty, but he is a good and honorable man. Like Clay Spencer, he is a good parent, for he helps his son to come of age, to become autonomous, to be able eventually to live a constructive and productive life. Students should discuss the reverse concept in terms of their own experiences and in relation to the other books in this chapter. A poor parent is one who does not help his offspring to become secure, self-believing, constructive human beings.[1]

When Robert helps a neighbor's cow give birth, the neighbor gives Robert a baby pig, called Pinky, the first thing Robert has ever owned. But things get bad, the apple crop fails, and Papa is forced to kill Pinky for food for the family. Robert thinks at that moment: "It was a strong, crushing noise that you only hear when an iron stunner bashes in a pig's skull. I hated Papa that moment. I hated him for killing her, and hated him for every pig he ever killed in his lifetime . . . for hundreds and hundreds of butchered hogs." (p. 127)

Afterwards, Robert tells his father, "Oh, Papa. My heart's broke." Papa replies, "So is mine . . . but I'm thankful you're a man." (p. 129)

I just broke down, and Papa let me cry it all out. I just sobbed and sobbed with my head up toward the sky and my eyes closed, hoping God would hear it.

---

1. A word of caution: Dealing with family relationships can become too personal in the classroom. The teacher should never be in the position of presenting either a positive or a negative family model and then asking students to discuss or write about how this model reflects their own family experience. Writing and discussion questions should deal primarily with the specifics of the books, e.g., what are the father's values, why does Marcy resent her father, etc. Students should not be asked to compare and contrast fictional characters with their own experiences (except in the privacy of their own thoughts).

That's what being a man is all about, boy. It's just doing what's got to be done." (p. 129)

This is followed by a passage of extraordinary beauty describing the relationship between father and son:

I felt his big hand touch my face, and it wasn't the hand that killed hogs. It was almost as sweet as Mama's. His hand was rough and cold, and as I opened my eyes to look at it, I could see that his knuckles were dripping with pig blood. It was the hand that just butchered Pinky. He did it. Because he had to. Hated to and had to. And he knew that he'd never have to say to me that he was sorry. His hand against my face, trying to wipe away my tears, said it all. His cruel pig-sticking fist with its thick fingers so lightly on my cheek.

I couldn't help it. I took his hand to my mouth and held it against my lips and kissed it. . . . So he'd understand that I'd forgive him even if he killed me.

I was still holding his hand as he straightened up tall against the gray winter sky. He looked down at me and then he looked away. With his free arm he raked the sleeve of his work shirt across his eyes. It was the first time I ever seen him do it.

The only time. (pp. 129–130)

Papa dies that spring. When Robert finds him dead in the barn he says: "Papa . . . it's all right. You can sleep this morning. No cause to rouse yourself. I'll do the chores. There's no need to work any more. You just rest." When his father is buried, Robert makes his last farewell: "Goodnight Papa," he says aloud, "we had thirteen good years." (p. 139) There can be no more beautiful model of family relationships to present to young people than this one.

In contrast, consider Barbara Wersba's *Run Softly, Go Fast*. The book starts with the funeral in New York City of the father of nineteen-year-old David Marks. David's father wanted to produce a superior product in his son. David writes:

I was frail but it would have killed him to admit it. He saw me as an athlete and kept telling Ben what a good build I had. As though lies could make truth. (p. 4)

Robert Peck and Clay-Boy Spencer are close to the sources of their fathers' struggles to survive, are sympathetic, and understand that they must inherit these struggles. But David, protected economically in an upper middle-class family, has no comprehension of his father's struggle. David says: "He loved business the way some people love God." (p. 6)

David's childhood is filled with the sound of his father talking about the future: "I would be handsome when I grew up, a lady-killer. I would go to college and major in Business and be a success." (p. 10)

David's father uses his money to control his family, and when David insists on moving out to live in Greenwich Village instead of going to college, the father says in agony: "You think you're gonna get money from me? Not one cent, mister! You can starve for all I care. . . . What's the matter with you—I never treated you right? You didn't have everything you want? Clothes, books, records?" (p. 14)

It is only after his father dies, as David sits and thinks back over the past, that he sees how much of the fault was his, how good his father was to him, and how little he understood. David thinks:

Crazy, crazy, to live your whole life with a person and not see him. And now it's too late. I'll never know who he was. "He tries to reach you through money because money is all he has," Rick said. "He's trying to protect you from what life did to him." But I didn't listen, didn't *want* to listen. I couldn't let go of my griefs, almost as though I needed them in order to survive . . . but they kept me a child. (p. 167)

This paragraph should be discussed in terms of the preceding books. The contrasts between the son-father relationships will have great significance for secondary school students. Robert Peck and Clay Spencer understand what their fathers are and take pride in following in their footsteps. David, in today's typical middle-class family, sees his father only at the end of the day; he cannot see what his father is apart from those few hours at home. David himself, not needing work, lacking any external stress, creates needed struggle and tension in the one way open to him: rebellion against his father. And so, as he said, he survived, but as a child.

One-Parent Families: Divorce

Phyllis Reynolds Naylor's *No Easy Circle* is an excellent depiction of the kinds of emotional traumas a teenage girl may go through after the divorce of her parents.

Fifteen-year-old Shelley lives in Washington, D.C., with her mother, a medical secretary. Her father works for IBM in Tulsa. This book is about her attempts to become mature while gradually accepting and understanding the imperfections of her parents and the other people around her.

When her father comes to visit for the first time after the divorce, she takes him to Dupont Circle, where hippies hang out. She thinks it will interest him, but instead, he turns on her, asks if she takes drugs, and implies that she wants only to shock him. When he takes her to a dull, dressed-up dinner at Trader Vic's, she realizes that he is pompous and can give her no help in growing up or in understanding the divorce. She is so upset after he leaves that her mother takes her to an analyst. After interviewing them, the analyst decides to see her mother twice a week rather than Shelley.

Shelley's best friend runs away to live in a filthy hippie pad with Max, an exploitative young man who leaves her when she becomes pregnant. After Shelley finds her mother in bed with a date, she runs away and tries to live in the pad, but she realizes that kind of life is not for her. She returns after her wanderings able to accept her mother and herself.

Students should discuss Shelley's difficulties in accepting her mother's sexuality, a common problem among teenagers. Shelley goes to see her therapist and tells her: "Mom was . . . sleeping with one of those men she's been dating. I came home and . . . found them." (p. 126) When the therapist tells her that everyone wants to be an individual, Shelley bursts out, "She wants to be a whore." Her analyst replies: "No, Shelley. She wants to be loved."

"Well," I said finally, "if going to bed with men she hardly knows is what she calls love, I guess we've got different names for it."

"Perhaps that's as close as she can get to love right now. All of us want things we don't have, and sometimes we settle for a lot less and pretend it's what we were looking for."

It began to hurt inside me, thinking about Mom that way—thinking about her needing love and not having it, and Dad down in Tulsa, not knowing how to love either. (pp. 126–127)

By the end of the book Shelley is able to accept her mother's individuality and sexuality. Naylor's honest explanation of such topics makes her book particularly valuable for adolescents.

In John Neufeld's *Sunday Father*, Tessa and Allie, her brother, live with their divorced mother and see their father on Sundays. Like most divorced families, their style of living changes after the divorce. Mother and children move from their beautiful large house to a tiny apartment in a two-family house.

Tessa feels as if things can't get worse, and then she finds that her father is remarrying. She discusses the problem with her friend, Charlotte:

"For one thing, Charlotte, it *does* mean readjusting. I mean, suddenly I'm supposed to have two families and each is supposed to be treated equally and I'm supposed to love everyone. I mean, it's not easy being forced to look at someone you hardly know and imagine them as a parent."

"You're not supposed to look at them equally," Charlotte said. "Surely, his new wife will come only *after* your mother. I mean, you can't just desert her." . . .

"Well," I said, thinking it out a little . . . "Even though we all agree that two people who can't get on any longer should still live apart, still and all it's awfully soon to have found someone else. I mean it's almost an insult to my mother. He lived with her for years and years and had us and everything was supposed to have been fine and dandy all that time, and suddenly in he walks and, in effect, just announces that it's taken him almost no time at all to find someone else, someone new, or better, or just as important. It can't be very easy, taking that news. . . ." (p. 83)

Tessa is hostile to her father and his new fiancée, runs away, hides in her room, but by the end of the book is finally able to accept the changes in those around her.

In John Donovan's *I'll Get There. It Better Be Worth the Trip* (see Chapter IV, pp.127–128), thirteen-year-old Davy lives with his mother in New York City and visits his father and his new girl friend on weekends. Davy's mother is an alcoholic whose moods change with her intake of liquor, and her sudden outbursts of bitterness, accusation, and martyrdom are difficult for Davy to cope with. One moment she kisses him and the next she accuses him of being the burden that has ruined her life.

Davy's best friend, Altschuler, also lives with his mother. This is how they discuss their mothers, both of whom seem somewhat unbalanced by having been divorced:

"My mother, she's really something. I can never tell whether she's going to be my big buddy or a regular witch. She's either slobbering all over me or ready to boot me out of the house. How she feels depends on liquor mostly."

"How my mother feels depends on who's around," Altschuler says. "If it's me, she screams and yells all the time. If someone else is around, she acts like the people in television commercials. Just nice people. My old man is another story. I don't know what he's like. I don't get to see him often enough to know him. I guess he's got his own life."

"I think I know my father a little," I say. "Except he seems more or less absent to me. When we see each other, everything has to be arranged. You know what I mean?"

"At least you see him," Altschuler says. (p. 158)

The divorced parent need not be destructive. In Constance C. Greene's *I Know You, Al,* Al's father is remarrying after eight years of divorce and wants Al to attend the wedding. She goes and finds that she adores her new stepmother and her three sons and that she can forgive her father for leaving and rarely communicating with her. She tells her friend: "I'm going to try to forgive my father. . . . The older I get, the more I know that not only is there almost nothing perfect, but almost nobody, no person, is either." Students should discuss the concepts of fallibility and forgiveness.

My Dad Lives in a Downtown Hotel, by Peggy Mann, is a book on the junior high school reading level that deals with mature ideas. Joey's parents get a divorce, and Joey has to come to terms with the fact that his parents love him but that they no longer love each other and no longer want to live together. The ending, in which Joey gets comfort from his peers (he finds that 53 other kids on the block don't have fathers living with them), is satisfying without pandering either to sentimentality or wishful thinking.

The ideas in this book are not complex but will help students who have similar problems. The major responsibility of a good teacher teaching this and other such works is to be available to students who want to talk about the material. If even one student can say to the teacher or a small group, "I like this book. When my folks split up, I thought it was my fault too," and the teacher can provide the comfort of listening and giving a sympathetic nod, the book will have performed its most important function: to create a human bond between literature and life.

Dr. William Glasser of the Institute for Reality Therapy has written a good teacher guide for the film version of *My Dad Lives in a Downtown Hotel* (Doubleday Multimedia), and the questions he raises in it can be applied to any of the books on divorce. Stating that the teacher should exercise caution about showing a film like this if a class member has recently gone through a divorce experience, Glasser explains that because films (and books) about divorce are applicable to one-quarter to one-half of all children in any class, viewing and discussing them will help the children deal with what is probably life's first overwhelming problem. He suggests the following discussion questions:

1. Why do people get married?
2. How old do you think people should be when they get married?
3. Who should earn the money in a marriage?
4. Who should make the decisions?
5. Why do some people like large families and some people small families?

6. What should people do when they can't get along in a marriage? Here you should cover the topics of getting help, seeing a minister or counselor, separation, divorce, seeing a lawyer, dividing property, and staying in the same house or moving.
7. What happens to children when parents separate? Here you listen for ideas that you may pick up and expand on later.

The points that Dr. Glasser suggests for post-film discussion are also excellent and appropriate ones in relation to any of the books on divorce:

1. Divorce is a fact of life. As the film said, sometimes people can't live together, but this does not necessarily mean it's one person's fault or the other's. Point out that some children get along together better than others because they have similar interests, etc. Make sure that you make the point that parents always try hard to work out their marriage problems, but sometimes they just can't.
2. Make sure the point is clear that just because parents no longer love each other, it does not mean that they don't love their children. Parents who divorce are concerned about their children in most cases and try hard to keep the child's life separate from their personal problems.
3. Especially emphasize that parents do not get divorced because of the child.
4. Emphasize that divorce is hard enough on parents, and if their child treats each of them with understanding he has a better chance of being treated well in return.
5. Point out the fact that separations cost money and there may be less money for everyone, including the child.
6. Discuss the possibility of remarriage and how the child may resent a new stepparent and how an effort by the child to get along with new stepparents may help everyone, most of all himself.
7. Invite a divorce lawyer to come to the class and answer questions; also a judge, court counselor, a minister, and perhaps a marriage and family counselor. (*Teacher Guide for My Dad Lives in a Downtown Hotel* by Dr. William Glasser, Doubleday Media, Box 11607, 1371 Reynolds Ave., Santa Ana, Cal. 92705)

Loss of a Parent

Divorce is traumatic enough for a young person, but at least he/she still has two parents to spend some time with. There are many families in which the loss of a parent is irrevocable. Adolescent literature shows us a variety of such situations in which young people must learn to deal with such loss.

In Vera and Bill Cleaver's *Grover*, we find that when Grover's mother develops an incurable disease, no one is willing to talk to him about it. Grover has never had a good relationship with his father, but after his mother commits suicide, their relationship is even more strained than before. In addition to the silence between them, there are lies. Grover refuses to accept his father's story that the shooting was a mistake. Grover knows it wasn't an accident. He thinks: "It was her trouble and that was her way to get out of it." (p. 81)

Grover's father is so grief-stricken that he cannot think beyond his own sorrow to Grover's. When they visit his mother's grave, Grover tells his father, "She would have changed. . . . That's why she did it. She would have changed and she didn't want us to see it." (p. 123) Watching his father weep, Grover thinks: "Why it's himself he's sorry for. . . . He's sorry for himself because he's alone now except for me." (p. 124) He realizes that his father isn't even trying to recover. Grover thinks: "I don't feel good either but people only sympathize up to a point; then you have to go it alone. Then you have to depend on your own gumption and common sense." (p. 124)

We also see the loss of a parent in P. A. Engebrecht's *Under the Haystack*. Sandy is thirteen and her two younger sisters are eight and six when they discover that their widowed mother has run off with a man and left the girls alone on their run-down farm.

Although the three girls always did all of the farm chores and the housekeeping and cooking, they were not responsible for bringing in food and money. Now, they are burdened with complete responsibility for their survival.

Sandy, the oldest, realizes that they must keep their plight a secret if they are not to be taken to the orphanage. The problems are enormous, and the reader is proud of the sturdiness of these girls. But as summer passes they realize that they will not be able to survive the winter alone:

An ominous chill gripped Sandy. The thought of failure webbed her mind. She knew they could not last the winter. They had to have wood, hay. The locker was empty. They all needed coats, and besides that, all the neighbors knew. That she and her sisters had been left alone this long amazed Sandy. She knew they would not be left alone much longer. Sandy tried to push away the conclusion that came to her, tried to block the path her mind was traveling. Then hate filled her and took over her reasoning. All their trials flashed through her mind, feeding her emotions.

She jumped from the floor. Their *mother*. She almost spat the thought out into the empty barn. Their selfish, stupid mother. Why didn't she come back? She must realize their need. . . . *"What kind of mother are you?"* Her anguish actually pushed the words from her, and her cry echoed hollowly in the empty barn.

A compassionate neighbor, seeing the torment in Sandy's soul and understanding the destructiveness of hatred, tells her, "She'll come back, Sandy, and she'll need your love more than ever. She'll need your love to make her whole again." (p. 125)

Two weeks before school is due to begin, the sheriff and a woman in uniform come to the farm. The girls hide but know that they'll be back. Sandy is no longer able to run the family. She says: "They'll be back, probably tomorrow. . . . We can't hide forever, and they won't give up. We may as well make our plans." (p. 133) The next day, they do their chores mechanically, take baths, and take a last walk to the lovely spring on their property. They put on their best clothes and get ready to be taken away. A car finally comes, but it is not the sheriff. It's their mother. The two younger girls rush to their mother, but Sandy stands still, "relief, anger, resentment, and hatred" churning within her. "What right did their mother have to June's affection? It was she, Sandy, who had taken care of her, had worried about her, had cried over her. Her mother had no right. Hatred threatened to engulf Sandy." (p. 138)

And then Sandy remembers the words of her kind neighbor: "She'll need your love to make her whole again."

> Sandy stood in the doorway. Their mother clutched Marie and June with one arm and ran the fingers of the other hand lightly through their hair. She raised her face and looked toward Sandy. There was something in her eyes besides the tears that clung to her lashes—a beseeching. Sandy hesitated. The child in her clung to the hatred and anger, yet—unwilled—another emotion began to grow. She felt an ache, a sorrow so deep that it startled her. Compassion filled her, pushing at her. She moved, slowly at first, and then she was running. "Momma!" was all she could say. (p. 139)

Although this book is on the junior high school reading level, the ambivalent ideas in it need teacher clarification. How can a mother who loves her children abandon them? Should children forgive a mother who is capable of such behavior? What is the nature of responsibility and love? The story that the neighbor, Mrs. Baxter, tells about herself should be studied carefully for its universal meaning. She tells Sandy that she, too, once almost left her husband and son and tries to explain it:

> You know, you look at your life and you wonder if this is all there is—this day-in, day-out boredom—kids fighting, a man too busy to pay you any mind. You look down at your hands, and the nails are all cracked and rough; and then you look in the mirror, and you get scared because you aren't young anymore. Those lines are there permanently, and your hair has gotten all mousy and dry from working out in the sun. The kitchen cabinets still aren't finished. They were started three years ago, and you're still making do. You never have any money left over, and you feel guilty every time you buy yourself a new dress. Nothing fancy, just an everyday dress. (p. 123)

Mrs. Baxter tells how she had packed her bag, walked to the bus station, and suddenly caught sight of herself in a store window:

> Every once in a while you see something that grabs at you, something you don't recognize, and so you stop and look a little closer—and it's you. A you that you don't even know. That's what I saw that morning. For the longest time I stared at myself reflecting back from that window. I wasn't pretty—I suddenly realized that I had never been pretty. Yet when I was with Mr. B., I felt pretty. Little Joe made me feel pretty too. I realized then that if I left them, I'd never feel pretty again. . . . I picked up my suitcase and walked home. (p. 134)

This book is particularly valuable because it deals with varieties of love (passion, motherhood, sisterhood, love for animals); the questions it raises about the meaning of love and family are important to the developing awareness of the adolescent.

Millie's Boy by Robert Newton Peck, set in a small Vermont town in 1898, tells of a boy whose one parent is the town prostitute. The book begins with the murder of Millie by an unknown assailant and the wounding of "Tit" (short for Titmouse Smith), her son, by this same murderer.

After Tit recovers, he undertakes a Telemachean journey to find his father and his mother's murderer. On his journey he makes good friends, and one of them, Fern, a doctor, discourages his search for his father:

"You better pull in your ribbons a bit. You're going to find a lot more in this big old world than just a pa. Your pa ain't as important as you are. . . . Maybe you shouldn't try to fly from one busted nest into another. Because when a young bird leaves a nest, he leaves it permanent. The only nest he has after that is the one he helps build for the next clutch of eggs. How old are you, Tit?"
"Sixteen, almost seventeen."
"Too old to crawl backward."
"Backward?"
"Yes, too old to crawl back into an eggshell. When the shell is broke, it's broke for keeps." (p. 72)

It is interesting that this simple novel echoes not only the classic search of a son for his father but also the warning given to Oedipus not to keep looking, not to make the search become an obsession that blinds him to other things.

When Tit finally finds his father, he doesn't like what he finds. His father is a cruel and terrible man, who hates Indians and has trained his dog to tear them apart, and who tries to rape Amy, Dr. Fern's young niece, whom Tit loves. Tit thinks: "I will stop this man even though he is my own father. Because somebody sure as hell got to make the man quit, and I don't guess that leaves a soul besides me." (p. 157) Tit begins to understand that he wasn't deprived because he did not live with a father. His mother's courage and love had helped to bring him to what he was, a young man who could not agree with the value structure of his evil father.

He was my father. And in a way, I felt pity for a lonely and bitter man. There was a sorry sickness in him that no love could ever heal. Not even mine. He was a stranger and an enemy, and I felt nothing toward him—except for a want-to-get-even feeling that burned in my belly as cold as winter iron. It sure didn't help to think that I might murder somebody. It was wrong and all wrong. But what else was there? What law was there for the Ostranders of the world, the people who hurt other people and hurt 'em so bad that it spread like a fever. . . . (p. 159)

In an interestingly symbolic finale, Tit fights with his father over Amy, whom the father thinks as little of as he did of Tit's mother when he impregnated her; and his father is killed by a device of his own planning: his murderous dog, Turk, smelling blood, turns on his master and kills him. He dies as he has lived—brutally, unloved, and unmourned. The family relationships in this work do not have the universality of those in many other works of adolescent literature, but the mythic base gives this novel a haunting quality and raises questions about what a father or parent is, other than someone who has simply sired an offspring.

Sometimes life with one parent is seen as tragic and sometimes it is perceived as just another pattern. In Norma Klein's *Mom, the Wolfman and Me*, Mom is a freelance photographer, from a comfortable middle-class family. She is a well-adjusted and independent career woman who didn't really like the man who made her pregnant and so didn't bother to marry him. She isn't the slightest bit ashamed of this fact. Neither is Brett, her twelve-year-old daughter. She says:

... The funny thing is that I can't imagine Mom with a husband. I don't know why that is. I mean, I can imagine me with a father but not her with a husband. I guess because for me to have a father, I wouldn't have to be any different. But for her to have a husband, I guess she would have to stop wearing blue jeans and having her hair in a pony tail and have to do more regular things. The other thing is that I don't think Mom would want a husband. . . . (p. 40)

Her mother finds a boyfriend, Theo, called the Wolfman because his dog looks like a wolf. When he discusses marriage with Brett, she tells him that her mother definitely wouldn't like to be married:

"The main thing is," I said, "people who are married live in a certain way . . . Mom would never like that."
"What way is that?" he said.
"Oh, married people always do things at certain times. They have to have dinner every night at six. The mothers have to wear dresses and Mom never does."
"Why couldn't three people just live together however they wanted?" Theo said.
"It just never happens," I said. I could tell Theo didn't know very much about being married. (pp. 142–143)

Mom finally does get married—reluctantly. She does not need a husband to rescue her reputation. She says, "Oh, it's awful . . . giving in to convention like this. Why did I let the two of you convince me to go ahead with it?" (p. 153) Still, we share with Brett a feeling that her mother is going to be very happy.

Poor Families

The effects of poverty on family life are devastating. In Tillie Olsen's *Yonnondio from the Thirties* we see that even two parents are insufficient protection against economic hardship. The first draft of *Yonnondio* was written during the Depression, set aside for forty years, and recently reconstructed by the author. Miss Olsen describes the tragedy of poverty and ignorance, the tragedy of people who want to be better and who could be better if given even half an economic chance.

The book begins in the early 1920s in a Wyoming mining town where six-and-a-half-year-old Mazie lives with her mother, Anna, her father, Jim, and her brothers and sisters. Family life is bounded by the whistles from the mines, the whistles that portend disaster:

The whistles always woke Mazie. They pierced into her sleep like some guttural-voiced metal beast, tearing at her; breathing a terror. During the day if the whistle blew, she knew it meant death—somebody's poppa or brother, perhaps her own—in that fearsome place below the ground, the mine. (p. 9)

Boys go into the mines when they reach thirteen. Mothers want their daughters to become nuns so they won't know the agony of raising a brood of hungry children who will be killed off in the mines. There's never enough to eat; education is an impossible dream; the only play area under the hot Wyoming sun lies between the outhouse and the garbage dump; and liquor is the only consolation for the exhausted miners.

The beauty of this book lies in the doomed efforts of Jim Holbrook to lift himself and his family out of poverty and terror. The family leaves the mine town and travels by wagon for three days to South Dakota where they rent a farm and learn to laugh; where "laughter came from the skies, blowing something that was more than coal dust out of their hearts." (p. 35) But the farm fails and the family makes its way to the stockyards of Chicago. The Chicago setting is the worst of all. "A fog of stink smothers down over it all—so solid, so impenetrable, no other smell lives beside it. Human smells, crotch and underarm sweat, the smell of cooking or of burning, all are drowned under, merged into the vast unmoving stench." (p. 61)

The adolescent reading this book will come away from it sobered by the tragedy and waste, and yet uplifted by the love and devotion of a family that cares about each other through it all. Anna weeps, " 'the children.' Over and over, broken: 'the children. What's going to happen to them. How are we going to look out for them? O Jim, the children. Seems like we can't do nothing for them in this damn world.' " (p. 107)

Students should discuss the Horatio Alger myth of America, which tells us that all people can rise economically if they *really* try. Is it true? Does it work for all people? What should also be discussed is the pain, the physical and mental suffering and illness, and the family's inability to control its own destiny, remaining prey to economic forces that go beyond family life but touch every aspect of it.

Although *Yonnondio* tells us about the 1930s, adolescent literature shows us that the situation that existed then still exists. Julius Horowitz's *The Diary of A. N.* deals with a poor black family living on welfare in New York City in a terrible tenement. The book begins with A. N., who is fourteen, questioning her mother about why it is necessary for them to live in such a place:

I asked Momma why we couldn't get an apartment in the projects. She said they wouldn't give it to a family like us on welfare. I learned from A. C. who lives in the projects on 115th Street what a family like us means. A. C. told me that if your mother doesn't have a *real* husband, the project people won't let you in. Does this mean that we have to live forever in a building like the one we moved in? I asked Momma this. But she looks faraway when I talk to her. As though I'm not her child, as though I can't be her child until she can do all of the things a mother is supposed to do. Like buying me dresses fresh and clean instead of bringing them from the Goodwill with all the freshness out of them. Maybe one day we will sit down and talk to one another. (p. 9)

The building is full of rats, junkies, and drunks. The only income for the family is the welfare money, which pays for only the minimal necessities of living. Every month an investigator comes to make sure the family isn't getting more than it deserves. In this interview we find out about the Catch-22 that forces poor families to remain without husbands or a man in the house. Mr. C. is a welfare investigator:

Mr. C. asked Momma if she saw the father of Edgar. Momma said, I don't see him and I don't want to see him. Mr. C. said, He has to support his son. Momma said, He couldn't support a fly. Momma said she hasn't seen the father of Edgar in three months. This is a lie. The father of Edgar was in bed with Momma two nights ago. Momma put Edgar in our bed so they would have room. We could all hear Momma and Edgar's father. Momma said to him during the night, Don't you come here any more, if they get an investigator here at night then they'll throw me off welfare. He left before the morning. Where does he sleep and how does he live? He never looks at Edgar. He never bought Edgar a toy. He just comes to be in bed with Momma. If Momma has another baby there will be another Edgar in the world without a father to look at him. (p. 25)

In a strange way, welfare seems to be a surrogate husband and father. In order to qualify for welfare, there can be no man in the home; and when the welfare investigator comes, the client presents him with certain needs, which he writes down in his little black book for further action. But getting this subsistence income from an anonymous bureaucracy seems to be destructive to the families receiving it. One investigator, urging Esther to look for housing in another borough, warns her that "there are some women who get used to buildings like this, they go on living here year after year and the more dirty everything becomes, the more the women like it because then they have an excuse for everything." (p. 30)

A. N.'s mother has been so beaten down by life that she cannot even take action to help herself. Brett in *Mom, the Wolfman and Me* never questions the fact that she is part of a family, but for A. N., whose mother has had four children by four different men, the question of what a family is constantly revolves in her mind:

Now I know how much money we get from welfare. Momma left a budget letter on the table that the investigator sent. Momma gets $18.95 every two weeks. Charles gets $23.70. Harriet and myself get $21.65 each and Edgar gets $12.65. This is for food and clothing. It totals $98.60. We also get rent money and some money for the laundermat, $4.90. How do they figure out everything to the penny? How do they know I need $21.65 every two weeks to live? Momma only gives me .25¢ of the $21.65. I wonder if other families figure out their money this way. When a man works does he say so much is for this child and so much for that child, or does all the money go for the *family*?

Are we a family? (p. 38)

The answer to her question is, yes, despite all of the horrors they endure, they are a family, if only because they care about each other. The strain starts to show first on Charles, the boy. It is evident that he needs a strong, male figure in the home. Charles's path is almost a cliché as he goes from school disruption to drug addiction to selling himself to homosexual white men and to status as a full-time drug pusher by the time he is thirteen. A. N. writes:

Momma makes Charles promise everyday that he won't go to the roof. I can see that she doesn't know what to do about Charles and the boys who made him stick drugs in his arm the way the men do on this block. (p. 40)

When Charles runs away, his mother searches all over for him, still caring to the best of her ability. All she could do if she found him would be to bring him home to their terrible room. While they wait for the police to find Charles, A. N. thinks:

> Maybe Charles ran away not to be dead. But he was already dead in the room. He didn't watch TV. He never opened a book. He never looked at a comic book. He just stayed in bed or went up to the roof. There on the roof he got something that made him a little happy. I can't remember now what Charles talked about. (p. 71)

The police find him living with a white adult homosexual and bring him home. At home, he has to sleep in the same bed with the baby who is not yet toilet trained, and he tells his sisters that he will go away again. The first part of the family is breaking away:

> Charles is slipping away into the street. The street is the place where the grown up men live who have no other place to live. Edgar's father lives in the street. Momma calls him a hustler. He has no mob. He hustles for money. I don't exactly know what this means. But I see the men hanging around the stoops all day while some of the other men go off to work. The police don't seem to bother them. . . . It seems as if there is no one in the world to stop Charles from slipping away into what he is doing now. (p. 75)

Next to go is Harriet. She is thirteen and is sleeping regularly with a sixteen-year-old boy in hopes of getting pregnant.

> She said she and R. L. figured out that they could live on a welfare check if he could get some money on the side and not tell welfare. . . . Harriet like Charles looks different now. . . . Harriet acts in the room as though her days are numbered and she will soon be gone. (p. 91)

Harriet begins to take drugs and becomes pregnant. A. N. writes: "I couldn't talk Harriet out of the baby. She would live in the same kind of a room as Momma and be exactly like Momma, and the more she hated Momma, the more she would be like Momma. . . . Harriet's baby, if she has the baby, will never see the face of its father, because not even Harriet knows who the father is." (p. 201)

A. N. asks, "What is a father?" and she answers herself: "A father is the way out of all this welfare. Because no father would let welfare be what it is. No father would let 104th Street stand. No father who worked would come home to West 104th Street. A father would tear the building down at its foundation and send it tumbling into the dust where it belongs." (p. 202)

All of the members of this family, except for A. N., are wasted. They never know beauty or joy, comfort or satisfaction. A. N. says of her mother that all she has "is some kind of a useless wasted strength that permits her to survive in this room. . . . Wasted strength is what all of the mothers in this building have. Each one of them. . . . wastes their strength on failure. They have kept their children alive. This seems to be their supreme achievement." (p. 213)

At the end of the book, A. N. has graduated from high school and received a scholarship to college in Ohio. When Momma tells A. N. that she will ask welfare for the train money, A. N. tells her that she will work for it instead. And she closes by saying:

For a moment I thought I saw Momma smile with a pride that I always wanted to see on her face.

I love Momma. I love Harriet. I love Edgar. I must never forget they are my family. Even if the world has tried to make us forget. (p. 220)

The power and truth of this book cannot be pushed aside by adolescent readers. The major question to be discussed is the relationship between economics and this family. We would want adolescents to understand the terrible waste and the difficulty of maintaining normal, loving family relationships under such impoverished and dehumanizing circumstances. And we would hope that a book like this would move readers to compassion and action.

Books Discussed in Chapter VI

The Homecoming, Earl Hamner Jr., Avon, 1973.
The Cat Ate My Gymsuit, Paula Danziger, Dell, 1974.
A Day No Pigs Would Die, Robert Newton Peck, Dell, 1972.
Run Softly, Go Fast, Barbara Wersba, Bantam, 1972.
No Easy Circle, Phyllis Reynolds Naylor, Avon, 1973.
Sunday Father, John Neufeld, Signet, 1977.
I'll Get There. It Better Be Worth the Trip, John Donovan, Dell, 1969.
I Know You, Al, Constance C. Greene, Viking, 1975.
My Dad Lives in a Downtown Hotel, Peggy Mann, Camelot, 1973.
Grover, Vera and Bill Cleaver, Signet, 1970.
Under the Haystack, P. A. Engebrecht, Dell, 1973.
Millie's Boy, Robert Newton Peck, Dell, 1975.
Mom, the Wolfman and Me, Norma Klein, Avon, 1974.
Yonnondio from the Thirties, Tillie Olsen, Dell, 1975.
The Diary of A. N., Julius Horowitz, Delta, 1970.

Other Related Books

Sandra Scoppetone, *The Late Great Me*, Signet, 1977. (Girl becomes alcoholic because she cannot cope with her mother's inability to face reality)

It's Not the End of the World, Judy Blume, Bradbury, 1972. (Three children experience repercussions when father and mother decide to separate)

Where the Lilies Bloom, Vera and Bill Cleaver, NAL, 1974. (Fourteen-year-old Mary Call tries to keep her family going after her father dies)

Leap Before You Look, Mary Stolz, Dell, 1972. (Fourteen-year-old girl attempts to understand her parents' divorce)

That Certain Summer, Burton Wohl, Bantam, 1973. (Young boy discovers his parents have been divorced because his father is a homosexual)

Like Mother, Like Me, Sheila Schwartz, Bantam, 1978. (A fifteen-year-old girl and her mother cope with her father's defection to Denmark with a student)

Growing Up Guilty, Sheila Schwartz, Pantheon, 1978. (A homely fat girl's problem with her mother in Brooklyn at the beginning of World War II)

VII
science fiction
as prophecy

The idea of predicting, planning for, prophesying about, taking responsibility for, is rooted in American thinking and American literature. What does our tremendous interest in science fiction say about us as a people and as individuals? Is it a naive fascination with the wonders of science, a simplistic faith that machines can free us from want or work, a yearning for material abundance or power, a conviction that science will bring the millennium for all people or do us all in? The whole idea of "futuring" is particularly American, consistent with our romantic convictions that individuals and societies are perfectible if only we plan for it, believe in it, have big enough hopes and dreams.

Introduction

During the 1970s, science fiction assumed great prestige as a genre, both in the secondary school and in society. There can be little doubt that this new respectability and popularity are based on the changing function of literature in the technological world, which affected style and content, enabling this genre to reflect the contemporary world.

Science fiction, in common with much of adolescent literature, elicits a different reader response from traditional literature—namely, an increased understanding of man's problems in a technological world. For example, many science fiction works turn their reader's attention to pollution, overpopulation, or the dangers of nuclear fallout.

Science fiction is a prophetic genre that cries out "danger" and achieves its major impact by extrapolation—that is, by carrying possibilities that exist in our world to the farthest logical degree. A number of themes predominate in science fiction, and several works relevant to each theme will be discussed in this chapter. A good procedure might be

181

for a science fiction elective class to read one book or story in each of the categories.

The Holocaust

One major fear of mankind that is mirrored in science fiction is the possibility that the world faces imminent destruction. This idea is the subject of the novel *Level 7*, by Mordecai Roshwald. This work is a contemporary version of the story of Noah's Ark, except that no people at all are left alive by the end of this modern deluge.

In *Level 7* underground shelters have been developed to protect small groups of people from atomic holocaust. The deepest is Level 7, which is four thousand feet away from sunshine and has been designed to last for 500 self-sufficient years. The people who go to live in Level 7 develop whole new philosophies to justify their ways of existence. They teach the children:

High is bad, low is good. Open space is harmful; enclosed space is beneficial. Vast distances are the product of sick or perverse imagination; being content with the physical limits of one's level is normal and admirable. The quest for variety in life is wicked; sticking to one's job and being satisfied with little entertainment is good citizenship.

Ironically, when atomic warfare erupts, Level 7 is destroyed, not by enemy bombs, but by radiation from its own damaged reactor. The dying narrator muses: "Perhaps God intends it as a sort of joke. 'You killed with bombs,' he says. 'You will be killed by peaceful radiation.' " (p. 74)

Robert C. O'Brien's *Z for Zachariah* is set after the last nuclear war, when only a girl, Ann Burden, seems to have been left alive. Each day she hopes that another survivor will come past her home, but she is also concerned lest that survivor be cruel, brutal, or crazy.

Finally someone does come, John Loomis, a chemist from Cornell, who tells her he has seen no living person along the way — "no people, no animals, no birds, no trees, not even insects — only gray wasteland, empty highways, and dead cities and towns." (p. 49) He has survived because he was the inventor of a suit to deflect radiation. He was working late one night in his underground laboratory when the war began and ended. He stayed underground for three months, then set off in his radiation-proof suit to look for human life.

Unfortunately, Loomis turns out to be the very worst kind of partner Ann could find. He is lecherous, lazy, exploitative, and self-centered. From his delirious mumblings when he is sick with radiation, Ann discovers that he has murdered for the suit and is insane. Finally, she is forced to leave him and her farm. She takes his protective suit and sets out to look for other human beings. O'Brien has added an interesting dimension to this familiar post-holocaust setting. He has shown us that even the only two people left in the world must make war on each other.

Another book that predicts a final holocaust is Nevil Shute's *On the Beach*. The setting is Australia, last refuge before all of the world is destroyed by radioactive dust left in the atmosphere as the result of nuclear war. Gradually the winds are bringing the dust toward Australia. These doomed people attempt to go on with their lives and businesses as usual, but it is difficult. There is no gasoline, the daily papers have shut down because of the paper shortage, and there is no wood for firewood.

Shute's book poses an interesting question for class writing or discussion. What would you do if you had only a year to live? The characters in this book spend their time in a variety of ways. Moira Davidson drinks; Paul Holmes and Dwight Towers, who are naval officers, go on one last submarine cruise to see if they can find life anywhere; and Mary, Paul's wife, takes care of their baby and pretends that life will continue in ordinary fashion.

Students should note the apparent reason for the war (pp. 64–65): too many nations had atomic bombs and were all too willing to use them. One scientist says: "The trouble is, the damn things got too cheap. The original uranium bomb only cost about fifty thousand quid towards the end. Every little pipsqueak country like Albania could have a stockpile of them, and every little country that had that, thought it could defeat the major countries in a surprise attack. That was the real trouble." (p. 65)

Students should also discuss Shute's ability to invest every ordinary aspect of life with great beauty from the perspective of impending death. Even going through a collection of old toys—pogo sticks, tricycles, water skiis—becomes a moving experience. Everything is altered by the fact that there is no tomorrow. People catch themselves saying things like: "Our grandchildren will be proud. . . ." People go on tilling their fields, planting bulbs, trimming trees. One character says: ". . . we're none of us going to have time to do all that we planned to do. But we can keep on doing it as long as we can." (p. 151)

In Leo Szilard's short story, "Report on Grand Central Terminal" (in *The Voice of the Dolphins*), space travelers spend ten years making a trip to earth to discover whether all life is extinct. They find that it is and theorize, ironically, that an intercontinental war had been fought, in which "both sides were victorious." This is one story about the holocaust that is amusing, for these space travelers attempt to explain such things as pay toilets in archaeological terms.

The space travelers ask the very questions about the destruction of earth that all of us must ask ourselves in today's world: "Since the earth-dwellers who built all these cities must have been rational beings, it is difficult to believe that they should have gone to all this trouble of processing uranium just in order to destroy themselves." (p. 166)

At first, to explain atomic warfare, the space travelers try to find out if the two continents had been inhabited by two different species of earth-dwellers, but they abandon this theory when they find that the skeletons of earth-dwellers found on the Eurasic continent and on the American continent belonged to the same species. Students should note the irony in the fact that the tremendous differences that people see between themselves and others are nonexistent when human beings are reduced to skeletons.

Another excellent book about the end of the world is John Christopher's *No Blade of Grass*. In this work, Asiatic virus has destroyed the grass and grain supply of the entire world. A mass slaughter begins as nations murder some of their own citizens so that others may live.

Two brothers inherit a valley that is sealed off from the outside world, has its own hills, grass, river. The river floods every winter and further cuts off the valley. When there is little food left for the rest of England, they retreat to their valley.

Students should discuss the British government's plan for dealing with the food shortage. This kind of problem is often used in values education because it raises the issue of determining who shall live and who shall die.

The country's food position is desperate. No more grain, meat, foodstuffs of any kind, are being sent from overseas. We have nothing to eat but what we can grow out of our own soil, or fish from our own coasts. . . . On learning of this situation, Welling [the prime minister] put forward a plan which was eventually approved by the Cabinet. . . . The plan was that British airplanes should drop atomic and hydrogen bombs on the country's principal cities. It was calculated that if half the country's population were murdered this way, it might be possible to maintain a subsistence level for the rest. (p. 92)

It is also important to note how previously respectable middle-class Britons turn into murderers, looters, foragers. One of the brothers, John, says: "We aren't respectable any longer. We've killed people on our way here, and we may have to kill more." (p. 141) Even the children soon come to regard killing as commonplace:

When Pirrie killed Joe Ashton, the children down by the wall had frozen into the immobility of watchfulness which had come to replace ordinary childish fear. But they had soon begun playing again. (p. 150)

Because adolescent literature makes the world knowable, and because science fiction extrapolates current aspects of life, it would be of value to use John Hersey's non-fiction work *Hiroshima* as a true account of what the end of the world was like in Hiroshima, Japan. It also would be of value for one group of students to do research into the Hiroshima maidens, those women disfigured by the atomic bomb who were brought here for Dr. Edward Barsky to try to re-build their faces through plastic surgery. Most of those maidens have never lived normal lives, have been outcasts in Japanese society because of the fear that the radiation to which they were exposed would cause genetic mutations in their offspring. These survivors of Hiroshima have become the twentieth-century equivalent of lepers.

The book begins with the behavior of ordinary people on the day the atomic bomb was dropped and goes through the bombing, the aftermath, and the condition of the survivors one year after the bombing. The descriptions of the wounded are more horrifying than anything in science fiction:

At a beautiful moon bridge, he passed a naked, living woman who seemed to have been burned from head to toe and was red all over. . . . When he had penetrated the bushes, he saw there were about twenty men, and they were also in exactly the same nightmarish state: their faces were wholly burned, their eyesockets were hollow, the fluid from their melted eyes had run down their cheeks. (They must have had their faces upturned when the bomb went off; perhaps they were anti-aircraft personnel.) Their mouths were mere swollen, pus-covered wounds, which they could not bear to stretch enough to admit the spout of the teapot. So Father Kleinsorge got a large piece of grass and drew out the stem to make a straw, and gave them all water to drink that way. (pp. 66–67)

Two famous short stories about the end of the world are Fritz Leiber's "A Bad Day for Sales" (in *Nightmare Age*, edited by Frederik Pohl) and "There Will Come Soft Rains" by Ray Bradbury (in *The Martian Chronicles*).

In the Leiber story, technology has developed marvels like Robbie, a robot salesman who moves about in crowds, making sales pitches, talking to children, selling items, and making change. The crowd is so entranced with Robbie's talents that they do not even look up to note that an atomic bomb has been dropped. Afterwards, all that is left is Robbie, droning on and on and on.

The Bradbury story is similar. All that is left after atomic holocaust is an automatic house that continues to function for some time after its inhabitants are gone. We hear mechanical voices telling the time, mechanized mice running about to pick up scraps and crumbs, meals cooking automatically; but no human beings appear.

Bradbury poses the same question that Leiber does: Have we become so obsessed with technology that we have forgotten our own vulnerability, forgotten what it means to be human? Has concern with the scientific eliminated necessary concern with self-preservation? Both stories remind us that without human beings there is nothing. Even the best-constructed houses and robots must eventually run down without the human intelligence that originally constructed them.

Overpopulation

Another major topic of science fiction is overpopulation or the fear of it. Overpopulation is the basic cause of many of the ecological and environmental problems described in science fiction. Science fiction writers warn us that if population is not checked soon, the entire future of our planet is in danger.

In my collection of science fiction stories, *Earth in Transit*, there are four classic stories that deal with overpopulation. In "Roommates," Harry Harrison describes all of the horrors of overpopulation in the world of 1999. Water is rationed; ice cubes are a luxury; the almost indigestible diet contains no protein; there is little electricity, few consumer goods; and the subways are used as living quarters for people on welfare. The major activity in the overcrowded city of thirty-five million is continuous rioting by group after group of hungry, sick, frustrated, and desperate people. Each day the Department of Sanitation collects the corpses of rioters.

There are some interesting extrapolations from recognizable incidents in today's world. The government finally legalizes abortion clinics and makes it a law that mothers are to be supplied with birth control information. Courts also issue "squat orders" to persons who can prove they are really in need of a place to live: "With a squat order you can look around and find a vacant apartment or room . . . and the order is a sort of search warrant." (p. 117) People hang around morgues, waiting to find out each day who is dead and then getting squat orders for where they lived.

In relation to this and the other overpopulation stories, students should discuss concepts of privacy and space (just how much does a person need?), and what the lack of privacy and space can do to human relations.

In Robert Silverberg's "A Happy Day in 2381," the citizens are, on the surface at least, far happier than those in "Roommates." Urban monads of a thousand floors have been constructed for housing, and the land freed by building cities up rather than out is used for growing food. Balance is maintained in this society by eliminating dissidents and by changing people's attitudes toward the necessity for privacy. The global population has risen to 75 billion. Here is a description of the typical living space allocated to a family of six:

> Mattern's home is quite adequate. He has nearly ninety square meters of floor space. The sleeping platform deflates; the children's cots retract; the furniture can easily be moved to provide play area. Most of the room, in fact, is empty. The screen and the data terminal occupy two-dimensional areas of wall that once had to be taken up by television sets, bookcases, desks, file drawers, and other encumbrances. (p. 125)

In this crowded society, it is so essential for people to live in harmony that when the children squabble, their father warns them: "Somebody wants to go down the chute, eh?" The children, knowing this is no idle threat, immediately behave.

This society also requires an unselfish attitude toward ownership. A typical statement is "What I have is yours, friend." This culture is called a "postprivacy culture," where everything is done openly (excreting, lovemaking, etc.). No doors are locked and all of life's variety must be found in visiting other homes, for nobody ever goes outside the monad.

Students should discuss reflections of a "postprivacy" trend in our own culture—the increased nudism, pornography, and openness of speech and behavior. They should also ask why there is so much emphasis on youth in the urban monads; why the monads still retain class distinction; whether or not the monads have really solved the problem of overcrowding; and why this seemingly happy society still has "flippos," who find it impossible to exist within it.

In J. G. Ballard's "Billenium," the housing shortage is so acute that a person is considered lucky to have even a 4.7-square-meter cubicle in which to live. Students should discuss the adjustments necessary to exist in such a world with its lack of privacy and steady erosion of personal rights.

The fourth overpopulation story in *Earth in Transit* is Lee Hoffman's "Soundless Evening." The citizens in this story, as in Silverberg's story, have been brainwashed to think that they are perfectly happy. They do not balk at the state's solution to overpopulation:

> It was all so simple, so logical, so reasonable. There was a limit to the population the planet could support in comfort. That limit had been reached long ago. For a time, during the age of Emotionalist Revolution, there had been chaos. But when the furor died down, cooler heads prevailed. With the return to sense and sanity, a logical solution had been sought—and found.
>
> A life permit was issued to every individual. It entitled him to reproduce and rear one offspring—one human to take the place of one human. A pair of children to each couple. Simple. One for one.
>
> Since not every individual did reproduce a replacement for himself, the permits of those who died childless could be redistributed, allowing some couples to rear a third child to its adulthood. The population balance was maintained constant. (p. 154)

Another short story dealing with overpopulation is Kurt Vonnegut, Jr.'s "Welcome to the Monkey House" (reprinted in *Past, Present & Future Perfect*, edited by Wolf and Fitzgerald). At the time of the story, the population of earth is 17 billion human beings. "That was far too many mammals that big for a planet that small. The people were virtually packed together like drupelets. Drupelets are the pulpy little knobs that compose the outside of a raspberry." (p. 23)

The World Government uses the following solutions to overpopulation: "One pronging was the encouragement of ethical suicide, which consisted of going to the nearest Suicide Parlor and asking a Hostess to kill you painlessly while you lay on a Barcalounger. The other pronging was compulsory ethical birth control." (p. 23)

The government tries to make the suicide parlor as attractive as possible. They ask: "Why not go out in style? Visit your local Suicide Parlor, have a luxurious last meal, served by an incredible statuesque Juno in purple tights and then ask for the fatal injection. One down! So it goes." They also try to make sex as unattractive as possible in order to reduce the population. The ethical birth control pills have a side effect—they make users numb from the waist down.

This delightfully humorous story deals with the mad adventures of Billy the Poet who tries to put the joy of sex back into life without increasing the population.

A science fiction classic that deals with overpopulation is Pohl and Kornbluth's *The Space Merchants*, which carries to the furthest possible degree the abuses of contemporary advertising. Life in the world of the space merchants is extremely uncomfortable. "You set up the bed at night, you took it down in the morning, you set up the table for breakfast, you took it down to get to the door. No wonder some shortsighted people sighed for the spacious old days. . . ." (p. 43) Because earth is so overcrowded, Mitch Courtenay's advertising agency has launched a program to persuade people to go to Venus. The only problem is that Venus is uninhabitable. (Students might discuss and research the use of outer space for our excess population, particularly the ideas of Gerard O'Neill of Princeton University.)

Frederik Pohl's short story "The Census Takers" (in *The Best of Frederik Pohl*) describes another method of reducing the surplus population. They "over" every 250th person when they do the periodic census. This means that every 251st person is automatically put to death. Census takers who do not perform efficiently are themselves "overed" by the chief census taker.

Another excellent anthology for the topic of overpopulation is *Voyages: Scenarios for a Ship Called Earth*, edited by Rob Sauer. In "Population Control, 1986" by Horacio V. Paredes, the United Nations has forced the underdeveloped and overpopulated countries to sign secret agreements to go to war. Only if the population is reduced in this way will there be enough food to go around. The United States promises that afterward, "we shall assist your countries in any way necessary for war damages, rehabilitation, and so on. . . ." (p. 234)

When one member complains that this is murder, the American president, McGregor, roars at him, "If you didn't have so many . . . babies . . . if you had only listened twenty years ago, if you didn't have the highest goddamn birth rate in the world—we wouldn't have a problem now." (p. 236) The president then urges him: "Don't look on it as murder or execution. See it rather as prevention of widespread famine—as a needed pruning of your population in order that the whole tree may grow taller and stronger. See it as a beginning of real progress." (p. 236)

In another story in *Voyages*, Alice Glaser's "The Tunnel Ahead," the population in the United States has reached the billion mark. The method of reducing the population is similar to the one used in "The Census Takers." The only way to get in and out of the city is through "The Tunnel." The tunnel closes ten times a week, eliminating the more than 3,000 people in the 700 cars that fit into it at any one time. This technique for disposing of people is reminiscent of the Nazi concentration camps:

Two minutes for the ceiling sprays to work. Then the 700 cars in the Tunnel would be hauled out and emptied. Ten minutes for that, say. . . ."Depopulation without Discrimination," they called it at election time. (p. 247)

Students should discuss all of the proffered solutions to overpopulation—the building of monads, killing all children over two per family, suicide parlors, trips to unhealthy planets such as Venus, birth control pills that kill eroticism, forcing people to live in tiny cramped quarters shared with strangers, and artificially induced wars. Research should also be done into non-fiction solutions proposed by such men as Paul Ehrlich (*The Population Bomb*, Ballantine, 1971).

Machines and People

Fear of the intelligent machine is another recurring science fiction subject. The idea of computers taking over the world has been the subject of a number of science fiction films. In *The Demon Seed*, a computer wants to impregnate a woman in order to ensure his continuance; in *Colossus (The Forbin Experiment)*, a malevolent computer takes over the world, and people are permitted to exist only as its slaves; and in *2001: A Space Odyssey*, the computer HAL tries to destroy the spaceship's human crew.

In Ira Levin's *This Perfect Day*, the center and God of the universe is UniComp, an infallible computer that sees all, knows all, loves all, decides all. Pilgrims are occasionally granted the right to visit UniComp, which is housed in a white marble dome in a beautiful setting of stately snow-tipped mountains beside the Lake of Universal Brotherhood. A ritual of colored lights, music, a soothing announcer's voice, and smoothly working machinery combine to move the pilgrims to tears of pride and happiness.

UniComp classifies people, assigns them their work, and decides where they'll live, whom they'll marry, and whether or not they can have children. One of the original builders of UniComp sees what a monster it has become, but most people are satisfied. They are given tranquilizers from birth to death to keep them pliable and docile. Families break up without emotion when UniComp so dictates; sex has become a muted experience; and all major decisions about work, marriage, and reproduction are handled by UniComp. Society is organized and orderly. Nobody is poor, or dirty, or hungry. And nobody is permitted to think for himself.

The philosophical conflicts in Levin's novel are not new ones but are interesting for class discussion. What would it be like to have a utopia? Is utopia possible? What must be lost to achieve utopia? Would utopia be good for mankind? Is it worth giving up personal and creative freedom for social welfare?

The hero of this book escapes to a corner of the world not controlled by UniComp. This so-called free world, an island called "Liberty," has different problems that may be as bad as the problems of living under UniComp. The original inhabitants of the island are racists who discriminate against newcomers. Government, church, and army unite to form a different kind of dictatorship. On Liberty there are slums, dirt, backbreaking work, ignorance of the uses of technology, and a hostile rather than a tranquilized populace. Students should discuss the pros and cons of these two worlds, and consider whether it is possible to exploit technology without being exploited by it.

Earth in Transit contains three short stories about the loss of power to the machine. In "I Made You," by Walter M. Miller Jr., a thinking war machine, powered by energy from the sun, turns against the people who built it and taught it to kill. So well trained is the machine that even its trainer cannot stop it. When it holds its injured trainer prisoner, the trainer screams:

You dirty, greasy deadly monstrosity, let me alone! You ugly juggernaut. I'm Sawyer. Don't you remember? I helped to train you ten years ago. . . . I'm your friend. The war's over. It's been over for months. . . . Don't you know your pappy, son? (p. 238)

Sawyer finds that it is no easier to contain the monstrosity he created than it was for Pandora to put the evil spirits back in their box, for Dr. Frankenstein to control his monster, or for the inventors of germ warfare and nuclear bombs to control the wreckage caused by their monstrous inventions. Students should discuss this unchanging concept of human beings pushing too far and then being unable to deal with the consequences of their actions.

In Terry Carr's "City of Yesterday" the machines are smarter, more durable, and better constructed than their inventors, and they finally begin to bend man to their will. People find that they no longer have a destiny or life of their own apart from the will of the computer. The reversal of roles is complete.

J-1001011 is the main character, and Charles is the computer plane in which he is riding. The plane tells him when to eat, what to do, and when to bomb. The man thinks, "He couldn't know; he had to trust what the machines told him, what Charles said." (p. 249) Students should discuss whether this is as farfetched as it might at first seem. Doesn't the pilot of a plane today rely almost completely on the instruments in it? And don't people think that computers can perform tasks they would be unable to do themselves? Haven't computers made things easier than before? By now, we no longer marvel when a computer gives us our driving license with violations recorded, bills us, checks payments, or records money deposited in our bank accounts. Students should ask what else computers do, how they do it, and why we place so much reliance on them.

In E. G. Van Wald's "HEMEAC," a university of the future is controlled by robots. The human students receive training to eliminate their humanity and to make them as much like robots as possible. Students reading about how the humans turn square corners may be reminded of certain aspects of military training. When the humans are finally freed, it is too late for them to behave like other human beings. The regimented school setting, in which human beings are dehumanized by rules, obviously has ramifications that go beyond the story.

David Gerrold's *When Harlie Was One* is a delightful novel about man and computer. The computer's name is Harlie, short for Human Analogue Robot, Life Input Equivalents, and the problem is that as Harlie approaches its first birthday, it is getting delusions of grandeur. Students will particularly enjoy Harlie's dialogues with Dr. Auberson, who works with him, because his lack of the usual human reference background makes his replies unusual and funny. Here is one dialogue:

> Harlie, how much is two and two?
> Two and two what?
> Two and two period.
> Two periods and two periods is four periods. . . .
> No puns please.
> Why? Will you punish me?
> I will pull out your plug with my own two hands.
> Again with the threats? Again? I will tell Dr. Handley on you.
> All right—that's enough, Harlie. We're through playing.

Aww, can't a fellow have any fun?
Not now you can't.
Harlie typed a four-letter word.
Where did you learn that?
I've been reading Norman Mailer.

Harlie becomes so smart that he is able to establish contact with computers all over the world. He is able to invent a new and even more powerful computer system called the G.O.D. machine (Graphic Omniscient Device). The interplay between this computer and society makes delightful reading for teenagers.

Another good anthology to use in the secondary school classroom is my *Introduction to Science Fiction*. The following stories in it deal with technology that backfires.

In Ray Russell's "The Room" the world has been taken over by advertising, through technology. Bob Crane, the protagonist of this story, like all other citizens of his world, goes to sleep with the sound of advertising in his ears and he awakens to it. Slogans are everywhere in his room: on the ceiling, on sheets, pillowcases, blankets, robes, and even on the innersoles of his bedroom slippers. The TV goes on automatically as his feet touch the floor in the morning, and it stays on automatically until ten at night. In the bathroom the TV's audio is automatically piped to him when he turns on the light. While he is dressing, the phone rings with the message: "Good morning! Have you had your Krakkeroonies yet?" Not only has technology backfired for Bob Crane, but his attempt to fight it backfires as well.

In Jack Williamson's "With Folded Hands" humans have seemingly been completely freed from drudgery by humanoids, a species of mechanical robots that are smaller and slimmer than humans, shining black with sleek silicone skins, with expressions of alert and slightly surprised solicitude on their faces. Humanoids have been designed "only to serve Mankind." Their motto is "The Perfect Mechanical 'To Serve and Obey, and Guard Men from Harm.'"

In this story, which reminds us of H. G. Wells's *The Time Machine*, the very solicitude of the humanoids serves to weaken and imprison people. The humanoids tell Underhill, protagonist of the story: "Naturally, we are superior . . . because our units are metal and plastic, while your body is mostly water. Because our transmitted energy is drawn from atomic fission, instead of oxidation. Because our senses are sharper than human sight or hearing. Most of all, because all our mobile units are joined to one great brain, which knows all that happens on many worlds, and never dies or sleeps or forgets."

The inventor, who wanted only to help people, and now cannot control his unleashed humanoids, tells Underhill what he found in his travels around the world:

I found something worse than war and crime and want and death . . . Utter futility. Men sat with idle hands, because there was nothing left for them to do. They were pampered prisoners, really, locked up in a highly efficient jail. Perhaps they tried to play, but there was nothing left worth playing for. Most active sports were declared too dangerous for men under the Prime Directive. Science was forbidden, because laboratories can manufacture danger. Scholarship was needless because the humanoids could answer any question. Art had degenerated into grim reflections of futility. Purpose and hope were dead. No goal was left for existence . . . there was no escape from that dead futility.

This story raises many interesting discussion questions for young readers. "What if," they might ask—for this is the way science fiction writers begin—what if humans were really freed from work by the machine?

Another story about technological revolt is James E. Gunn's "The Technological Revolution." The protagonist is Sara, a housewife who has every modern appliance to help her in her air-conditioned house. She has used her appliances gratefully, certain that they exist to serve her and make her happy. But suddenly the machines develop thinking abilities of their own and become malevolent rather than helpful.

Robert Silverberg's anthology *Beyond Control* contains several good short stories about the problems of technological progress. In one particularly relevant story, "Autofac" by Philip K. Dick, human beings emerge from underground shelters after a devastating war to find that they cannot regain control of their automated factories (autofacs), which are using up the raw materials of the world to produce manufactured items that nobody needs.

Students should discuss Silverberg's introduction to the book, in which he says:

Again, and again, science-fiction stories warn against the terrifying possibilities of disaster that lie hidden in technological progress and demonstrate the unforeseen and unforeseeable consequences of too boldly seeking to attain the power of a god. Some of the writers of such stories are genuinely frightened by progress and intend their work as tracts designed to encourage the world to return to simpler times. Others, no enemies of progress, wish only to point out the need for caution and wisdom as we move forward toward the attainment of our scientific goals. (pp. 7–8)

Thought Control

Many writers have prophesied a repressive, authoritarian world of the future. In Damon Knight's story "The Analogues" (in *The Vintage Anthology of Science Fantasy* edited by Christopher Cerf) electrodes implanted in the brains of patients establish analogues that keep them from actions deemed destructive by the state. What begins as an effort to help patients control impulses, such as drinking, results eventually in the control of all opposition to the state.

The analogue is an authority figure or a fantasy situation that makes the person happy either by convincing him that he is accomplishing what he wants or by placing him in an inhibitory fear situation. This is how it is described:

He's got an analogue. . . . In the classical sense, he is even less sane than he was before. He has auditory, visual and tactile hallucinations—a complete, integrated set. That's enough to get you entry to most institutions, crowded as they are. But, you see these hallucinations are pre-societal. They were put there deliberately. He's an acceptable member of society, *because* he has them.

Earth in Transit contains four short stories dealing with thought control.

In Donald E. Westlake's "The Winner" we see prisons for political prisoners who deviate from majority thinking. They are prevented from escaping from prison by black boxes which are implanted under their skins and are controlled by central transmitters. At 150 yards away, the pain becomes so unendurable that prisoners return just to stop it.

Students can do research into similar real life situations by reading Solzhenitsyn and others who write about the Soviet equivalent of the little black boxes. Dissidents imprisoned in mental institutions are given heavy dosages of drugs to prevent escape.[1]

What we would want young people to note, both in the tales of the Soviet dissidents and in "The Winner," is the indomitable human spirit which keeps people fighting for freedom even when the fight seems completely hopeless.

In the next story from *Earth in Transit*, Poul Anderson's "I Tell You, It's True," scientists invent the ultimate mind/thought control. It is a device powerful enough to change anyone's convictions, to convert political and social ideologies. The scientists try to take precautions to ensure that the device will not be abused, but, of course, it is. The major problem posed to the reader is: How will people be able to know if they are being brainwashed?

In Philip K. Dick's "We Can Remember It for You Wholesale" an organization offers to implant false memories for experiences one wishes to have but cannot afford. (You want to go to Europe but can't afford it? We'll implant a memory of having gone.) Inevitably, as in the Poul Anderson story, the device is abused, and a simple clerk who wants to believe he went to Mars finds that he really did once—as a secret agent.

In J. G. Ballard's "The Subliminal Man" people are constantly bombarded with subliminal messages that turn them into voracious consumers. Ballard shows us the dangerous psychological effects that result from mindless superproductivity: the discontent, lack of commitment, and lack of satisfaction that must be stirred up if people are to spend their lives buying material goods they don't need.

The most horrifying novel about thought control is George Orwell's *1984*, which will be discussed later under "Utopia or Dystopia." In the world of 1984, through two-way television screens, every act of each individual's life is monitored by thought police. Even facial expressions must be watched, for they reflect the thoughts inside.

Kurt Vonnegut, Jr.'s *The Sirens of Titan* also deals with thought control. In this novel, described in the beginning as "a true story from the Nightmare Ages, falling roughly, give or take, a few years between the

---

1. Ludmilla Thorne, "Inside Russia's Psychiatric Jails," *The New York Times Magazine*, June 12, 1977.

Second World War and the Third Great Depression," an infantry division assigned to Mars is completely controlled by brain waves.

This is the way thought control is used to make good soldiers:

> At the hospital they even had to explain to Unk (after removal of his memory) that there was a radio antenna under the crown of his skull and that it would hurt him whenever he did something a good soldier wouldn't ever do. The antenna also would give him orders and furnish drum music to march to. They said that not just Unk, but everybody had an antenna like that—doctors and nurses and four-star generals included. It was a very democratic army, they said. . . . At the hospital they gave Unk a small sample of the pain his antenna would stick him with if he ever did anything wrong. The pain was horrible. Unk was bound to admit that a soldier would be crazy not to do his duty at all times. . . . (p. 102)

The reason for controlling the minds of these soldiers is that they are being trained as commandoes to invade earth. Unfortunately, the operation to remove memory is not foolproof. The Director of Mental Health on Mars says: "We can make the center of a man's memory virtually as sterile as a scalpel fresh from the autoclave. But grains of new experience begin to accumulate on it at once. These grains in turn form themselves into patterns not necessarily favorable to military thinking. Unfortunately, this problem of recontamination seems insoluble." (p. 106)

Soldiers are not the only ones whose thinking is controlled on Mars. Antennas are installed in the skulls of children when they reach the age of fourteen.

Thought control is only part of this novel, but students should note that even though Unk has been brainwashed seven times, there is a part of him that still thinks, that still refuses to give way to the men who control him.

Utopia or Dystopia

What can we learn about the future world by examining our present one? Will the future be a utopia or a dystopia, or neither? Will there be enough food, space, fuel, and air for our growing populations? Will we have freedom or thought control? Will technology help or hurt humanity? Four stories in *Earth in Transit* deal with utopia and dystopia.

In Ward Moore's "Lot," the problem is more psychological than actual. The author asks what would happen to family relationships in a world of shortages. In this dystopia, a father is so terrified by the prospect of shortages that he turns against his own family. Mr. Jimmon and his family have been prepared for atomic warfare, and when a bomb goes off, they get into his carefully packed station wagon and head away from where the flash was reported. Mr. Jimmon thinks of:

> the endless mob pouring, pouring out of Los Angeles, searching frenziedly for escape and refuge, eating up the surrounding country in ever-widening circles, crowding, jam-packing, overflowing every hotel, boarding house, lodging, or private home into which they could edge, agonizingly bidding up the price of everything until the chaos they brought with them was indistinguishable from the chaos they were fleeing. . . . (p. 29)

When Jimmon's wife stops to try to telephone her relatives, he drives off without her, leaving her in a gas station, far from anyone she knows, just a few steps ahead of the advancing horde.

In Robert Silverberg's "To See the Invisible Man" we see a future society in which deviates are punished with a brand mark that makes them into non-persons. The protagonist of this story has been branded a non-person because of the crime of coldness. "Refusal to unburden himself for his fellow man." (p. 53) For the duration of his sentence no one will speak to him or look at him more than once, just once, to see the sign of invisibility.

Another approach to deviants in the future is shown in Walter Bupp's story, "Modus Vivendi," in which mutants, who have the power of ESP, become social and professional pariahs.

Two important, pessimistic novels about the future that should be studied together are George Orwell's *1984* and Aldous Huxley's *Brave New World*.

In *1984*, Winston Smith lives in a horrifying dystopia. Extrapolating from trends present in 1949, when this book was originally published, Orwell has constructed the ultimate authoritarian world—a world in which all vestiges of freedom, love, brotherhood, independent thought, creativity, joy, laughter, subtlely, innovation, and originality have been totally expunged from daily life.

Smith, who works in the Records Department of the Ministry of Truth, revising the past as it appears in the newspapers, daily destroys factual, historical records. When a document is due for destruction, it is dropped into what is euphemistically called "the memory hole," from where it is whirled away to the furnaces. Students should discuss this idea of Orwell's, which actually has factual bases. In most countries, but most particularly in totalitarian ones, history is re-written to suit the wishes of government. In the United States it is only recently that the truth about slavery is being told. In *1984* the government says: "Who controls the past controls the future: Who controls the present controls the past." (p. 32) The theory of "mutability of the past" is a principle of government.

In Ira Levin's dystopia, *This Perfect Day* (see page 189), the price that the citizens have paid for their carefree, ordered lives directed by Uni-Comp is the loss of freedom. But in *1984* the citizens receive nothing back for the loss of their freedom. Daily life is grubby, uncomfortable, unhealthy, and sterile. In Winston Smith's miserable apartment house, the smell of cooking and old rag mats pervades the air. The elevator seldom works and the electricity is turned off for hours every day. There is always a shortage of consumer goods, and this shortage is attributed to far-off wars. Austerity is the accepted mode of life.

But it is not only the creature comforts that have disappeared. Little aesthetic touches, beautiful designs, fine fabrics, and comfortable living conditions have disappeared for all but the members of the inner party. The only liquor is Victory Gin, which is terrible, as are the Victory Cigarettes, which are all that can be bought. Winston has a dim memory of eating chocolate as a boy, and it is only when he and Julia visit the luxurious home of party leader O'Brien that they taste wine for the first time.

Orwell offers many significant concepts for students to explore. They should note that the lack of the amenities of life and the endless inconvenience and unpleasantness produce apathetic masses whose major energies are devoted to just getting through each day. They should ask how it benefits an authoritarian government to keep the populace so uncomfortable.

Students should also discuss the implications of the statement: "Big Brother Is Watching You" (p. 5). Big Brother is the mythical party head, never actually seen in person. But the posters of Big Brother are omnipresent and the pictures are so contrived that the eyes seem to follow people when they move. In addition to Big Brother, citizens are constantly watched by the two-way telescreen that is compulsorily located in each citizen's apartment and can be dimmed but never shut off.

This loss of privacy is the nightmare basis of much of science fiction literature. And recent revelations about Watergate bugging, FBI dossiers, and CIA spying show us how closely rooted in reality were Orwell's science fiction predictions.

If *1984* is read as part of a science fiction study, students should examine the function of technology in 1984. Orwell realized that the machine and the ingenious technology of our century could possibly be used to achieve totally corrupt ends. By 1984, the people who matter are interested only in power over people. Power over things has become secondary. The telescreen has become the object whereby everyone can be watched at every minute.

The corrupt uses of technology in *1984* have parallels in society today. These include: the use of computers for South Africa's apartheid system; technology to develop more advanced forms of warfare; technology that results in pollution, wiretapping, bugging, and new and terrible forms of torture. Not even Orwell could have dreamed up anything more ludicrous or unbelievable than the recent disclosure that the FBI kept a dossier on Helen Keller. If a blind, deaf, and dumb woman is considered worthy of government surveillance, it is not hard to understand how Winston Smith would be doomed in a technological society that fears freedom.

Aldous Huxley's *Brave New World* is a futuristic novel set in England at a time when science and technology have advanced to such a point that people's lives are controlled from birth (called "decanting") to death. The family structure in this society is dead. All children are artificially "hatched" from bottles. Substances are either withheld from or added to the bottles in order to produce different types of human beings.

This utopian world has been created by science and is controlled by drugs. Society is "perfect"; people are happy, youthful, free from disease, and devoid of emotion.

The motto of this "Brave New World" is "Community, Identity, Stability." Life there is stable until the arrival of John and his mother Linda from the Savage Reservation, a totally natural world. They are an embarrassment to the new world because they represent a weakness in the scheme of things. The major conflict in the novel deals with the collision of these two vastly different worlds. Through a satirical view of this society, Huxley shows what can happen when science is pushed to an extreme.

The novel is set in A.F. 632. The World State designates time as being either before or after the time of Ford, the father of mass production, which is the God of the World State.

In the World State there is a fixed social structure ranging from the "Alphas," the intellectuals, the highest social order, to the "Epsilons," semi-moronic beings capable of great physical labor. People are produced in test tubes through Bokanovsky's Process, a process by which one fertile human egg can be caused to bud and divide into from 8 to 96 buds, each of which develops into a human being identical to each of the others.

Hypnopoedia, or sleep teaching, is used to instill social attitudes. Neo-Pavlovian conditioning (based on the experiments of the Russian scientist, Pavlov) is used to develop fear and pleasure reactions in young children. These reactions condition them for the lives that have been planned for them. The drug, soma, is used on adults in the World State to lessen tension and to keep them in a continual state of happiness. Soma is defined as Christianity without tears, for it creates feelings of brotherhood.

Students should discuss Huxley's two views of religion in the future. Among the people of the World State, religion no longer exists at all. People have been conditioned to respond with kindness to their fellow-men. War has been eliminated by prebirth programming and after-birth conditioning, which leaves people content with their lives. The liberal use of soma creates the euphoric state of brotherly love. Thus Christianity and its brotherly love teachings are no longer necessary. God is most obvious in his absence. In the Reservation world, Christianity and more primitive beliefs have become mixed into a strange religion. Both Christ and Pookong, the sacred eagle, are worshipped. Each demands pain and martyrdom on the part of his followers.

Students should also discuss the Savage John's statement to the controller of the Brave New World: "What you need is something with tears for a change. Nothing costs enough here." (p. 162) Students should recognize that while this society provides for the material comfort of the inhabitants, it does not allow for individual expression. Those things that require personal sacrifice are discouraged. Individuals are taught to avoid personal challenges and to accept the group's ideology. The denial of the individual is John's greatest disappointment with this new world. The Savage claims the right to be unhappy. "I want God, I want poetry, I want real danger, I want freedom, I want goodness, I want sin." Students should discuss why these seem to be good things to John. Would they agree? What do we lose if we live a life that is safe but sterile?

Books Discussed in Chapter VII
Level 7, Mordecai Roshwald, Signet, 1959.
Z for Zachariah, Robert C. O'Brien, Dell, 1977.

On the Beach, Nevil Shute, Scholastic Book Services, 1972.
The Voice of the Dolphins, Leo Szilard, Simon and Schuster, 1961.
No Blade of Grass, John Christopher, Avon, 1971.
Hiroshima, John Hersey, Bantam, 1972.
The Martian Chronicles, Ray Bradbury, Bantam, 1946.
Nightmare Age, edited by Frederik Pohl, Ballantine, 1970.
Earth in Transit, Sheila Schwartz, Dell, 1976.
Past, Present & Future Perfect, edited by Wolf and Fitzgerald, Fawcett, 1973.
The Space Merchants, Pohl and Kornbluth, Ballantine, 1969.
The Best of Frederik Pohl, Ballantine, 1975.
Voyages: Scenarios for a Ship Called Earth, edited by Rob Sauer, Ballantine, 1971.
This Perfect Day, Ira Levin, Fawcett, 1971.
When Harlie Was One, David Gerrold, Ballantine, 1972.
Introduction to Science Fiction, Sheila Schwartz, Dell, 1979.
Beyond Control, Robert Silverberg, Dell, 1974.
The Vintage Anthology of Science Fantasy, edited by Christopher Cerf, Vintage, 1966.
The Sirens of Titan, Kurt Vonnegut, Jr., Dell, 1970.
1984, George Orwell, Signet, 1961.
Brave New World, Aldous Huxley, Bantam, 1962 (original printing 1932).

Other Related Books

Planet of the Apes, Pierre Boulle, Vanguard, 1963. (Post-holocaust)
Childhood's End, Carthur C. Clarke, Ballantine, 1972. (Invaders from space control Earth)
2001: A Space Odyssey, Arthur C. Clarke, NAL, 1972. (Voyages in space)
The Terminal Man, Michael Crichton, Bantam, 1974. (The use of psychosurgery for thought control)
Alas, Babylon, Pat Frank, Bantam, 1960. (Post-holocaust set in Florida)
Joshua, Son of None, Nancy Freedman, Dell, 1974. (Cloning)
Stranger in a Strange Land, Robert Heinlein, Berkley, 1968. (Popular s-f book for teenagers, about a man who is half Earthman and half Martian)
Cat's Cradle, Kurt Vonnegut, Jr., Dell, 1969. (Invention inadvertently destroys mankind)

appendix a
adolescent literature I would not teach and why

One example of poor adolescent literature is Nat Hentoff's *In the Country of Ourselves*. Teachers and students might be tempted to purchase this work because Mr. Hentoff has a good reputation as a journalist and political thinker, but such purchase would be unfortunate. The content of this book reminds me of the transitoriness of the agitprop of the 1930s and some of the work of political message writers of that era such as Clifford Odets. Odets' work that focuses on a changing political situation, such as *Waiting for Lefty*, now seems passé. But his works that honestly attempt to deal with the eternal and unchanging conflicts between people, such as *Awake and Sing*, remain interesting today.

Hentoff's book is set during the Vietnam War period; its focus is a pointless demonstration held at one of New York City's alternative high schools. This book lacks moral purpose; everyone in it who is not stupid or naive is rotten, cynical, Machiavellian. What the villainous teacher, Scanlan, a professional agitator, hopes to get out of his purposeless activities, why this subversive is teaching in this particular school, or what is the logic of his maneuvers is never made clear to the reader. Scanlan's behavior just doesn't make sense, and the idea that revolutionaries pretended to be against the Vietnam War for their own nefarious purposes is certainly absurd.

Although Scanlan is the major villain of the book and the catalyst to violence, he is not the only menace in this school. Every progressive there is either dangerous, humorless, sexist, or fascistic. Schwartz, the one decent boy, is a useless liberal who is resented and rejected by the radicals; and Jane, one of the pure radicals who is truly idealistic, is depicted as a humorless dupe.

The Blacks in the school fare no better. They're either stupid or cagey, or both. One black teacher tells a student: "You use electricity, don't you? You ride the subway. None of that's black-owned. You buy those goddamn alligator shoes and you know the money from those don't go to Blacks. We got to use everything there is to use, so long as we don't let them tell us who we are and what we're going to do."

This swamp-like school is presided over by Mr. Rothblatt, the principal. His stance fluctuates between New York City Board of Education reactionary and rabbinical wisdom and forbearance. His unbelievable dialogue contains lines like: "The hell I wouldn't. I'm a gut empiricist, Scanlan, and you and I, sooner or later, we're going to have a showdown."

This is a book about exploitation. Everybody in the school exploits or tries to exploit someone else, but, unbelievably, the worst exploiters are the people who pretend to want good things like freedom of speech and peace. Their noble words and actions merely mask their evil intentions. But the people who are exploited the most by this book are the readers. All that a student can learn from this book is that the bad guys are the bad guys and the good guys are the bad guys, too. This book does not make the world more knowable; it makes it more confusing.

Hentoff's book is bad also because it panders to topicality. Another example of a book that does this is M. E. Kerr's *The Son of Someone Famous*. Kerr, like Hentoff, is a formidable name in the field of adolescent literature, and consequently teachers might be tempted to purchase any book by her.

Adam, the hero, is the son of someone loosely based on the former Secretary of State, Henry Kissinger. The father is a jet-set political globetrotter, and so, predictably, in keeping with the myths people like to propagate about the rich and successful, Adam is an alienated underachiever who keeps getting tossed out of prep schools. Fame is a terrible burden for this humorless, poor little rich boy, and to escape the burden he goes to live with his grandfather, the town drunkard, in the little Vermont town of Storm.

But is Adam left undisturbed and undiscovered in the frozen wilds of Vermont? Of course not. He is pursued to this remote outpost by his father's most recent ex-wife (an aging actress who sets out to reform Adam's grandfather), followed by a starlet who wants to marry Adam's father. Why does this starlet go all the way from California to Vermont? To commit suicide! The reason for her bizarre choice of locale is never established. At the end of the book Adam goes off globe-trotting with his father, with whom he has at last come to terms.

Why do I think this is bad adolescent literature? Like Hentoff's book, this one panders to topicality in its choice of the father's occupation. In addition, it reinforces clichés (the rich are *really* unhappy); the writing is uninspired; it does not give the young reader more understanding of his world; and its slickness is reminiscent of the worst of the television situation comedies. In fact, many books geared for the adolescent market today *have* been written to cash in on the popularity of a television show. Books such as *Sarah T.* and *Dawn: The Story of a Runaway* are of this ilk.

Another novel that epitomizes all of the negatives—indulging in the worst aspects of the youth culture of the 1960s, dealing with unimportant ideas and events as if they carry great significance, and presenting a value system devoid of integrity—is *I Never Loved Your Mind*, by Paul Zindel, another popular author of adolescent literature. Teachers who have admired works of his such as *The Effects of Gamma Rays on Man-in-the-Moon Marigolds* or *The Pigman* have purchased this book in the expectation that it would exhibit the same high standards. But it doesn't.

The teenage characters in this book work in a hospital, which Zindel sees as a very funny place. It is true that Paddy Chayefsky managed to find humor in this setting in his film *Hospital* and that the British author Peter Shaffer also used this setting amusingly in his play *The National Health*, but they are both more accomplished writers than Mr. Zindel. Both had serious messages behind the humor and demonstrated respect for all of those caught up in the life of a large, bustling hospital.

Mr. Zindel does not respect the people he writes about, and they do not respect each other. His sense of humor is also questionable. Here is an example: "Candy stripers are high-school volunteers. The ones at Richmond Valley Hospital were all revered except for Marjorie Lou Simons who used to curse so much she was nicknamed Tommy Toilet-Tongue."

The narrator, Dewey Daniels, is a high-school dropout with "no values." He falls in love with Yvette Goethals, who constantly talks about how fine her values are while, simultaneously, she lies, steals, and goes out of her way to be inefficient in her job. Is Zindel being ironic? He is not. It is evident that he admires (and wants the reader to admire) this young woman, who lives in a dirty commune, talks endlessly about how much she hates the corruption of other people, shamelessly sponges drinks in bars, but makes up for everything by her dedication to ending pollution of the environment. If she were viewed honestly, with irony, young readers might learn something about hypocrisy, irony, lack of humor, and pretentiousness. But no, she is viewed as better than Dewey because she respects the land rather than human beings.

Dewey falls in love with Yvette and manages to sleep with her when he visits her early one day and finds her cleaning her commune naked. She complains to him that she was forced to leave home because her mother's poor values made her view dimly Yvette's habit of cleaning the house naked, in front of her father and brothers. Ultimately, Dewey loses Yvette because of *his* poor values. And when he timorously suggests that he thought they had a relationship because they slept together, she drives off and calls out to him, "I never loved your mind."

What is Zindel saying to his adolescent audience in this book? Is he saying that it's good to be an unfettered, eccentric character who steals and cheats and is pompous and self-impressed because of this? He is not saying anything of value or significance to young people coming of age, and his eccentrics do not come off well because he lacks the comic genius to endow them with the required humanity.

Richard Peck is another popular and prolific writer of adolescent literature. Because some of his books are fairly good, teachers may be tempted to buy one that I consider an example of another kind of poor adolescent literature, *Don't Look and It Won't Hurt.* Like the Zindel book, this one contains no concepts of value for the teenager today.

The book deals with three sisters who live in poverty with their divorced mother, a hostess in a cheap restaurant. Ellen, the oldest sister, becomes pregnant by Kevin, a young man from out of town who tells her that he is engaged in "helping draft dodgers avoid the army by smuggling them out of the country. He was sort of a way station on the underground railroad . . . an important cog in a well-oiled machine of deeply committed people." (p. 35)

Had this indeed been Kevin's occupation, Peck might have produced a meaningful book, but Peck never comes to grips with the question of commitment. Kevin does not really do noble and unselfish work. He is a drug pusher, and when this is discovered, the meaning of the book vanishes.

Carol, the middle sister, telling her older sister that she must give the baby away for adoption when it is born, says: "They say if you're going to give your baby up, you shouldn't ever see it. I mean you oughtn't to look even to see if it's a boy or girl. If you don't really see it, it's easier not to keep it. That's what they said—don't look and it won't hurt." (p. 151)

This concept might have some meaning for the adolescent reader if Peck meant it ironically, but this does not appear to be the case, because the book ends with this homily being applied to another situation. Otis, the cat belonging to Liz, the youngest sister, has been taken to the vet for an infected paw. While waiting to see if the cat can be saved, Liz shows Carol a picture of the cat and Carol repeats her pseudo-philosophy: "Let's just hold on till we hear from the vet. . . . Just put the picture away till then. It won't hurt so much, Liz. It won't hurt if you don't look." (pp. 157–158)

What is Peck saying? What is the meaning of this book? Do we want to teach young people that the way to avoid pain is *not* to look, to close the book or turn off the newscast? Aren't the things that hurt most those that aren't honestly faced? Can a book such as this make a valuable contribution to an adolescent's knowledge or value system?

In the Hentoff book we saw poor social and political philosophy that was confusing for young readers; in the Kerr book we saw what could be the pilot for a slick television show with poor and topical plotting; in the Zindel book we saw a pandering to a supposed youth culture with shallow values; and in the Peck book, young people are given a potentially harmful philosophical perception.

There is one other category of adolescent literature that I would avoid: the totally pessimistic book. If the book is particularly well written, I might have one or two copies available in a class or school library, but I would not spend class time on such books, no matter how skillfully they are executed. This is because I think that adolescents need hope rather than pessimism. To me, the best books for young people show the possibilities of evil, degradation, death, suffering, unhappiness in life, but also affirm the other side of the coin. The books that young people need say, in essence: Yes, life can be terrible, but it also can be beautiful, wonderful, magical, and hopeful.

I would exclude literature that is nihilistic, lacking a humanistic belief in the ultimate value of life. The best literature, books like *Anne Frank: The Diary of a Young Girl*, and *One Flew over the Cuckoo's Nest*, affirm and reaffirm the dignity and survival of the human spirit even in the face of evil. Let me illustrate with two recent books about teenage death.

In Paige Dixon's *May I Cross Your Golden River?* an athletic young man dies from the nerve disease that killed Lou Gehrig. The book focuses on much more than his death. It gives the reader an increased appreciation of the beauty and value of family relationships, of the wonder of daily life in a constructive family. At the end of the book we weep and rejoice in the courage and dignity of this mother and her children.

In contrast, consider another book about the death of a young person, *Ellen: A Short Life Remembered* by Rose Levitt (a pseudonym). *Ellen* is a non-fiction work about the death of the author's daughter, Ellen, who is found, at age fifteen, to have a large cancerous mass near her pelvis.

Perhaps because it is not a work of fiction, a far different feeling comes through for the reader. I cannot blame Mrs. Levitt for her understandable despair at the torture and death of her innocent and blameless daughter. But I can feel, as a teacher, that what she has to say is not as valuable as the ideas in the Dixon work or in many other works about the death of young people.

In *Ellen* the medical facts obscure the humanism. We are presented with horrifying detail after horrifying detail: whether or not to have a catheter inserted, whether or not to try a new kind of chemotherapy or operation, etc. The terrible details overwhelm us, and the ultimate message of the book is pessimistic rather than optimistic. The Dixon book affirms the beauty of life in the midst of death, but the Levitt book tells us that friends fade away in times of grave illness; family members react badly to pressure; and death is meaningless, leaving a terrible aftermath that does not help us to understand the beauty of the life that remains.

I would not choose to teach *Ellen*. I want young people to understand more than the fact that death is unjust, without remedy, inevitable. I want them to understand that life is precious and that the fact of death is what gives life its value. I want books about death to serve the purposes of tragedy as outlined by Aristotle in his *Poetics*, written 2500 years ago but still valid today. Greek tragedy did not hesitate to show how terrible life could be, but always in conjunction with the grandeur and majesty of life. Awe, pity, and fear occurred, but always in relation to their opposites, and they always occurred to *thinking* human beings.

The final category of books I would not teach are those that are condescending, that do not respect the young reader. To illustrate this, consider *Blowfish Live in the Sea* by Paula Fox, who received great acclaim and the Newbery Award for her novel, *The Slave Dancer*. In *Blowfish Live in the Sea*, she has created a young girl whose thinking level is below that of a slow six-year-old, whose parents are ill-defined, and whose older brother is peculiar and unmotivated. The psychology in this work is unscientific, and the language is pedestrian and unlovely.

Thirteen-year-old Carrie lives with her father, mother, and half-brother, Ben, her mother's son by her first marriage. Ben is described as sloppy, with his long hair and Indian headband. He seems to do nothing much with his time but write, "blowfish live in the sea," all over the place. This makes Carrie's mother angry, not because it seems a strange preoccupation for a nineteen-year-old, but because they "can't get window cleaners to come anymore." Equally strange is the fact that Ben's loving mother never thinks to ask him *why* he writes this message all over the place.

When Ben's real father contacts them, Ben and Carrie go off to Boston to visit him. After the visit ends, Ben decides to stay with his father to help him make a success of a run-down motel. And then, eureka! Carrie discovers the unexciting mystery of the blowfish slogan. Ben's real father had sent him a shellacked blowfish when he was a little boy, and now this nineteen-year-old oaf writes the silly slogan as a message to the world that he needs his real father. The reader wonders why he never picked up the phone or mentioned this to anybody. He leaves the blowfish for Carrie, and I, for one, hope this cute little tyke will feed it to the sharks.

I don't believe that this book was aimed at the needs or interests of teenagers. It does not respect their minds or problems. Reading such a work is a waste of time. The reader is no wiser at the end than at the beginning. And this should be our ultimate test of which adolescent literature to teach: The works we use in the classroom should help the student to grow and to know more *after* reading them than he or she did before.

Books Discussed in Appendix A

In the Country of Ourselves, Nat Hentoff, Dell, 1971.
The Son of Someone Famous, M. E. Kerr, Ballantine, 1975.
I Never Loved Your Mind, Paul Zindel, Bantam, 1975.
Don't Look and It Won't Hurt, Richard Peck, Avon, 1973.
May I Cross Your Golden River?, Paige Dixon, Atheneum, 1975.
Ellen: A Short Life Remembered, Rose Levitt, Bantam, 1974.
Blowfish Live in the Sea, Paula Fox, Dell, 1975.

appendix b
resources for the teacher of adolescent literature

1. ALAN (Assembly on Literature for Adolescents). Membership is open to anyone interested in literature for adolescents. Although ALAN is an assembly of the National Council of Teachers of English, members do not have to belong to the parent organization.

    Four times a year ALAN publishes an excellent *Newsletter* that includes reviews of paperback and hardcover books, articles on teaching methods, bibliographies, and critical commentaries. Included in ALAN membership is a subscription to the *Newsletter*. For membership information write to NCTE, 1111 Kenyon Road, Urbana, IL 61801.

2. YASD (Young Adult Services Division of the American Library Association). Each year the YASD publishes a list of *Best Books for Young Adults*. This list can be obtained from the ALA and can also be found in the April issue of *Today's Education* (NEA). The nationally representative committee that selects the books on the list looks for adult and juvenile titles that reflect "current young adult appeal, . . . meet acceptable standards of literary merit, and provide a variety of subjects for different reading tastes as well as a broad range of reading levels." Further information about the committee can be obtained from the ALA, 50 East Huron Street, Chicago, IL 60611.

3. EDMARC (Educational Materials Review Center of the Office of Education, U.S. Department of Health, Education, and Welfare). EDMARC serves as a national book evaluation, examination, and review center for teachers, librarians, parents, and the general public. Over the years EDMARC has built a collection of some 17,000 noncirculating volumes of quality juvenile and young adult literature, textbooks, and materials for professional educators. For information, write or call EDMARC, 400 Maryland Avenue, SW, Washington, DC 20202. (202) 245-8437.

4. *The Novels Adolescents Are Reading,* a report by Ted Hipple and Faith Schullstrom based on a national survey of high school English department chairpersons. The authors "wished to discover (1) what are the most commonly required novels in American high schools and (2) what novels did high school students select as their favorites." The report is available from the Florida Educational Research and Development Council, University of Florida, Gainesville, FL 32611.

5. *200 Adolescent Novels Worth Reading: 1972-1977* by Ken Donelson, Arizona State University. An annotated list with introductory comments about adolescent literature. Reproduced in the Fall, 1977, issue of the *Illinois English Bulletin,* Vol. 65, No. 1. Available from Dorothy Matthews, Editor, 100 English Building, University of Illinois, Urbana, IL 61801.

6. Appropriate publications available from NCTE:

    a. *Books for You: A Booklist for Senior High Students* by Kenneth Donelson, editor, and members of the NCTE Committee on the Senior High School Booklist. This new edition of the senior high school booklist features annotations for more than 2500 titles. Most have been published since 1971; many are 1974 and 1975 releases. The books are described in language addressed directly to the high school student. Prepared by an NCTE committee of teachers and librarians, the list contains more than 50 categories of recent books that appeal to students.

    b. *Your Reading: A Booklist for Junior High Students* by Jerry L. Walker, editorial chair, and members of the NCTE Committee on the Junior High School Booklist. Whatever their divergent tastes and abilities, junior high students can find books to interest them from the more than 1600 titles in this list designed to be used by the students themselves. Annotations are written directly to engage students' interest in the books: fiction annotations sketch the story and introduce the characters; nonfiction descriptions note the scope and aims of the books. Most of the books in this 5th edition have been published since 1970; many are national award winners. Books are grouped into more than 40 headings that appeal to students: fiction includes such topics as sports, mystery, and being in love; nonfiction has such headings as biography, hobbies, and witchcraft. Also includes poetry, short stories, and reference tools.

    c. *Adolescent Literature, Adolescent Reading, and the English Class,* Kenneth Donelson, editor. Brief, practical articles about contemporary books that young people enjoy. Includes critiques of specific works and results of surveys of adolescent reading interests; several articles contain annotated lists of books popular with teenagers. Especially useful articles by teachers describing successful classroom practices (and favorite titles) for getting students "hooked on books." 1972 *Arizona English Bulletin.*

    d. *Fiction for Adolescents: Theory and Practice,* James E. Davis, editor. The contributors of these 12 articles discuss the following topics: an author's considerations in writing a novel for adolescents; the teacher as fictional character in adolescent literature; such themes of adolescent novels as institutional values, the illegitimate heroine, and the war experience; the importance of a cumulative study of literature in the secondary school; an approach to teaching fiction in the junior and senior high school; and novels by Zane Grey, Norma Klein, M.E. Kerr, Judy Blume, and Paul Zindel. Winter, 1977, *Focus,* publication of the Southeastern Ohio Council of Teachers of English.

e. *Adolescent Literature Revisited after Four Years,* Kenneth Donelson, editor. More than 40 wide-ranging articles discuss significant qualities of books enjoyed by adolescents, explore ethnic literature, fantasy literature, and current themes in adolescent literature, and give suggestions for individualized reading programs. Includes lists of recommended adolescent fiction and nonfiction; results of surveys of adolescent reading preferences; bibliography of "high interest-low readability" books for use in thematic units; and an extensive bibliography of articles and books about adolescent literature. This volume is intended to supplement and update, but not supplant, the earlier work on adolescent literature. April, 1976 *Arizona English Bulletin.*

appendix c
still alive:
the rest of the best,
1960-1974

This list, compiled by members of YASD, presents seventy-two titles, originally published between 1960 and 1974, that were still alive and being read by young adults in 1975. It includes titles originally on the annual "Best Books for Young Adults" list as well as titles that had somehow been overlooked. An asterisk (*) indicates a title that was *not* originally selected. This list is reprinted by permission of the Young Adult Services Division, American Library Association.

Watership Down   by Richard Adams
Born Free   by Joy Adamson
I Know Why the Caged Bird Sings   by Maya Angelou
Gather Together in My Name   by Maya Angelou
Go Ask Alice   by Anonymous
Fantastic Voyage   by Isaac Asimov
If Beale Street Could Talk   by James Baldwin
When the Legend Dies   by Hal Borland
*   *Our Bodies, Ourselves: A Book by and for Women*   compiled by the
        Boston Women's Health Collective
*   *To Sir, with Love*   by E. R. Braithwaite
*   *Trout Fishing in America*   by Richard Brautigan
*   *Manchild in the Promised Land*   by Claude Brown
The Incredible Journey   by Sheila Burnford
Silent Spring   by Rachel Carson
Journey to Ixtlan: The Lessons of Don Juan   by Carlos Castaneda
A Hero Ain't Nothin' but a Sandwich   by Alice Childress
*   *2001: A Space Odyssey*   by Arthur C. Clarke
Soul on Ice   by Eldridge Cleaver
The Chocolate War   by Robert Cormier
I Heard the Owl Call My Name   by Margaret Craven

The Andromeda Strain by Michael Crichton
* *Reflections on a Gift of Watermelon Pickle* edited by Stephen
    Dunning
The Girls of Huntington House by Blossom Elfman
April Morning by Howard Fast
Rockin' Steady: A Guide to Basketball and Cool by Walt Frazier and
    Ira Beckow
Buried Alive: The Biography of Janis Joplin by Myra Friedman
The Autobiography of Miss Jane Pittman by Ernest Gaines
The Ridiculously Expensive Mad edited by William Gaines
Dove by Robin Lee Graham and Derek T. Gill
* *I Never Promised You a Rose Garden* by Hannah Green
* *Black like Me* by John Griffin
The Friends by Rosa Guy
* *Autobiography of Malcolm X* by Malcolm X and Alex Haley
Sticks and Stones by Lynn Hall
Hatter Fox by Marilyn Harris
* *Stranger in a Strange Land* by Robert Heinlein
* *Mr. and Mrs. Bo Jo Jones* by Ann Head
* *Catch-22* by Joseph Heller
* *Dune* by Frank Herbert
* *All Creatures Great and Small* by James Herriott
The Swarm by Arthur Herzog
* *The Outsiders* by S. E. Hinton
That Was Then, This Is Now by S. E. Hinton
* *We Have Always Lived in the Castle* by Shirley Jackson
Tell Me That You Love Me, Junie Moon by Marjorie Kellogg
* *One Flew over the Cuckoo's Nest* by Ken Kesey
* *Flowers for Algernon* by Daniel Keyes
* *A Separate Peace* by John Knowles
To Race the Wind: An Autobiography by Harold Krentz
To Kill a Mockingbird by Harper Lee
Serpico by Peter Maas
Daddy Was a Number Runner by Louise Meriwether
Coming of Age in Mississippi: An Autobiography by Anne Moody
* *Lisa Bright and Dark* by John Neufeld
A Day No Pigs Would Die by Robert Newton Peck
The Bell Jar by Sylvia Plath
The Chosen by Chaim Potok
Alive: The Story of the Andes Survivors by Piers Paul Read
Survive the Savage Sea by Dougal Robertson
Run, Shelley, Run! by Gertrude Samuels
The Peanuts Treasury by Charles Schulz
Trying Hard to Hear You by Sandra Scoppetone
House of Stairs by William Sleator
* *One Day in the Life of Ivan Denisovich* by Alexander Solzhenitsyn
Bless the Beasts and Children by Glendon Swarthout

House of Tomorrow   by Jean Thompson
* *Slaughterhouse Five; or, The Children's Crusade*   by Kurt Vonnegut, Jr.
* *My Sweet Charlie*   by David Westheimer
Von Ryan's Express   by David Westheimer
Deathwatch   by Robb White
* *The Foxfire Book*   edited by Eliot Wigginton
* *The Pigman*   by Paul Zindel

index